Posthuman Rap

POSTHUMAN RAP

Justin Adams Burton

OXFORD
UNIVERSITY PRESS

OXFORD
UNIVERSITY PRESS

Oxford University Press is a department of the University of Oxford. It furthers
the University's objective of excellence in research, scholarship, and education
by publishing worldwide. Oxford is a registered trade mark of Oxford University
Press in the UK and certain other countries.

Published in the United States of America by Oxford University Press
198 Madison Avenue, New York, NY 10016, United States of America.

Library of Congress Cataloging-in-Publication Data
Names: Burton, Justin Adams.
Title: Posthuman rap / Justin Adams Burton.
Description: New York, NY : Oxford University Press, [2017] | Includes
bibliographical references and index.
Identifiers: LCCN 2016059026 (print) | LCCN 2016059694 (ebook) |
ISBN 9780190235451 (alk. paper) | ISBN 9780190235468 (alk. paper) |
ISBN 9780190235475 (updf) | ISBN 9780190235482 (epub)
Subjects: LCSH: Rap (Music)—History and criticism. | Rap (Music)—Social aspects.
Classification: LCC ML3531 .B87 2017 (print) | LCC ML3531 (ebook) |
DDC 782.421649—dc23
LC record available at https://lccn.loc.gov/2016059026

9 8 7 6 5 4 3 2 1
Paperback printed by WebCom, Inc., Canada
Hardback printed by Bridgeport National Bindery, Inc., United States of America

For Kathryn

My One and My Only

CONTENTS

Preface   *ix*
Acknowledgments   *xi*

Introduction: Pre-Echo—Monsters in the Mix   *1*

1. Posthuman: "Completely Outside Our Present Conception
   of What It Is to Be Human"   *15*

2. "Cheap and Easy Radicalism": The Legible Politics
   of Kendrick Lamar   *45*

3. Sonic Blackness and the Illegibility of Trap Irony   *69*

4. Party Politics: Rae Sremmurd's Club as Posthuman Vestibule   *101*

Epilogue: Posthuman Sub-Bass   *129*

Notes   *133*
Bibliography   *139*
Index   *151*

PREFACE

Between the time I received a peer review report for the complete draft of this book and the time I submitted the final manuscript that incorporated the suggestions from that peer review, the United States elected Donald Trump as its president. Trump ran on a platform that involved very little policy detail but that trucked in racial violence, xenophobia, anti-Muslim ideology, and masculine aggression. As I type this preface, we're still a little more than a month and a half out from Trump's inauguration, and several things about the way the United States works might be noticeably different by the time *Posthuman Rap* is in print, after Trump's first hundred days in office. If his promises are to be believed—and from this vantage point, it's the safest way to proceed—Trump will pursue the withdrawal of health insurance from millions of people, a registry of Muslims in the United States, a dragnet to aid in the deportation of immigrants, the construction of a wall on the United States' southern border, and the consolidation of further violent power under a militarized police force.

My best guess is that *Posthuman Rap* will read like a book written in the middle of the Trump regime. The anti-blackness that contextualizes the posthumanity of Nicki Minaj, Rae Sremmurd, and rap artists will likely come into sharper relief during Trump's presidency. But I wrote the book before the 2016 election, and this is an important point. While much of the liberal/Democratic hand-wringing over Trump's ascension involves a certain disillusionment with a system that was believed to have progressed past the kind of racist politics that helped elect him, Trump does not represent anything new in US politics. If the Trump era turns out to be as bad for marginalized groups as many fear, it won't be because Trump broke the system. It will be because a broken system created someone like Trump. While it's absolutely alarming that we have now consolidated so much power behind white supremacist authoritarianism, and the conditions of existence will worsen for many in the United States and across the globe because of that, we'll be best served if we remember that the kind of ideology Trump rode to power has persisted since before the United States existed.

Here's why that matters: people have been finding ways to construct and affirm their humanity in the face of white supremacist, anti-queer, ableist political violence for centuries. *Posthuman Rap* tunes in to some of that work, and the critical theory I engage points to even more. Those who are disillusioned, who see Trump as a fundamental break from the United States' standard operating procedure, would benefit from taking their cues from the theorists and activists who have already been working against or outside of white supremacist cisheteropatriarchy—outside of systems that are tipped in favor of whiteness, strict gender binaries, normative sexuality, and the dudes. These kinds of theorists and activists would be doing this work regardless of who's president. This is not necessarily a matter of formalizing political power but of recognizing that formalized political power is part of the problem in a system that thrives on inequity. The way forward, then, may not follow an expected path, and the kind of posthumanism I explore in this book imagines ways of being human that exist outside of the norm, that follow unexpected paths, that don't register as audible to the kind of formalized politics that flow in the mainstream.

ACKNOWLEDGMENTS

This is my first book, so I have a lot of people to acknowledge. I'll be ignoring any play-off music from the Oscar orchestra.

It starts and ends with Kathryn Adams Burton, who has been every definition of support possible: emotional, intellectual, financial. I've learned from Kathryn how to think critically, how to think deeply, and how to think generously. She's shaped my understanding of the world, thought through and strengthened any ideas I have, and is, in that way, directly responsible for anything good you find in this book. And far beyond this book, I have learned from Kathryn what love and forgiveness and commitment and passion and joy are. Some of it I wish I hadn't learned the hard way. I owe Kathryn my life, which I offer with the promise to make it count for her. For us.

Academia is weird, and there's no making it through without solid mentors, colleagues, friends, collaborators, and co-conspirators. My initial love for writing and the humanities was a gift from two of my high school teachers, Ms. Ivey and Mrs. Andrews. Jeff Hopper wrote me the recommendation letter that unlocked graduate study for me. Once at Rutgers, my first and lasting mentor was Nanette de Jong, who made it OK for me to study popular music. I remember a short meeting with her turning into several hours as we sat at a table outside the College Avenue Au Bon Pain. She was trying to get me to write clearly: I'd write a paragraph, she'd ask me what it meant, then cross it out and tell me to write it better. Write, cross out, repeat. There are probably still some unnecessarily dense passages in here, but if any of it is clear, you have Nanette's patience to thank for that. The outside reader for my dissertation, Mark Katz, worked overtime in his role, offering insight as I wrote, writing letters when I needed them, and introducing me to Suzanne Ryan at Oxford University Press and Mary Francis at University of California Press. Mark's generosity made the transition from student to assistant professor much easier than it otherwise would've been.

The first pitch I had accepted for publication was for the *Oxford Handbook of Mobile Music Studies*. Chris Doll, who joined the Rutgers faculty while I was finishing my dissertation, recommended me to the editors, who took a chance on me. My first draft was lousy, not because I wasn't trying but because I simply didn't understand what I was writing about. Jason Stanyek and Ben Piekut, the editors of the volume, told me they couldn't publish what I'd submitted, which stung. They also told me they'd like me to take another shot at a chapter, which was incredibly kind. I'm grateful to them not only for the second chance but also for telling me how that first chapter came up short. I was trying to write about posthumanism, and their critique pointed me toward a path that I've found much more satisfying.

Once at Oxford, I landed with Norm Hirschy as my acquisitions editor. If I could create an acquisitions editor in a lab, it'd come out just like Norm. This has been a years-long process, from pitch to proposal to proposal to proposal to, well, we're here now, aren't we? Norm has not only been patient every step of the way, but he is supportive in a tangible way. His feedback is incisive, and he has a gift for efficiently delivering some book-changing thoughts. I have trusted him completely with this project and am looking forward to more in the future.

Popular Music Studies is an interdisciplinary brew, and I've had the pleasure of plugging into several different networks in the field. The International Association for the Study of Popular Music, US Branch (IASPM-US) folks are my home base. IASPM-US was the first conference to accept one of my papers, and when they were looking to expand their Web presence several years ago, they set me loose at iaspm-us.net, where I had the opportunity to curate several postings from scholars across the field. It was an invaluable experience that put me in touch with scholars I otherwise wouldn't have had the excuse to meet. Bekka Farrugia, Barry Shank, Karl Hagstrom-Miller, and Eric Weisbard helped me find my footing in the organization. Later, Kwame Harrison would let me mess around on his conference program committee, which was a launching pad to the conference program committee I'd co-chair a couple years later with Ali Colleen Neff. That conference was in Louisville (it was an icy mess—a record-setting cold spell for the city), and it was an absolute joy to coordinate it with Ali and Diane Pecknold. It's also at IASPM-US conferences where I met Luis Manual-Garcia, Travis Gosa, and David Font-Navarrete, whose support has been important over the years. When I took over the Web editor position, Jason Lee Oakes made the handoff. We'd later find ourselves on a hip hop panel together at the joint IASPM-US/POP conference in New York, and before we knew it, we were co-editing the *Oxford Handbook of Hip Hop Music Studies*. You should be able to get your hands on it a few months after

Posthuman Rap is out, and it's going to be good because Jason is an excellent collaborator who has put all of his considerable editorial skill into the volume. As home base, IASPM-US has provided me with a place to try out ideas and talk through all manner of pop music nerdery with friends and colleagues.

While I was editing the IASPM-US Web site, I had the pleasure of first conspiring with the *Sounding Out!* (soundstudiesblog.com) crew. Jennifer Stoever and Liana Silva have consistently offered me space since then to work on my ideas and my writing. When they started running a series of guest-edited posts, they, along with Aaron Trammell and Neil Verma, let me curate a set that loosely revolved around EDM trap (as in the Electronic Dance Music version of trap, which isn't exactly the same as the Southern hip hop version of trap I deal with later in the book) and included some of my early engagement with Karen Barad's theory of agency (which was central to one of the proposals for this book but didn't make it into the final cut). Jenny and Liana are ridiculously gifted editors who make my writing infinitely better than it otherwise would be. Working with *Sounding Out!* has been one of my favorite and most satisfying things.

The American Musicological Society and Society for Ethnomusicology (SEM) have also offered space for development and exchange. I fell into an ecomusicology crowd that has proven to be particularly fun. Rachel Mundy and Kate Galloway have always been particularly gracious in creating space for accidental ecomusicologists like me, and they've been a delight to work with on a variety of projects. It was also at an SEM that I met Kyra Gaunt, who joined Travis Gosa at a hip hop conference I co-hosted (shout-out Brea Heidelberg and Mickey Hess!) at Rider University.

Speaking of Rider, it's a much better place because of Laura Luck, who welcomed me when I first came to fill out paperwork to adjunct and who has brought countless smiles to my face in the years since. This book has advanced from a proposal in need of reworking to a finished manuscript with the aid of summer fellowships, which provided some financial support to focus exclusively on the book during summer months. While it was in process, the Rider musicology reading group—Eric Hung, Sharon Mirchandani, Samantha Bassler, Dana Gorzelany-Mostak, Amy Kimura, Carolann Buff, and Steve Allen—read and critiqued the proposal and introduction on a couple of occasions, offering feedback that helped me hone my argument quite a lot. Rider also hosts a writing camp each summer, which is just ten people sitting around a conference table all typing on various projects. It's stupid how helpful that is. It's also a wonderful way to connect with faculty from across campus as we thrive on each other's presence while performing what can otherwise be some of the loneliest academic work there is.

Other early readers of the proposal were Rachel Mundy's "After Humanism" seminar at the University of Pittsburgh. I'm not only grateful to Rachel for adding me to her syllabus, but also to her students for reading closely and offering terrific feedback on my project. It's changed quite a bit since then, and that conversation was an exciting step in the book's progression. My own classes have also been a party to this book. I haven't assigned any of the readings to them (ahem, yet), but I've worked out my ideas in class with my students. Especially in the courses "Black Music in America," "Gender and Sexuality in Hip Hop and R&B" (just rolls of the tongue, doesn't it?), and "Welcome to the Dirty South," I've talked with my students about readings that are in this bibliography and listened with them to some of the music that I analyze here. Thanks to my students for keeping me on my toes and being game enough to come along for the ride, even when some of what we were doing together was still fairly speculative.

I love peer review. Like, mention peer review to me, and watch the idealist emerge. *Posthuman Rap* has been read by at least five different anonymous peer reviewers across its stages of development, and they've all shaped the final product in varying ways. No lie, some of that feedback hurt, but all of it helped me get this where it is now. Peer reviewers: thank you for the time and energy you put into this. I hope you like what came of it all.

I wouldn't have half my thoughts about southern hip hop if it weren't for Ali Colleen Neff. Her *Let the World Listen Right* is a tent pole in southern hip hop studies, but more than that, Ali has pushed me to engage this music on several fronts, whether it's a formal collaboration, an exchange of rough drafts, a late-night conversation at our house or hers, or just her head nodding vigorously up and down when I get something right during a conference presentation. She's worked with my students, nudged me to work harder and better, and been a true friend to our whole family.

At Rider, I've had the good fortune of being able to work alongside Brea Heidelberg as I navigate the tenure track. We teach the "Gender and Sexuality in Hip Hop and R&B" class together, and we also worked with Mickey Hess on the hip hop conference Rider hosted. But more than any particular work that needs to be done, Brea is always right there to celebrate an accomplishment, no matter how minor, and to brainstorm how to fix a problem, no matter how huge. Sometimes colleagues are friends, and I lucked out in this case.

Finally, my family. My parents, Ken and Diane Burton, showed me how to read and ask questions, and when it was clear music was my thing, they shelled out for lessons and instruments. My mom taught me a good bit about how to think about gender, too, which doesn't mean she endorses the material in here. My older sister, Jennifer, has always been the smart one, and she provided a model for me to follow when it came time to study and work hard. My othermother, Christie Robison, showed me how to think deeply, creatively. Kathryn's parents, Carol and Glen Adams, have treated me like I am their very own kid—it's a display of openness that has taught me a good deal about how to love. My siblings-in-law, Thomas, Jane, and Ross, all intersect with my work in different ways. Ross has always heard good music before I have, Thomas is a great sounding board for theories about art and praxis, and Jane will work and talk politics anytime, any-place. Our family has shaped this book in big abstract ways, and they've also cleared space for me to write, helping with kids or preparing dinners or just holding everything down while I bang out a couple thousand words. There aren't words to express my gratitude.

Then there are Emmett and Evers. I think I don't care if they ever read this book. They infuse my life with a special kind of joy that keeps me work-ing when work is hard and reminds me to step away from work when it becomes too consuming.

I'm thankful to everyone I've mentioned here for the roles they've played in helping shape this book. The good stuff is good because of all of these people.

Introduction

Pre-Echo—Monsters in the Mix

First things first, I'll eat your brains.
                    Nicki Minaj, *"Monster" (2010)*

Nicki Minaj's voice rips through the soundscape about two-thirds of the way through Kanye West's "Monster" (2010).[1] Rising from her lower register, it's a track-altering encounter. The beat, which is already sparse, is reduced to an 808 that thuds out a sort of clavé rhythm with a faint tom echoing behind it.[2] At the end of every measure, a percussion fill gives the impression that the rest of the beat is ready to join, but as long as Minaj lurks in that lower register, the instrumental can't really find itself. It's as if her sonic presence remains monstrous enough that the beat doesn't know how to proceed.

Well, *kinda* Nicki Minaj's voice rips through the soundscape about two-thirds of the way through Kanye West's "Monster." She infamously takes on a number of alter egos, and this particular section belongs to Roman Zolanski, a queer misfit frequently at odds with his mother, who says things Minaj doesn't want to, and who here engages in a back-and-forth with another alter-ego, Harajuku Barbie (Ganz 2010). But it isn't actually the alter egos I'm too concerned with right now. Rather, I want to return to the other two moments in "Monster" when the beat reduces itself to this specific point: pre-echoes. To best understand what kind of monster Minaj is, it's helpful to hear how these pre-echoes respond to the monsters she's surrounded by.

Before listening closely to those pre-echoes, let's first consider the instrumental track more broadly. "Monster"'s large-scale structure is fairly simple:

Vocal Prologue (Bon Iver)	0:10[3]
Intro (Rick Ross)	0:31
Hook (Kanye West)	0:41
Verse 1 (West)	1:02
Hook (West)	2:14
Verse 2 (Jay Z)	2:34
Hook (West)	3:25
Verse 3 (Nicki Minaj)	3:46
Instrumental Interlude	5:05
Epilogue (Bon Iver)	5:26

"Monster"'s instrumental, though, is less predictable. It's built from four basic parts that are turned on or off over the course of the song. Borrowing from production terminology, I'll call these four basic parts "stems," which refers to groups of audio tracks that are processed and mixed together prior to final mixing. The instrumental stems in "Monster" combine in varying and largely unpredictable ways throughout the song. It's the unpredictable part that matters here and that ultimately complicates our experience of the large-scale form. Usually, when we hear songs whose instrumental stems are triggered separately in the mix, it's an additive process, where different components of the instrumental track sound in sequence until they coalesce into a whole. Once the full instrumental is established, the track is often pared down in some sections and played fully in others for contrast and to signal different sections of a song. "All of the Lights," the track that immediately precedes "Monster" on *My Beautiful Dark Twisted Fantasy* (2010) and that is also a West-led production, provides a good example of this.

"Lights"'s beat includes six stems, which are introduced in a fairly straightforward additive sequence during the song's opening pre-chorus and hook (sung by Rihanna). Table I.1 visualizes what is audible: the instrumental adds a new part periodically until the last four measures of the hook realize the full instrumental track, which returns (except for the midrange "oooooh") for the entirety of the second and third instance of the song's hook. In this way, the additive process of introducing the stems also marks the large-scale form. The hook is where the

Table I.1 "ALL OF THE LIGHTS" PRE-CHORUS (M1–4)
AND OPENING HOOK (M5–16)

		Main Horns	Strings/Synth	Descant Horns	Kick + HiHat	Snares + "Woo!"	Midrange "ooooooh"
m1–2	1:09	■					
m3–4	1:16	■	■				
m5–8	1:23	■	■	■			
m9–12	1:36	■	■	■	■		■
m13–16	1:50	■	■	■	■	■	■

Table I.2 "ALL OF THE LIGHTS" FIRST VERSE (M17–24)
AND PRE-CHORUS (M25–28)

		Main Horns	Strings/Synth	Descant Horns	Kick + Hihat	Snare + "Woo!"	Midrange "ooooooh"
m17–20	2:03	■	■		■		
m21–24	2:17	■	■	■	■		
m25–28	2:30	■	■		■		

full instrumental plays alongside Rihanna's vocals. In contrast, Kanye's two verses are the territory of a pared-down instrumental that receives a small additive moment (the addition of the descant horns halfway through the verse) that pushes the song back toward the pre-chorus and hook (Table I.2).

In "Lights," the stemmed instrumental track works in conjunction with the large-scale form: we could follow the structure of the song even if we were listening to an isolated instrumental with no vocals. Theoretically, "Lights"'s isolatable stems *could* be combined in random ways, but they aren't. Instead, they follow a predictable pattern of additive build that leads from one section of the song to the next.

"Monster" is different. Though, as I show above, the form of the song is a familiar verse/hook alteration, that form is almost entirely inde-cipherable if we were to listen to the instrumental track on its own. "Monster"'s beat combines its stems in unpredictable ways, ultimately unsettling the form of the song. Table I.3b maps out the shifting combinations of the beat over the course of "Monster," pinpointing four primary stems, three of which sound in modified versions at various points in the song. The two stems heard most in the song—*kick* and *synth*—each

Table I.3a PERCUSSION OF "MONSTER" ("C" IS THE CYMBAL, AND "K" IS THE KICK DRUM)

	1	2	3	4	5	6	7	8	9	10	11	12	13	14	15	16
C					■								■			
K	■			■			■			■			■			

revolve around a modified clavé rhythm in a four-measure loop, while the cymbal and vocal loop fill in some of the leftover space. Table I.3a shows the percussion combo. Table I.3b shows "Monster"'s stems:

> *Kick*: four-measure loop; low resonance, like a thud; modified clavé rhythm (Table I.4a and b); background echoing midrange percussion figure.[4]
> *Cym*: crash cymbal on 2/4 of each measure.
> *Synth*: four-measure loop; combination of two synthesizer (synth) sounds; one (which dominates measure 1 (m1)&3) is crunchy and outlines a modified clave rhythm; the other (which dominates m2&4) is a rising figure that sounds like a mallet instrument.
> *VL*: four-measure vocal loop; indecipherable as speech.

The light gray sections of I.3b indicate an alteration of the instrumental, as described below.

- In all instances of light gray *Kick* with the exception of m120–27, the kick drum doesn't include the echoing midrange percussion hits that accompany the kick during the rest of the song.
- In m21–32, 49–51, and 53–60, *VL* isn't looped; instead only the downbeat of *VL* is played every fourth measure.
- In m100–102, only the downbeat of the synth is played every measure.
- In m120–27, a piano riff accompanies the kick; this section is longer on the album version than it is on the video version.

In addition to the stems shown in Table I.3b the instrumental is occasionally overlaid with applause (m6.4–8, 16.3–17, 32, 73–75.2, and 92.4–93.2) and periodically punctuated by a roar (end of epilogue and m68) or scream (end of epilogue), while a piano riff pipes up in the epilogue. Comparing I.1 and I.2 to I.3 shows that the sonic experience of "Monster" isn't as straightforward as listening to "Lights." After what seems like a formulaic

Table I.3b BEAT OF "MONSTER"

(Artist)		Kick	Cym	Synth	VL
Bon Iver	prologue				
R Ross	intr 1–4	■	■		
Kanye	hk 5–8	■		■	■
	hk 9–12	■	■	■	■
	v1 13–20	■	■	■	
	v1 21–32	■	■	■	■
	v1 33–36	■	■	■	
	v1 37–39	■	■	■	■
	v1 40	■	■	■	
	hk 41–48	■	■	■	■
Jay Z	v2 49–51	■		■	■
	v2 52	■	■	■	■
	v2 53–56	■	■	■	■
	v2 57–60	■		■	■
	v2 61–63	■	■	■	■
	v2 64	■	■	■	■
	v2 65–67	■		■	■
	v2 68	■	■	■	■
Kanye	hk 69–76	■		■	■
Nicki (R)	v3 77–80	■		■	■
	v3 81–84	■	■		
	v3 85–88	■			
(B) (R@91)	v3 89–92	■		■	
(R)	v3 93–96	■		■	
(B) (R@99)	v3 97–99	■		■	
(B)	v3 100–103	■		■	
(R)	v3 104–106	■			
	v3 107				
Instr	108–11	■	■	■	■
	112–13	■	■		■
	114–15	■			■
Bon Iver	epi 116–19	■	■		
	epi 120–27	■			

build (not unlike "Lights"'s) through the Rick Ross introduction and Kanye opening hook, the stems come and go rather mysteriously.

A few broad generalizations are possible, though. As the main percussive element, the kick drum persists in some form throughout the song except in instances when the entire instrumental track is dropped. The synth is the next most pervasive element. After laying out for the first eight measures of Kanye's and Jay Z's sections, it remains a steady part of the beat for each of them with the exception of eight measures in the middle of Jay Z's verse. In other words, the synth behaves as if it can only join the instrumental once it recognizes the rapper's flows. Meanwhile, both the vocal loop and cymbal hits come and go with little discernible rationale in the Kanye and Jay Z verses. Finally, though not identical, the last sixteen measures of both Kanye's and Jay Z's verses include a small build to the hook, and the hook includes all four stems each time it is sounded from m9 onward and at the beginning of the instrumental section at m108.

But when Nicki raps? The already slippery beat turns downright elusive. As with the first appearance of the other rappers, Minaj's run opens with no synth accompaniment. She launches into her verse alongside the kick drum, then the cymbal joins after four measures, but that's it. After another four, the instrumental reduces itself to just the kick again so that Minaj spits twelve bars—three times as many as Kanye and Jay Z open with—before the synth finally shows up. Here's where the alter egos matter, less because of who they are and more because of how they sound. It's at Minaj's thirteenth measure that she slides from Roman's deep, throaty voice to Barbie's light, breathy one. And wouldn't you know it? That's when the synth finds its entry, too. Neither last. Roman interrupts Barbie after three measures (m91), and the synth disappears shortly after. It makes one last attempt to glom onto the beat at m100 (at another Barbie section), but the effort is timid, as the synth can only be heard in clipped form on the downbeat of each measure. By the time Roman takes over again, all the instrumental can muster is six measures of the modified kick (no echoes) before the whole thing drops out for Minaj's final couplet. The vocal loop never manages a peep; it's in the hook just before and the instrumental just after Minaj's verse but nowhere in between.

In a song about monsters, Minaj proves the most monstrous of them all, cowing the beat and chasing off both the hook and her fellow rappers (they never come back). Certainly the instrumental proceeds with caution around the other rappers, all of whom, like Nicki, are self-proclaimed "motherfucking monster[s]." But when her voice hits the track, she destabilizes everything further. Why? Who are these monsters, and why does the instrumental relate to them differently?

Kanye and Jay Z are playing stock characters in a neoliberal white supremacist patriarchal farce. They are the rapacious black men who waste resources and require constant surveillance and, ultimately, punishment. Indeed, it's surveillance and punishment that guarantee their wastefulness can be transformed into wealth for white supremacy through militarized police forces and the prison industrial complex. This is familiar ground for Kanye, especially, whose œuvre frames him as a conspicuously consumed conspicuous consumer. As I've written elsewhere, Kanye and Jay Z would return to this general theme of surveilled and punished black masculinity a few months later on their collaborative album, *Watch the Throne* (2011). There, they bury ruminations on black masculine precarity under fantastic and often ridiculous caricatures of unchecked and insatiable appetites.

"Monster" is the dark side of those appetites, where verbal references to "rape, murder, and pillage," are overlaid with visuals of dead women littering the grim opulence of some horror movie's castle set. The rappers go unpunished for their misdeeds within the parameters of the video, but the level of surveillance they experience suggests imminent demise. The first time Kanye sings the hook, which opens with "gossip, gossip," his back is to a metal grate, as hands with blood red nails grope at his face and naked torso. Soon after, the vocal loop joins the beat, the indistinct voices from outside the castle plotting their way inside. Throughout the Kanye and Jay Z sections, "Monster" depicts black masculinity as, on the one hand, dangerous and, on the other, something that can be capitalized on. As Kanye reminds us in the other half of the hook, he's got "profit, profit," and the hands reaching through the gates, the angry villagers at the door, the voices organizing an assault outside—they move against the male rappers not just to claim vengeance but to seize their profits. The instrumental mirrors this pose: it reduces itself to a minimal combination of stems for each rapper's entrance (*kick* for Kanye, *kick* and modified *VL* for Jay Z), as if proceeding with caution because of the danger they pose. As Kanye and Jay Z become legible as black masculinity that can be plundered for "profit, profit," the instrumental track calls in all of its resources (its stems) and begins to circle and close in on the rappers, never moving uniformly or predictably, proceeding with care in the presence of monsters, only reaching full force in the hook, when Kanye ironically drops the constabulary line, "Ima need to see your fucking hands."

It's different with Minaj. The instrumental doesn't know how to proceed with her because her performance doesn't maintain the kind of legibility Kanye's and Jay Z's performances do. In Savannah Shange's analysis of Minaj's "strategically queer" performance of her gender and sexuality, she notes that Minaj's femme presentation is her most legible; in the words of rapper Cazwell, "People like a pretty girl no matter who she sleeps with" (Shange 2014, 39; Ganz 2010, 6). Indeed, it's in the moments when she is performing as Barbie that the "Monster" instrumental, which provides the synth to accompany the Barbie lines, begins to advance on her the way it did Kanye and Jay Z. She may be a pretty girl to her fans, but she's just another financializable black body to the profiteers at the gate.[5] The instrumental can't fully close in, though, because Roman, a black stud performance emanating from a femme body, is harder to place. Ultimately, Minaj allows her alter egos, especially the stud Roman and femme Barbie, to collapse on each other, as Shange details in her analysis of another Minaj track:

> On "Stupid Hoe," she uses a Roman-esque voice to tell Lil Kim to "suck my diznick," an insult congruent with the battle rap framing. Nicki's gender performance in the song takes a turn when in her "own" voice, or what she calls "Nicki" in her interviews, she belts out in a sugarsweet alto melody: "Oooh, dick in yo face, I put my dick in yo face, I put my dick in yo face, yeah!" (Maraj [Minaj] 2012). Because she sings in a very different register than the no-nonsense battle rapper who spits bars on "Beez in the Trap" and the rest of "Stupid Hoe," the "dick-in-yo-face" serenade emphasizes the juxtaposition between her polished, coy, femme presentation and hip hop's long-established discourse of fellatio as a tool of denigration, from the "deez nuts" era onward. Especially with such an extended, passionate riff, Nicki gives us time to imagine not only her having a dick, but putting it in our faces, thereby conjuring the queered queer scene of a black femme top whose sexual aggression belies the pillow princess archetype. (Shange 2014, 40)

The same transfer of persona occurs in "Monster" as Roman and Barbie don't so much interrupt each other as shift fluidly in and out of earshot. Minaj's run from Barbie starting in m89 and ending as Roman in m92 is a performance of gender unfixed enough to chase away the advancing *Synth* stem. The fluidity with which Minaj swaps out alter egos eventually results in a dropped bar. The phrase at m97 is only three measures long—the first two Barbie's, the last Roman's—and the disruption of the structural meter is such that when Barbie does take hold again at m100, the synth only feebly attempts to join in, landing on the downbeat for three measures before giving up entirely. Minaj's Roman/Barbie trans-performance has left the structure of the song and the work of the instrumental unintelligible, and all that's left over her final four measures is the bare kick drum.

Minaj's queer performance in "Monster" marks her as illegible. The advancing instrumental that carefully, in starts and stops but with ultimate conviction, comes for Kanye and Jay Z can't make heads or tails of Minaj. In fact, while Barbie's voice seems to resonate in a range audible to the hostile ears at the gate, Roman's, in the moments of transfer from one persona to the other, only registers long enough to scare away the instrumental, then vibrates the rest of his verse queerly out of earshot. Minaj is a monster; so is Kanye, and so is Jay Z. But in "Monster," Kanye and Jay Z perform a monstrosity that is legible enough to be pulled into neoliberal capital, their surveillance, containment, and possible deaths all profitable to the mainstream. Minaj, meanwhile, in "*claiming* the monstrosity" that Hortense Spillers traces through African-American configurations rooted in New World slavery, "places her[self] . . . *out* of the traditional symbolics of female gender" (Spillers 1987, 80).

OVERVIEW

This is a book not just about monsters but about the broader social population made up of monsters and others who place themselves out of traditional symbolics: it's a book about the posthuman. Where most writing about the posthuman, especially in relation to popular music, revolves around human-technology hybridity, I theorize posthumanity along the same lines that I analyze Minaj in "Monster." Following critical race and queer theory, *Posthuman Rap* defines the posthuman not in relation to or as an evolution of liberal humanism but as—and these words from Sylvia Wynter guide this project more than any other words do—a way of existing "completely outside our present conception of what it is to be human" (Wynter in Scott 2000, 136). The result isn't anything definitive, a closed category called "posthuman" that is easily identifiable or authenticated. Rather, I pursue here a narrow argument about how posthumanity is sounded especially in rap subgenres. Following Eve Sedgwick, I'd call it primarily "weak theory," as my case studies are embedded in a set of genre aesthetics that condition specific kinds of performance so that resonating out of earshot, as Minaj manages in "Monster," doesn't boil down to a single musical strategy repeatable across a broad selection of musical genres (Sedgwick 1997, 11–13).

Still, the book's argument hangs on some fixed theoretical points that work in concert with the sonic aesthetics I analyze in the case studies. Chapter 1 establishes these theoretical tent poles. Posthuman is inextricably tied to notions of "human," and I start from this observation in order to critique posthuman literature that, even as—and, in fact, because—it attempts to pull away from the gravity of liberal humanism, often simply reinforces all of liberal humanism's problems in its configurations of the posthuman. I turn from there to other possible humanisms, especially

Sylvia Wynter's "embattled humanism," as a way to think about posthumanism specifically as a move "completely outside our present conception of what it is to be human." That present conception? For Wynter, it's Man1 and Man2, the latter of which I call neoliberal humanism. Neoliberal humanism defines subjects according to their ability to be formed according to market logic; it defines the human as one whose very existence funnels capital back to white supremacist cisheteropatriarchy (think white straight dudes desperate to protect their power), to the powers that be and have always been. The result is a posthumanism found in the exceptions to neoliberalism's market logic, those who don't produce and reproduce as they should and who, following Weheliye's theory of *habeas viscus*, vibrate queerly out of range, like Minaj's performance in "Monster."

Chapters 2–4 then put this theorization into action. If illegibility is a marker of the posthuman, then legible politics are likely to be entrenched in mainstream discourse in a way that ultimately locks power and resources in a feedback loop that feeds those who already have a good deal of power and resources. In Chapter 2, I consider the problematic nature of legible politics by reading a strain of public reception of rapper Kendrick Lamar. Chapter 2 is light on music analysis precisely because the reception of Kendrick as a political rapper hinges primarily on his lyrics. I read this reception alongside Lester Spence's work on black parallel publics and Jared Sexton's theory of contemporary multiracialism. Spence's analysis of hip hop is a historical one, as his catalog spans 1989–2004, and I use the reception of Kendrick as a way of expanding Spence's work to apply to contemporary music. The structure of Kendrick's black parallel public matches Spence's theory, but the details of how that parallel public works have shifted since 2004. Specifically, I place Sexton's theory of multiracialism in the context of post-race ideology to hear the ways Kendrick's ostensibly black radical lyrics are received as the impetus to dissolve black solidarity in favor of an anti-black multiracialism. It's Kendrick's easy legibility as political that results in his music being put to work for neoliberal humanist purposes.

Having examined Kendrick as an example of how a parallel public functions in concert with neoliberal market logic, I turn to trap in Chapter 3. Trap, I argue, is the exception to Kendrick's parallel public, the performance of sonic blackness that registers as either apolitical, scary, or both. Here I think with Nina Sun Eidsheim and Loren Kajikawa regarding the way trap sounds a certain kind of blackness and, along the way, lay down an account of trap's sonic aesthetics. In contrast to Kendrick's readily received politics, trap resonates outside of political discourse and, through a series of performative ironies, stakes out space for the posthuman, "outside the ground of the orthodox body of knowledge" (Wynter in Scott 2000, 136).

Chapter 4 considers what might fill this space, what unorthodox bodies might build on this unorthodox ground. Listening to Rae Sremmurd and their penchant for partying in the context of ongoing state-sanctioned violence against black bodies, I argue that the rap duo's club is a posthuman vestibule, attached to the world of neoliberal humanism and un-naïvely aware of the dangers inherent in that attachment, but also offering the possibility of existing outside of that dangerous world. L.H. Stallings fuels much of my analysis of queer performances that happen in black clubs and black strip clubs like the one Rae Sremmurd build, and by returning to the sonic aesthetics mapped in Chapter 3 and welcoming Nicki Minaj back into the mix, we're able to hear how they party in a way that doesn't work the way it's supposed to, and, in so doing, create the possibility of a posthuman existence apart from neoliberal humanism.

Posthuman Rap is an argument that builds from cover to cover. I've written each chapter so that it can be sectioned off from the rest and read with a focus on the discrete argument contained in it. But these aren't chapters that are individual case studies falling under the umbrella of posthumanism. Rather, each builds on the previous one so that the book should best function if it is read in sequence, as a journey that lands us in Rae Sremmurd's club, a posthuman vestibule where we can party more freely and hear the music more clearly if we've travelled through the rest of the book to get there. The cover-to-cover argument narrows the scope of what's in *Posthuman Rap*. Though we'll listen to a good deal of music and trace the history of many of the sounds that make trap so trappy, there are also some really worthwhile pursuits related to the topic that would prove to be excursions that take me too far off the path leading to Rae Sremmurd's club and which are therefore not included here.

For instance, Chapter 2 focuses on Kendrick Lamar, whose music has become a touchstone for social consciousness movements like #blacklivesmatter and who works at the intersection of a number of genres whose sonic combination produces fascinating results. A comprehensive analysis of Kendrick Lamar is necessary, and, in fact, I anticipate that hip hop studies and related disciplines will provide rich and numerous analyses of his music in the coming years. While Chapter 2 should contribute to that discourse, it isn't and doesn't try to be (and couldn't be, given the length) a comprehensive analysis itself. Rather, I am focused in Chapter 2 on a particular thread of discourse *surrounding* Kendrick, as that discourse is part of the geographic context of Rae Sremmurd's posthuman club. Chapter 2, then, doesn't include analysis of Kendrick's music or a sympathetic account of what kind of useful political work his music might do, not because those aren't important but because they don't contribute to the argument I'm building in *Posthuman*

Rap. Elsewhere, I've written about posthumanism (*JMHP* 2014; *Sounding Out!* 2014) and embattled humanism (*Shima* 2016) and plan to continue working with the theoretical framework posthumanism affords. My publications on this topic so far began their lives as ideas in *Posthuman Rap* but proved outside the scope of the book's narrow argument. The book is not a comprehensive account of posthumanism or a comprehensive account of the music and musicians included here; there's tons more to say. My first graduate advisor, Nanette de Jong, is an ethnomusicologist, and she explained her approach to her work to me as being part of a larger ethnomusicological project. That larger project she described as a building, and her work would be a brick here or some mortar there that contributed meaningfully to the structure but would best make that contribution if she remained keenly aware that what she was doing was never the building, just a piece of it. I love that analogy and have held onto it ever since. And in the spirit of any good trapper, I have a brick to sell you.

There's a good deal of music analysis in this book. Not every reader will have the music theory background to follow a few of the finer points, but I use visuals that are intended to make the analysis accessible to a broad readership, and I bookend the more detailed analysis with a summary of what's happening that is also meant to provide accessibility for a variety of readers. My approach to analysis is the result of musicological training that I'm putting to use in an interdisciplinary context. I think sound is important, so I talk about it whenever I can, sometimes in technical music theory terms but often with descriptive language that is meant to capture the experience of the sound that makes sense to music specialists and non-specialists alike. The musical elements I focus on most in my analysis are *timbre, texture, rhythm, frequency,* and *structure.* Timbre describes what a sound sounds like; it's why you know a trumpet is a trumpet without seeing it. Texture describes the combination of several timbres together, and my primary interest in rhythm in popular music analysis involves identifying patterns as they repeat and change across a song or a genre. Frequency has to do with pitch, but I don't tend to do as much work with melody and harmony as I would if this were a book about classical music. Instead, I think about frequency in terms of ranges: low, middle, and high. Finally,

Table I.4a STANDARD CLAVÉ RHYTHM

1	2	3	4	5	6	7	8	9	10	11	12	13	14	15	16
■			■			■				■		■			

Table I.4b STANDARD CLAVÉ RHYTHM CONTRASTED WITH KICK DRUM FIGURE IN "MONSTER"

	1	2	3	4	5	6	7	8	9	10	11	12	13	14	15	16
clavé	▓			▓			▓				▓		▓			
"Monster"	▓			▓			▓			▓					▓	

structure refers to the way a song is organized, how we get from the beginning to the middle to the end. You'll find these terms in the book some, but more than that, you'll find me discussing sound without explicit reference to these five elements. Hopefully this brief guide will prove helpful for readers who haven't done exactly this kind of analysis before.

It's not just an interdisciplinary audience that shapes my analysis; the critical theorist in me finds it important to listen in a social and political context. This means that I try not to include musical observations—no matter how nerdily gleeful they might make me—that don't directly intersect with the social and political argument I'm advancing here. The result is an argument that depends on both political and sonic evidence to hold up. Sound, in this context, doesn't just exist, waiting for someone to hear it; it *does work*. My discussion of the sonic aesthetics of trap in Chapter 3 is the most obvious instance of this approach in the book, as the sounds of trap aren't just something to bump to but an integral part of a posthumanist project that builds an existence outside of neoliberal humanism.

So this is a book about one kind of posthumanism and the way we might hear it in contemporary rap music that often isn't perceived to have much depth or purpose. It's rooted not in technological hybridities or the cyborgs and androids that are so often synonymous with the posthuman; rather, it's grounded in critical race and queer theories and takes as its task the outlining of a way of being in the world that does not entail a permanent relationship with systems of oppression, violent figurations of the human, and institutions that mean you harm. Please make sure all gold teeth and fangs are securely fastened, and let's hear how monstrous we can be.

CHAPTER 1

Posthuman

"Completely Outside Our Present Conception of What It Is to Be Human"

I didn't want to go for what I call a cheap and easy radicalism.
Sylvia Wynter *(Scott 2000, 158)*

The prefix "post" often obscures as much as it clarifies. Perhaps because we like to use them so much, words that start with "post" can be vague and misleading. Postmodern, postracial, postsoul—they seem to arise in moments of change, beginning life as chronological markers (when "post" just means "after this other thing") before entrenching. Soon enough, they're conceptual terms we're stuck with, regardless of the ultimate relationship between "post" and the word that follows. Scholars and cultural critics then face the never-ending task of piecing everything together, determining what a given "post" term does (and doesn't do) even as the concept continues to emerge as so many cultural practices.

These "post" terms often stick, though, for good reason (Appiah 1991, 341–42). The coupling of history (where "post" means "after") and material practice (whether, say, modernity, coloniality, structuralism) can help us tune into the matter at hand without letting past, present, and future alternatives get out of earshot. "Post" terms remind us of what has been and what else there might be. At the limits of "post" terms, which fail to definitively name a set of practices and instead gesture toward a bunch of activities and concepts that seem to fit together with each other but not seamlessly with what came before, we can critique the systems in which these histories and practices try to adhere. In this way, "post" terms are like sticky notes, little brightly colored markers we leave across the social landscape to let us know where we need to come and think for a bit.

This book responds to the call of just such a sticky note about one of those "post" terms—posthuman. Posthuman theory is nothing new, and like other "post" terms posthuman often points in a number of different directions at one time. Such variability in meaning is no surprise; after all, what posthuman means depends quite a bit on what one's idea of human is. While many use posthuman simply to refer to a state of being that embellishes and extends the human body through technological means, this particular notion captures only a fraction of the term's potential. Robocops and androids may be posthuman—smartphone users and drones, too— but not only because they represent a blending of human and technology. A more robust account of the posthuman includes not only physical but also cultural and social dimensions of what it has meant to be human (and, of course, decades of feminist, critical race, and queer theory have shown the physical is itself culturally determined). Specifically, posthumanity, at its best, critiques and redresses the more traditional constructions of human that have historically privileged whiteness, masculinity, heterosexuality, capitalism, and able-bodied-ness over other dispositions, constructions that have left many on the periphery of humanity if not locked out altogether. I say "at its best" because I want to be clear from the outset: I'm interested in a very specific kind of posthumanity—the kind that makes the world less violent for those who aren't white, those who are queer, those who are expected to remain at or beyond the margins of society. So as we listen together to recent rap music in the pages of this book, I'll be critical of the strands of posthuman discourse that recenter white ableist cisheteropatriarchy, that fail to account for the work of women of color, that place faith in traditional regimes that route power and privilege and resources to some (remember the white ableist cisheteropatriarchy from before?) and away from others.

At the same time, I listen to and engage rap as popular music in this book not only to critique problematic constructions of the posthuman but also to tune into posthuman discourse and practice that reconsiders or altogether turns away from traditional assumptions about the boundaries and the limits of human-ness. The posthumanity that I'll constantly foreground is that which intersects with feminism, critical race theory, post- and anticoloniality, queer theory, and Afrofuturity. This is purposefully not an account of all the kinds of posthumanism there are, as I don't have the space to deal with all of them, and some are just Descartes and Kant dressed up for robot prom. Rather, what I'm interested in here is the kind of posthumanity that actively reconstructs what has long been a violently restrictive category: human.

RECONSTRUCTION

Reconstructing systems with violent histories can be a fool's errand. One must give time and energy to a concept that means you harm, must turn toward a totalizing force and pay it the attention it craves, must busy oneself with the work always asked of women and queer people and people of color: explain to the dominant culture what is so patriarchal/white supremacist/heteronormative about that culture, then suggest how to do it better. A reconstruction project risks recentering the oppressive system it's working against. Which is, in fact, why systems of violence and oppression invite critique from those they violently oppress: hegemony grows more hegemonic when critiques of it fall short (Sexton 2008, 12–13). One response to this is to say, well, screw it.

Middle fingers in the air at humanity could certainly follow from something like what Alexander Weheliye sketches in his discussion of Toni Morrison's *Beloved*: "once your animal characteristics have been measured against human ones in the pages of the plantation ledger, desiring the particular image of humanity on the other side of this very ledger seems, to put it mildly, futile" (2002, 24). Note that it isn't the achievement of this particular image of humanity that's futile but the very desire: it's easy enough to be that basic, but what's the point of wanting to be? This question gets at the underlying disposition of a good deal of posthuman and related theories, including antihumanism and Afrofuturism. While the latter, like Morrison, critiques humanism from a position of blackness—or treats it as "the other side of this very ledger," as Weheliye puts it—the former often proceeds as a critique from within, antihumanism voiced by those humanism often actually recognizes as human.

Like posthumanism, antihumanism isn't a singular field of thought but rather sprawls across several different philosophical movements, each taking aim at the liberal humanist subject from a different vantage point. My goal here isn't to sketch out a history of antihumanism. Rather, I want to work specifically at the intersection of humanism, antihumanism, and posthumanism. A helpful starting point is Rosi Braidotti's overview of antihumanism in her book, *The Posthuman* (2013). Because her ultimate aim is to demonstrate the continuities and fissures between antihumanism and posthumanism, a close read can expose some assumptions that embed themselves in critiques from within. Specifically, Braidotti's post-humanism is what I'm calling a Eurocentric model (apparent in writing from N. Katherine Hayles, Donna Haraway, and Karen Barad, among others), which I argue recenters the liberal humanist subject in its efforts to dismantle it.

Braidotti, while indebted to the academic tradition of antihumanism, finds it ultimately lacking in its ability to decenter the liberal humanist subject. As Braidotti traces the contours of a variety of antihumanist perspectives, she notes that what holds these antihumanisms together is a critique but not "complete rejection" of humanist thought and value (2013, 30). This amounts to what I mention above: a turn to that which means you violence in order to give it the attention it craves. For Braidotti, antihumanism simply positions itself in binary opposition to humanism, creating a system that will always wash out in favor of the always already hegemonic (white, able-bodied, cishetero). Posthumanism, grandly and optimistically for Braidotti, "marks the end" of this binary in order to fashion new alternatives unsurprisingly indebted to poststructuralism, postmodernity, postcolonialism, and a host of other "post"s that emphasize complexity over duality (37). Still, Braidotti's Eurocentric posthumanism is deeply rooted in antihumanism, and, perhaps because of this, her construct of the posthuman similarly recenters liberal humanism despite its efforts not to.

Let's go back to this idea, with slight changes: what posthumanism and antihumanism mean depends quite a bit on what one's idea of humanism is. Though Braidotti acknowledges that a variety of humanisms exist, she only squarely deals with the kind of humanism that traces through Protagoras, da Vinci, Descartes, Kant, Hegel—the kind of humanism that defines the Enlightenment subject, shapes liberal democracies, colonizes the globe, and defines "not-human" at least as passionately as "human": liberal humanism. Certainly this kind of humanism aspires to be a totalizing force, covering over, colonizing, and eradicating any other notions of the human that may exist. One problem with Braidotti's account is that she *allows* this totalization: "Complicitous with genocides and crimes on the one hand, supportive of enormous hopes and aspirations to freedom on the other, Humanism somehow defeats linear criticism. This protean quality is partly responsible for its longevity" (2013, 16). Beyond pointing out the vast difference between the tangible terror of genocide and the relatively vague notion of "hopes and aspirations to freedom," I might add that granting liberal humanism this much power also contributes to its longevity. In fact, a cornerstone of this book is the belief that "hopes and aspirations to freedom"—as well as any material realization of them—are the result of humanisms other than liberal humanism. For now, I want to point to Braidotti's tendency to privilege liberal humanism as she critiques from within, sketch out some antihumanist "critiques from without" that draw on critical race and queer theories, then consider the kind of alternative humanism that is embedded in the work of Sylvia Wynter (which overlaps significantly with the humanist theories of Sartre, de Beauvoir, Fanon, and Foucault). This intersection of humanisms and antihumanisms is where I'll situate the book's discussion of popular music and posthuman theory.

ANTIHUMANISMS

Braidotti opens *The Posthuman* by troubling liberal humanism, observing that not everyone is now or has been before human—"that creature familiar to us from the Enlightenment and its legacy" (1). Her goal in highlighting the limits of liberal humanism, though, isn't to point to other kinds of humanism that have always countered or simply existed outside of liberal humanism's reach, but to suggest that posthumanism is a *progression through and past* liberal humanism: "after the postmodern, the post-colonial, the post-industrial, the post-communist and even the much contested post-feminist conditions, we seem to have entered the post-human predicament" (1). This mirrors N. Katherine Hayles's 1999, *How We Became Posthuman*. Braidotti and Hayles each position the posthuman as something that emerges or evolves from liberal humanism; it's an advanced state of existence that improves upon the past, a harder/better/faster/stronger approach to ontology.

The teleological bent of Braidotti's and Hayles's posthumanism presents two main problems. First, it recenters the liberal humanist subject. If posthumanity is primarily a way of configuring oneself *after* liberal humanism, then those who enjoyed privilege as liberal humanist subjects will have first dibs on posthuman privilege, too. This is the crux of post-identity politics: 1) invite a select few groups who have traditionally experienced violence or oppression at the hands of a dominant institution (like patriarchy or white supremacy or liberal humanism) to enjoy new access to privilege, then 2) use that new access to praise the generosity and progressiveness of the dominant institution, while 3) doubling down on violence and oppression directed at those who aren't part of the select few groups. In crediting liberal humanism with "hopes and aspirations to freedom," Braidotti—and the Eurocentric model more broadly—sets up liberal humanism as the source of what counts as good in posthumanism. Which leads to the second main problem of a teleological posthumanism: it overlooks alternative humanisms that have always pulled away from, pushed against, or existed with complete apathy for liberal humanism. Specifically I want to consider here the collection of artistic and theoretical work that can be combined under the heading of Afrofuturity alongside the kind of queer world-making envisioned in Lee Edelman's *No Future*, each of which function as a kind of antiliberal-humanism. I'll conclude this section by turning toward the work of Sylvia Wynter to map out an alternative humanism and consider how posthumanism might be located within the humanist/antihumanist/alternative humanist nexus.

If Eurocentric antihumanism and posthumanism work *through* liberal humanism, Afrofuturism and some queer antihumanisms push squarely *against* it. Afrofuturism, a term Mark Dery coined in the early 90s but that encompasses a multimedia tradition that precedes the term and that has been theorized extensively—most notably by Alondra Nelson—since, works with some familiar tropes but often to unfamiliar ends (Dery 1993). Mark Sinker captures this in his rumination on Sun Ra's account of alien abduction (1992, 30–31). Where most who have been abducted by aliens return to Earth with purpose—this is the classic sci-fi self-satisfying fantasy, a white Jesus, armed with the knowledge of an alien race, saves the world and gets the girl (in no particular order)—Sinker notes that, in Ra's own telling, he politely declines the aliens' request to save Earth. Tellingly, Ra seems completely sold on the aliens' description of Earth as a deeply messed-up place; he just swerves a bit, choosing instead of saving Earth to gather a few like-minded friends and split. Sun Ra's music, his mythology, his lifelong performance all lead back to this basic premise: [surveys Earth, turns to whomever can hear] "Look at this dump. Let's get out of here."

And this impulse to get out is at the heart of much Afrofuturism. Writing in the wake of the June 2015 mass murder in a Charleston, South Carolina, AME church, Chris Taylor notes, "The future of a white politics is the undoing of any futurity, the dissolution of the world" (Taylor 2015). Antihumanism has, time and again, identified the ways liberal humanism is synonymous with (cisheteropatriarchal) white supremacy, and though Taylor wasn't speaking directly of Afrofuturity, his point resonates with Afrofuturism all the same: a black future must be forged apart from whiteness, apart from liberal humanism, apart from whatever concept of "human" stood on the so-called master's side of the plantation ledger. Or, to borrow from Kodwo Eshun, "The human is a pointless and treacherous category" (1998, 00–005). Because of this treachery, instead of fighting against liberal humanism, instead of rebuilding the human, instead of aspiring to be human, Afrofuturism works *against* liberal humanism in the way a rocket's engine pushes one out of orbit: liberal humanism is simply the leaving ground for blasting into space, to some more hospitable abode. The point isn't to attack and thereby risk recentering liberal humanism but to exit its gravity, to leave and never come back. If some liberal humanist Earth is scorched during takeoff, so be it.

Lee Edelman's *No Future* is a queer antihumanism that pushes against liberal humanism in a different way. While Afrofuturism looks for a way out, NoFuturism (that's my term; please don't blame Edelman) digs in. In the interest of "redefin[ing] such notions as 'civil order' through a rupturing of our foundational faith in the reproduction of futurity," Edelman figures queerness as a way of operating within a political system of white ableist cisheteropatriarchy in order to constantly disrupt and negate from within (2004, 17). Recognizing the Child as the symbol of the liberal humanist future, Edelman configures queerness so that it functions in direct opposition to this future. Queerness, then, embodies a death drive. If Afrofuturism launches itself out of liberal humanism's gravity, NoFuturism propels itself to the center of liberal humanist ideology, ironically occupying social and political space in ways that don't reproduce, that undercut the future, that rupture liberal humanism from the inside out.

To this cluster of antihumanisms, I want to add what Sylvia Wynter calls "embattled humanism." In this nexus—the overlap of Eurocentric antihumanism and posthumanism, Afrofuturism, NoFuturism, and embattled humanism—I will nestle the theory of the posthuman that I'll explore while listening to rap in the pages of this book.

EMBATTLED HUMANISM

In my original proposal for this book (as a matter of fact, no, you may not read it), I framed posthumanism in completely antihumanist terms. Liberal humanism, I reasoned, is bankrupt, a system that withholds the category of the human for a very few, extends some privileges of that category to a few more, and extracts those privileges through horrific violence all while hiding behind some abstractions about freedom. Any worthwhile notion of posthumanity, I argued, would run as far away from *that* as (post)humanly possible. I was maybe kinda right; it depends on what your definition of "*that*" is.

In preparing this manuscript, I found myself returning time and again to Sylvia Wynter's insistence on the term "human."[1] Wynter clearly has no use for liberal humanism, but her work is nonetheless devoted to the ontological category of the human. It's this insistence that points to a gap in Braidotti's account of liberal humanism and antihumanism; it's this insistence that calls race, especially, into an intersectional account of the (post)human; it's this insistence that undermines liberal humanism's totalizing claims; it's this insistence that resonates with the kind of existentialism Sartre and Beauvoir theorized; and it's this insistence that means a full account of the posthuman can't just pull from antihumanism. There are different kinds of humanism—a straightforward enough point, sure, but one that manages to elude most writing on posthumanism nonetheless.

In mapping out one different kind of humanism—existential humanism—Sartre appeals to the category of the human as the only one we have: "The only universe that exists is the human one—the universe of human subjectivity" (2007, 52). Like antihumanists, Sartre finds nothing worthwhile in liberal humanism. His appeal to the category of the human is not so much as one that is immanently worthwhile but just the one we have by virtue of a shared ontological condition. Braidotti, in *The Posthuman*, pulls humans together under the umbrella of species—a move similar to Paul Gilroy's "planetary humanism," which sheds identity politics in favor of a species-oriented sameness (Will Smith alien-fighting films receive understated approval) (Gilroy 2000, 17, 366). In defining the posthuman as "a qualitative shift in our thinking about what exactly is the basic unit of common reference for our species, our polity and our relationship to the other inhabitants of this planet," though, Braidotti again casts the posthuman as teleological (it's a *shift*), as proceeding from a kind of humanism (specifically, liberal humanism) that she describes too monolithically (2013, 2). Sartre's appeal to a shared ontological condition is in the interest of mapping nonliberal humanisms; Braidotti's appeal to species actually overlooks these other kinds of humanisms.

One of Sartre's primary goals in "Existentialism is a Humanism" is to unsettle the reliance of humanity on an outside arbiter, to map out how nontheism can produce ethical relationships and how the absence of deity from the ontology of humanity is essential to these ethics. This nontheism is a crucial move because it undermines one of the foundations of liberal humanism: a theologically based teleology that makes the human seem like a fixed category, a prescriptive one. Instead of teleology, Sartre sketches existential humanism as always moving toward "a future that is waiting to be created—a virgin future" (29–30). Existential humanism, then, is humanism because human subjectivity is the only way humans perceive the world. The connection among humans isn't a sociocultural imperative, as liberal humanism demands (for instance, the experience of whiteness is taken as standard in liberal humanism) but a way of existing as a particular type of animal. Splitting the species from the social and cultural allows existential humanism to imagine different ways of being human that don't take liberal humanism as the starting point.

Of course, the liberal humanist subject is no longer actually theological by the late 20th century, even if that late 20th century liberal humanist still pays lip service to theology in the interest of political expedience. Sylvia Wynter, theorizing from a position of anti- and post-coloniality, points to a different cultural imperative that Man uses to bind the species together:

> Now, up until the end of the eighteenth century in the West, the conception was primarily *political*; up until the fifteenth century it was primarily *religious*. What I'm saying is that it is the bioeconomic conception of the human that we inscript and institute by means of our present disciplines and their epistemic order, as Foucault shows so incisively, that determines the hegemony of the *economic* system over the social and political systems—even more, that mandates the functioning of the capitalist mode of production as the everyday expression of that hegemony. (Scott 2000, 160)

It isn't religion or politics that is the blunt instrument of Man but late capitalism. Wynter sketches here a rough overview of neoliberal biopolitics, where all actions—including being alive—are reduced to rational economic decisions. Here, money and power and privilege route back to ableist cisheteropatriarchal white supremacy not by means of overt theft and genocide, as the Western colonizers did it, but by setting the background conditions of the economy so that those who have always had power and money will attract more simply by "playing by the rules" (Fraser 2014, 60–62). This is neoliberal humanism, updated strategies to uphold the power dynamics of the old system, and I'll come back to it in the next section.

For now, I want to focus on the need to grapple with history and its ramifications head-on, as this is what sticks for Wynter, what causes her to return over and again to the category of the human. She doesn't fault capitalism itself with the imbalance of power but the discourses that institute, regulate, and normalize neoliberal biopolitics, that give it its mandate. Here, again, I want to note a subtle but crucial departure from Braidotti's anti- and posthumanism. Where Braidotti frames liberal humanism as *actually totalizing*, Wynter, by way of highlighting the discourses surrounding late capitalism, suggests that even if Man "overrepresents itself as if it were the human itself," *it doesn't have to be this way*, that a different way of talking about and framing the human is possible—in Wynter's words, a way that is different from "the normative order of the present organization of knowledge"—that liberal humanism isn't actually totalizing (2003, 260; 1984, 38). In her analysis of Glissant, Wynter gathers his major themes around a discursive uprising.

> I want to propose here that this uprising is directed not only at our present order of discourse and its founding Word of Man, as the word of the human conceptualized as a selected being and natural organism, but also at the tradition of discourse to which its specific discourse of Man belongs: that is, at the tradition on whose basis, from 1512 onward, Western Europe was to effect the first stage in the secularization of human existence in the context of its own global expansion and to lay the basis of the plantation structure out of which the contemporary societies of Glissant's Antilles, as well as the specificity of their Antilleanity, as he insists and reinsists, was to emerge. (1989, 639)

It's a revolution that doesn't demand to be assimilated into existing power structures but rather dismantles the way people understand and talk about the world—not only in the present moment but back to the historic roots of that understanding and talk—that allows those power structures to exist. Like existentialist humanism, Wynter's embattled humanism slices the cultural imperative away from the species in order to stake a claim in *a* humanism that isn't just a teleological evolution of liberal humanism. For Glissant, it was the liberal humanist subject that had to be removed to make way for an alternate kind of humanism; for posthumanism, it's the neoliberal humanist subject that gets cut.

Why mess with a word like "human" at all? The short answer is the same reduction we could make of existentialist humanism: that's the only word, the only framework we've got. Importantly, in Wynter's work, this idea is shaped by her own experience of colonial politics. Citing Mais, Césaire, and Fanon, Wynter describes the postcolony as exactly that—a place that used to be a colony and must be reckoned with as such: "you know that you cannot turn your back on that which the West has brought in since the fifteenth century. It's transformed the world, and central to that has been humanism. But it's also that humanism against which Fanon writes ... so that is embattled [humanism], one which challenges itself at the same time that you're using it to think with" (Scott 2000, 154). The point here isn't that there is intrinsic value in humanism; rather, it is simply a historical fact that humanism has shaped the past, present, and foreseeable future. It is a *part* (not a totalizing whole) of what made a colony a colony and what makes a postcolony a postcolony. Elsa Goveia, in excoriating an Eric Williams book, stresses this same idea in outlining a social/cultural/historical study of "the white colonists, the free people of colour and the negro slaves as joint participants in a human situation that shaped all of their lives" (1964, 51). Liberal humanism, in this case, is part of that equation; it sets, for instance, this term "human" that we are left to grapple with. It isn't, importantly, the whole equation, though, since "all of [slavery's] complexity" admits other ways of being human, other humanisms. What Goveia and Wynter point to is a question that runs through subaltern studies: how to speak and think of oneself when the words and the education are fashioned by Man? Embattled humanism is an ongoing grappling with this question, where the battle is "the central ethnoclass Man vs Human struggle" (2003, 261). The reason Wynter settles on any kind of humanism at all has to do with her assessment of late capitalist discourses.

If neoliberal biopolitics sets economic background conditions so that money and power flow to those who have always had it, and if this economic ontology is propped up and enabled by discourses that permeate cultural, political, and—and this last point is especially crucial in Wynter's work—educational venues, then one significant piece of power that Man wields is the ability to determine which discourses count (and, by extension, which discourses don't).[2] One needn't tangle with Man to establish a new discourse of being human—indeed, a great many humanisms exist that don't care what Man thinks. But if you want some of Man's stuff? Say, the resources that increase your chances of living outside prison walls? Or of surviving an altercation with police, who are otherwise empowered by the state to execute people in the street? Or of living free from a social imperative that requires you to suffer in order to be legible? Well, that requires a confrontation. So the slightly longer answer to why mess with "human" at all is that economic power yields material results, and when those results are devastatingly violent for so many, not only is a new discourse required but also a reckoning of how power is distributed through liberal humanism's use of the word "human."

A reductive but useful explanation of embattled humanism is this two-pronged approach:

1) Be human in a way that can exist apart from liberal humanism. No teleology or evolution, please: if the starting point is liberal humanism, or if neoliberal humanism is centered by this discourse, then it's a nonstarter.
2) Dissolve neoliberal humanism so that it can't choke off other ways of being human.

The two prongs are dependent on one another but not the same: 1 doesn't acknowledge Man, while 2 squarely faces him. Antihumanism works as an evolution of liberal humanism, while Afrofuturism busies itself with 1, and NoFuturism is concerned primarily with 2. But embattled humanism folds together the goals of Afrofuturist (be human separate from Man) and NoFuturist (disrupt the systems that support Man) sorts of discourses. Keeping the two prongs separate ensures the safety of one should the other fail: one can be a different kind of human even if liberal humanism persists. This overlap is crucial for the way I situate the posthuman in *Posthuman Rap*.

NEOLIBERAL HUMANISM

So all these things—Eurocentric antihumanism, Afrofuturism, NoFuturism, existential humanism, embattled humanism—these are ontologies that fashion a different human than the one liberal humanism conjures. As I outline in the previous section, each employs distinct strategies and can be situated in differing relationships to liberal humanism (should one so choose to situate, but part of the point is why bother doing anything in service of liberal humanism), and it's the not-liberal-humanism part of each that are pertinent to this book. That's where these ontologies pool together—think of it as the overlapping section of a Venn diagram—and where posthumanisms thrive.

This is the part of the book where I'm supposed to define posthumanism for you. The problem is as I stated it above, though: one's concept of the posthuman depends on one's concept of the human. And here I've gathered a few humanisms together so that we can swim out into the mix and hear what bubbles up. In other words, a firm definition isn't coming. Wait! Don't put the book down! Rather, in *Posthuman Rap* I approach the posthuman as a series of possibilities that remain speculative, open, audible in the musical examples collected here without coalescing into anything prescriptive. My approach to the posthuman is heavily indebted to Wynter's conceptualization of "ontological sovereignty."

> Now, we know about political sovereignty, especially with the rise of the state. We know about economic sovereignty, with the dominance of the free market all over the world, together with its economic organization of reality. We do *not* know about something called *ontological* sovereignty. And I'm being so bold as to say that in order to *speak* the conception of ontological sovereignty, we would have to move completely outside our present conception of what it is to be human, and therefore outside the ground of the orthodox body of knowledge which institutes and reproduces such a conception." (136)

The problem, of course, is that "mov[ing] completely outside our present conception of what it is to be human" or "outside the ground of the orthodox body of knowledge" isn't exactly easy. The notion that we live in a world so deeply messed up that we cannot even name the extent of its fuckedness is central to much critical theory. Wynter gestures toward this idea in her constant return to education, which determines the parameters of what we can and can't know and, like social media "like" buttons, consistently encourages us to accept what we have as good enough, to forget what the alternatives might be, and to always perform in service of strengthening the parameters that limit us in the first place.[3] Stuart Hall, in "Media Power" (1974), identifies a similar constriction of the boundaries of discourse in his critique of political media, which often present two opposing sides in order to give viewers the impression that they are in the midst of a full debate, even as those two opposing sides benefit from and strengthen each other while pushing all other possible positions off-screen, deleting them from the page, muting them in the mix. This is precisely the bind I've discussed throughout this chapter so far: how to step outside of a discourse or ontology that aspires to totalization? Or, as Adorno describes the work of music, how do we create "schemata of the known for what has never been" (2006, 102)?

So far I've been tracking alternate humanisms and describing them in relation to liberal humanism. And posthumanism is often described in these sorts of terms, as something that relates most directly to liberal humanism. For Braidotti, for instance, "Posthumanism is the historical moment that marks the end of the opposition between Humanism and anti-humanism" (37). And Hayles tracks "models of subjectivity sufficiently different from the liberal subject that if one assigns the term 'human' to this subject, it makes sense to call the successor 'posthuman'" (6). I'm unconvinced that liberal humanism is the most pertinent reference point for the posthuman. While the alternative humanisms I've touched on so far can be effectively framed as not liberal humanisms, one of the ways I want to situate posthumanism in this book is primarily in relation to neoliberal humanism. Or, if alternative humanisms are a way of existing in the context of liberal humanist hegemony, posthumanisms are a way of existing in the context of neoliberal humanist hegemony.

When Wynter invokes "the bioeconomic conception of the human," she's broadly describing what I'll call here neoliberal humanism (Scott 2000, 160). I'm using this term specifically to gather together some of the ways neoliberal politics shape the dominant notion of contemporary humanity, with free market logic at its core. Lester Spence's description of neoliberal governmentality locates the intersection of the human and the market: it attempts "to simultaneously shape individual desires and behaviors and institutional practices according to market principles, while simultaneously *creating* the market through those individual and institutional desires and behaviors." (12). Neoliberal humanism fashions the human and the market in the image of one another, so that one's life can be governed by cost:benefit ratios (think of how we "invest" in relationships or jobs or communities), where even our leisure time is spent in service to producing profits for Facebook or Twitter or the club as an investment in our own human capital. Importantly, neoliberal humanism also folds together human and institutional desires so that, as presidential nominee Mitt Romney reminded us, "Corporations are people, my friend" (Rucker 2011). Or as the US Supreme Court has ruled, individuals can essentially incorporate themselves in order to fund elections at historically exponential rates ("Citizens United versus Federal Election Commission," 2010). This folding together of individual, corporate, and market yields two specifically neoliberal humanist formulations: post-identity and exceptions.

Put most simply, the "post" in post-identity shifts the blame for power inequity from institutions to individuals. Are you poor? Incarcerated? Have below-average test scores? Exhausted? Dealing with chronic illness, pain, or disability? Well, that's all on you. Post-identity politics relegate race, gender, sex, ability, class, and the like to a bygone era of identity politics, where minority groups coalesce around an identity marker like those listed above and apply pressure for political change. One of the core strategies of identity politics is to demonstrate that institutions—governments, corporations, schools, societal norms—operate in a way that benefits some more than others (and some none at all) and to lobby for changes in policy or practice that are meant to level the playing field.

Neoliberal humanism short circuits identity politics primarily by setting market logic as the standard for both corporate and individual well-being. If the market is embedded everywhere, in "spaces, institutions, and bodies," as Spence puts it, then things like white supremacy, sexual normativity, patriarchy, ableism—these are all *discursively* pushed to the background as healthy bottom lines become the measure of all things (12). I italicize "discursively" to emphasize the fact that white ableist cisheteropatriarchy is absolutely still at play, but neoliberalism frames social discourse—Wynter's "disciplines and epistemic order"—so that the primary question is not how one identifies but whether individuals and institutions are maximizing their capital. Of course, those background conditions guarantee that the game is rigged.

Jared Sexton's critique of multiracialism in *Amalgamation Schemes* and Robin James's theory of multiracial white supremacist patriarchy in

Resilience & Melancholy are complementary accounts of how the neoliberal game is rigged and also how this bends back to individuals being held responsible for systemic or institutional problems. Sexton's account of multiracialism doesn't use the explicit framework of post-identity, but I want to read it as such here. Sexton critiques multiracialism in part because it positions itself as a blending together of formerly separate categories—black, brown, and white—in a supposedly progressive step forward for race politics. As Sexton points out, though, "The political effects of multiracialism are neither a fundamental challenge to the living legacies of white supremacy nor a defiance of sexual racism in particular" (1). It is anti-black and anti-queer. How? Sexton tracks the ways multiracialism, with its focus on blendedness, ends up pathologizing blackness as inert, unchanging, dangerous, while at the same time codifying sex—the route to multiracialism—as a reproductive act that allows no room for any sort of queer desire.

James's multiracial white supremacist patriarchy (MRWaSP) outlines the same kind of process. In short, as liberal modes of policing and maintaining the color line—excluding minorities in order to protect white ableist cisheteropatriarchy—become increasingly unprofitable, MRWaSP actually grows stronger by inviting minorities into its ranks (12–18). Not everyone, of course, but enough to diffuse charges of racism, sexism, homophobia. Recent US political history includes overt instances of this sort of rhetoric: Barack Obama's election signaled a fully post-racial society, while the legalization of gay marriage marked a gayer country. One way neoliberal humanism discursively pushes identity to the background is by pointing to "successful" minorities as indicators that the field has been leveled and anyone truly can succeed. The logic that turns systemic problems into something individuals are responsible for goes something like this: 1) Barack Obama is president, so 2) surely the United States is not racist, and 3) it is therefore your fault if you aren't upwardly mobile. Or, 1) gay people can get married, so 2) surely the United States is not homophobic, and 3) it is therefore your fault if you don't find happiness and fulfillment in a relationship. Neoliberal post-identity at all turns denies systemic problems and reframes them as individual ones: white supremacist patriarchy is over, y'all, so welcome to post-feminism and post-racism, where any violence you experience must be a figment of your imagination or else is simply a coincidence that you gotta overcome. Good luck with all that, k?

In addition to forcing individuals to shoulder the responsibility for institutional problems, neoliberal humanism creates what Spence calls "exceptions"—those who are too dysfunctional to be formed according to market logic (2011, 15). The examples above are again instructive: Obama's politics are far from a radical black tradition, his presidency marked by market logic (bank bailouts, health reform that creates an insurance marketplace, and an immigration/deportation policy that falls back on who could create capital and who couldn't), and his rhetoric marked by multiracialism (blaming black fathers for all sorts of societal ills, an "on the one hand/on the other" approach to all recountings of the US's violent racial history). This is the complement of what I'll discuss in more detail below, Spillers's formulation of how skin color works as a physiognomic sleight of hand masking racial inequity. In this case, the president's skin color works as a physiognomic sleight of hand *revealing* something that *looks* like racial equity but that actually strengthens neoliberal humanism not only by fortifying neoliberal policy but also by making it appear inclusive. Similarly, gay marriage recognizes a narrow sliver of queer desire that most closely mirrors heteronormativity, strengthening systems of sexuality that privilege reproduction and monogamy while pushing other queer desires further from privilege and resources. Falguni Sheth calls these exceptions "pariah groups" and tracks the way former pariah groups are incorporated into the mainstream imaginary as part of the process by which that mainstream can "manage, control, discipline, or terrorize the new, emerging outgroup" (2009, 136). In each case, those who don't comport with neoliberal market logic are rendered exceptions, incapable of contributing to society and therefore undeserving of society's resources.

This divvying up of resources according to who deserves it is biopolitics, the political management of life and death. Spence identifies three main categories of what I'm calling neoliberal humanism: "those perfectly formed according to market logic, those able to be re-formed according to that logic, and the exceptions unable to be re-formed" (15). The biopolitical consequences of being an exception can be dire: increased surveillance and detainment; physical removal from things like healthy food, clean water, education, and other resources that can be the difference between poverty and subsistence; psychic removal from mainstream politics and art. Wynter demonstrates clearly the way an exception becomes endangered in her analysis of the acronym NHI—No Humans Involved—which, we learned in the wake of the Rodney King trial, the LAPD used to describe "any case involving a breach of the rights of young Black males" (1994, 42). Here, having been removed from the category of the human, young Black men were also removed from the right to live. I'll revisit this category of exception in my discussion of bare life and *habeas viscus* ("you will have the flesh"), but I want to wrap this overview of neoliberal humanism by locating the overlap between some posthumanisms and the second group, "those able to be re-formed according to [market] logic." This group is where post-identity flourishes, where a former pariah group overcomes its minority identity to thrive in the neoliberal mainstream.

Post-identity works to maintain power differentials. Spence theorizes this in the realm of parallel publics, where those who have been marked as exceptions argue for their inclusion in the mainstream and, in so doing, push others further away from power and resources. Post-identity is, in other words, a neoliberal humanist paradigm, a biopolitical instrument that wreaks havoc on the precariat. And posthumanisms that start from liberal humanism—which neoliberal humanism readily admits was racist and sexist and ableist and homophobic—are post-identities, strategies that pull liberal humanism back into the realm of power and resource, ontological constructs that reinforce Man. If the main thing a posthuman is is a not liberal humanist, then it shares quite a lot in common with neoliberal humanism, which is also squarely not liberal humanist, opening pathways for formerly excluded minorities to move into range of formerly withheld biopolitical resources. Part of what props up post-identity is a flattening of history, when the weight of privilege that compounds over time is unaccounted for. Race or gender or disability or queerness can only be "overcome" in post-identity if people haven't accumulated and passed along massive wealth and power over centuries of gaming the inequities that accrue along these lines. For Spillers, it's these inequities, these centuries of violence that become "hidden to the cultural seeing by skin color" (1987, 16) so that making diversity virtuous requires a collective forgetting or ignorance of the historical weight of white privilege and racialized and gendered violence. Part of my argument in *Posthuman Rap* is that posthumanism that recognizes liberal humanism as the only kind of humanism, that mistakes hegemony for totalization, is guilty of a similar historical flattening and ends up building a post-identity posthumanity that feeds neoliberal humanism instead of imagining paths out of its destructive administration of life and death.

What I'm arguing for here isn't some brand new account of neoliberal biopolitics in conjunction with the posthuman; most writers, including Braidotti, formulate the posthuman with neoliberalism in mind. Rather, what I want to press in *Posthuman Rap* is the idea that if we don't start from alternative humanisms like the ones I've sketched above, then posthumanism is just another neoliberal post-identity that replicates old power inequities in new ways.

To be sure, Wynter frames embattled humanism with a keen awareness of the difference between liberal humanism and neoliberal humanism, even if she doesn't use the same terms. She theorizes a demarcation between Man1 and Man2, where Man2 is roughly *homo œconomicus.* Wynter doesn't call Man2 neoliberal humanity, but I take her dividing line that separates the "bioeconomic conception of the human" from previous instantiations as a recognition that Man2 is neoliberal and Man1 liberal. Wynter is particularly instructive here, as she continues to use the term humanism—not posthumanism—in the shadow of Man2. The lesson is that nothing is fixed, no terminology clearly agreed upon or necessary, no ontology easily separated from a closely related one. In *Posthuman Rap,* I'll read embattled humanism as at times a humanism that is the starting point for a certain kind of posthumanism, at other times as a posthumanism itself. I'm less interested in disciplining embattled humanism and more interested in thinking about and listening to posthumanity outside the framework of liberal humanism. Wynter and embattled humanism are integral to that task.

So it's not a definition, but I can offer a description of the kind of posthumanism I'm concerned with in this book.:

1. Posthumanism that *starts* from a humanism situated somewhere in the overlap among Eurocentric antihumanism, Afrofuturism, NoFuturism, and embattled humanism (itself closely connected to existential humanism).
2. Posthumanism whose relationship with neoliberal humanism parallels the above humanisms' relationships with liberal humanism.
3. Posthumanism that tries to move "completely outside our present conception of what it is to be human . . . outside the ground of the orthodox body of knowledge," "making a schemata of the known for what has never been."
4. Posthumanism that is sounded in popular music.

There's a real tension in the third and fourth points. Popular music— and the rap I listen to in these pages is absolutely popular music—exists so squarely within the "orthodox body of knowledge" that it's *named* for it: this music is so easily known that everyone loves it. In many ways, popular music is popular because it works from a schemata of the known for what has *always* been. The rest of this chapter, then, will be an exploration of this tension. I'll start with Alexander Weheliye's theory of habeas viscus in conversation with Wynter and Hortense Spillers in order to tease out some preliminary thoughts on what it means to move outside the present conception of "human," then conclude with how popular music fits into this and how I'll be listening in the pages of this book.

Hortense Spillers introduces "hieroglyphics of the flesh" in her (still) groundbreaking 1987 essay, "Mama's Baby, Papa's Maybe." From this endlessly evocative phrase Spillers spins an account of gender and race that traces the marks, "the lacerations, woundings, fissures, tears, scars, openings, ruptures, lesions, rendings, punctures of the flesh" that are "hidden to the cultural seeing by skin color" (67). Or, in white supremacist patriarchy, skin color works as a physiognomic sleight of hand masking racial inequity (as in the Moynihan Report that Spillers initially bounces off of in "Mama's Baby"), masking the cultural and physical processes of the Middle Passage, chattel slavery, Jim Crow, the prison industrial complex that render blackness as pathological, as existing outside social norms. Here's Spillers's difference between flesh and body, then: the flesh is antecedent to the body, a "zero degree of social conceptualization" that exists in the denial of personhood (67). The hieroglyphics of the flesh persist in Spillers's theorizing. Beyond emancipation, beyond the point flesh is recognized as a citizen body, the "phenomenon of marking and branding actually 'transfers' from one generation to the next" (Weheliye calls this a "pesky potential") maintaining the racial hierarchy that fuels white supremacy (Spillers 1987, 67; Weheliye 2014, 40).

Weheliye's 2014 *Habeas Viscus*—"you will have the flesh"—is titled as a deliberate play on the difference between flesh and body and as a way of pointing out the juridical distance between flesh and body. The body is human; the body is protected by law; the body is, in fact, *created* by law, a citizenship founded rather than found by its founding documents. The flesh? Not so much. The flesh, as Spillers puts it, resides in "the vestibule of a colonized North America" (67), marked and cordoned off but unprotected by law. Weheliye brings this vestibular flesh to a discussion of Agamben's "bare life," the biopolitical detritus of society that is destined for death. Critiquing Agamben's and Foucault's reliance on "fortress Europe" for their conceptualization of bare life and specifically Agamben's use of the Nazi concentration camp as the exemplar of bare life (where bare life is not just social but physical death), Weheliye suggests that Spillers's account of "hieroglyphics of the flesh" can open a different kind of bare life, one rooted in the Middle Passage and new world slavery.

Weheliye uses the term "racializing assemblages" to highlight the critical distance between Agamben's bare life and Spillers's flesh. An assemblage isn't emptied and left for dead, life made bare; rather, it is created and maintained as an integral part of racial hierarchy: "the ether that holds together the world of Man" (40). Man may well intend flesh to be an emptying out of personhood, a "clearing zone of indistinction," but Spillers and Weheliye find the flesh to be so much more. Because flesh is integral to white supremacist racial hierarchy—the supposed lack that highlights Man's personhood—it "stands as both the cornerstone and potential ruin of the world of Man" (44). Vestibules are funny things: they may be passage in or out, and Spillers and Weheliye theorize vestibular flesh as a space where humanness can be figured apart from Man, "a stepping stone toward new genres of human" (Weheliye 2014, 44–45).

So here we are, back around to Wynter's ontological sovereignty, flesh as "outside the ground of the orthodox body of knowledge." The play on "orthodox body" is too good to pass up. As I read Wynter, she means orthodox to modify "body of knowledge," essentially an orthodox discourse. But vestibular flesh also exists outside of the ground of orthodox bodies, bodies fashioned so that their race, gender, sex, ability are orthodox—bodies that read as bodies and not flesh, bodies whose knowledge becomes orthodox. Wynter calls the places where humanness is fostered apart from Man "demonic ground," and recalling Spillers's reading of gender and race in "Mama's Baby," we might ask what sorts of flesh dance on those demonic grounds. Part of Spillers's point with "Mama's Baby" was to insist on paying attention to racialized gender—or gendered race—in order to better track the "transfer" of the hieroglyphics of the flesh in black women's bodies, especially. These hieroglyphics etch black femininity as monstrously desexualized and hypersexualized all at once, and they produce an "enforced state of breach" when kinship becomes unsettled through the property relations of enslaver and enslaved, through a matriarchal lineage that is itself illegitimized by orthodox bodies. By formulating race and gender together, Spillers notes that black women's bodies have never been orthodox, and Weheliye's *Habeas Viscus* roots itself in black feminism as both ontology and epistemology, theory of flesh and theory from flesh.

Vestibular flesh will be central to the posthumanism I trace here, and I want to firm up how I understand relationality to work in the vestibule. The underlying principle here is that flesh *can* have relationships with any number of things, including neoliberal humanism, but it is not *required* to. So when Spillers claims gender as that which the Middle Passage and slavery denied, she is pitting flesh against Man *as one strategic possibility*. Thinking back to the two-pronged approach of embattled humanism can be helpful here, as this is theory of flesh used to undermine Man's racial and gender hierarchies. The point, as Spillers is careful to spell out, isn't to achieve some predetermined gendered space within the ortho-dox world but to gain "the *insurgent* ground of female social subject" (80). Insurgency comes not just through black women claiming a gender desig-nation that has been denied but also through black men gaining feminin-ity, "the power of 'yes' to the 'female' within" (80). "Mama's Baby" maps a queer futurity whose counter-logic is meant to disrupt Man's future; it's an example of vestibular flesh as it relates to Man's world. But the ves-tibule leads *out*, too. What I'd like to suggest as fundamental to embat-tled humanism and the posthumanism that extends from it is that flesh can exist with knowledge of neoliberal humanism (no naiveté or igno-rance here) *but no relationship with it*. The idea is to be human apart from neoliberal humanism in a way that doesn't depend on the destruction of neoliberal humanism. The queer femininity of "Mama's Baby" may well be the undoing of (neo)liberal humanist racial and gender hierarchies, but it also can be its own humanness regardless of its effects on anything else. If we're heading toward Rae Sremmurd's posthuman vestibule in this book, then this delicate theoretical slice that differentiates between (post)humanism that *targets* (neo)liberal humanism and (post)humanism that *exists apart from* (neo)liberal humanism is crucial. Part of it is what I laid out above: posthumanism framed as an evolution of the liberal humanist subject is a nonstarter. The vestibule allows for insurgency and apartness, but it doesn't really do evolution.

Weheliye distills habeas viscus similarly, as "relational modes of being in the flesh," that which is "heard, seen, tasted, felt, and lived in the ethereal shadows of Man's world" (122, 138). Being and knowing through habeas vis-cus is a route out of Man's ontology, a departure through the vestibule that brings into earshot fleshy humanness that survives and thrives in (follow-ing Wynter) unorthodox ways. In *Posthuman Rap*, I explore these relational modes of being primarily as they are *heard* in the context of Man's neoliberal world. In her read of Weheliye, Robin James notes the sonic potentiality of habeas viscus. If sight is a markedly Modern sense (here she cites Mulvey's cinematic gaze and Fanon's "Look! A negro!"), then flesh may register in other sensory planes, escaping Man's all-surveilling eye. Of course, picking a different sense isn't enough. *How* one is heard matters: "From the perspec-tive of the human as Man, the flesh radiates with queer vibes, with lively movements that nevertheless appear as, perhaps we should say, static and undead because they oscillate at frequencies . . . that Man can't recognize as his own" (James 2014). The queer futurity that spins out of Spillers's gender work → queerly vibrating flesh. *Posthuman Rap* turns an ear to what queerly vibrating flesh might sound like in the realm of rap music.

Posthuman Rap listens to rap music as popular music in the posthuman vestibule. Though I focus primarily on rap, the goal is to hear how (a kind of) popular music sounds ways of being human outside neoliberal humanism. Why popular music? There are a few things about popular music that recommend it as a medium for understanding the posthuman. Beyond, of course, my effort to get tenure.

Popular Music as Politics

At the heart of critical theory and cultural studies approaches to popular culture—the kinds of approaches that inform this book—is the firm belief that the popular is political. In "Notes on Deconstructing the Popular," Stuart Hall puts this about as plainly as possible when he urges that analysis of popular culture should always start from the "double movement of containment and resistance" (1998, 443). Within this containment and resistance is politics, the ongoing struggle over and negotiation for power. Hall's larger point is that popular media is not, on the one hand, *just* a tool for capitalist elites to indoctrinate the masses, nor is it, on the other, *just* a vehicle for radical expression and representation to be used by the masses in opposition to those capitalist elites. It's all that, often simultaneously.

If liberal humanism and neoliberal humanism are the dominant ideologies I have described them to be, then we will surely find them reflected in popular media. This is one way ideologies maintain dominance, by forming the background conditions of our everyday mundane interactions with the world around us, by vibrating in the ubiquitous soundtrack of contemporary life—this is Hall's containment. But, because, as Hall puts it, "ordinary people are not cultural dopes," we are also able to hear much more than just dominant ideology in our music (1998, 446). This is the heart of queer theory, reading or projecting or vibrating yourself—or someone like you—into a cultural object that, at its most benign, doesn't have you in mind or, at its most malignant, wishes to erase you. Following Hall's terms, if ignorance or erasure is containment, queered readings are resistance, and neither cancels the other out. Instead, multiple interpretations proliferate, each with a different political weight and resonance. Pop music listeners generate these multiple interpretations through their use and reperformance and consumption of music, while critical theorists suss out the politics of what and how music means.

In *Posthuman Rap*, of course, I'll focus my attention primarily on the dominant ideologies of liberal and neoliberal humanism, tracking the ways rap sounds containment and resistance in these registers. Because the politics of popular culture are never either/or, the question here isn't "Is this music posthuman?" Rather, it's "How is posthumanism sounded in this music?" Framing analysis in these terms helps to keep in view the ongoing and unequal struggle among dominant and vestibular conceptions of the human.

Popular Music as Sound

Weheliye, in his 2002 article on posthuman voices in R&B, names one of his goals as the desire "to realign the hegemony of visual media in academic considerations of virtuality by shifting the emphasis to the aural," to pull the focus of posthuman discourse in the direction of sound (21). "Feenin" starts this work, and *Habeas Viscus* extends it somewhat, though by 2014, Weheliye finds posthumanism an inadequate discourse for his work on sound and black feminism. I've outlined above where I find the overlap between *Habeas Viscus* and posthumanism, and I'll return to Weheliye throughout the book. Weheliye's own dissatisfaction with posthumanism parallels and informs my own; in bringing his work into conversation with posthumanism, I don't so much wish to recast his work as posthuman as much as I want to use his work as part of a larger critical intervention in what posthumanism is and does.

Alongside Weheliye's contributions, Robin James has offered the most on posthumanism and aurality, especially in her work on Beyoncé and Rihanna. In "Robo-Diva" (2008) and *Resilience & Melancholy* (2015), James first explores the musical performance of nonhumanness as a specifically black feminist strategy, then digs into the ways the posthuman can bend resources away from white supremacist cisheteropatriarchy. Like Weheliye, James often operates outside of posthumanism and has voiced skepticism about the discourse, but much of her work resonates with the kind of posthumanism I map in this book, and a close account of sound is central to her analysis of pop music.

Why sound? For Weheliye, the history of sound reproduction technologies presents a negotiation of presence and absence, being and not-being, human and posthuman that runs counter to the cyber theory that is central to much posthumanism. Instead of a growing gulf between humanity and posthumanity—the kind of great evolutionary break Hayles and Braidotti theorize—Weheliye finds humanness to be central to configurations of the posthuman as disembodied voices that are re-presented in musical record-ings. For James, sound is the neoliberal episteme, the structuring logic of big data and deregulated capital, the separation of signal from noise. Sound makes sense to neoliberalism, so the *way* one sounds—whether in earshot of neoliberal humanism or not—becomes crucial to an account of vestib-ular flesh. So, paying attention to sound means listening for ways of being that often run counter to visual and linguistic logic and simultaneously tuning to the signals, noises, and queer vibrations bouncing around and outside of neoliberal humanism.

As for explicitly shifting posthuman discourse to the aural, there isn't a ton beyond Weheliye and James. Auner (2003), Shaviro (2005), Hofer (2006), Middleton (2006), and David (2007) all listen to popular music alongside posthumanism, and while each tackle different genres and employ somewhat different definitions of the posthuman (David, for instance, uses the term pejoratively), they all ultimately rest on a notion of posthumanism that proceeds from or is wholly defined against liberal humanism. Middleton's use of "voice" as a pure representation of the self is emblematic; an "authentic" self is thought to lurk beneath various tech-nological shells and mods, and that self, once we peel through the layers, turns out to be remarkably similar to the same white straight dude who's been screwing people over for centuries. Of course, one needn't explicitly invoke the posthuman to be germane to the discourse. Plenty of literature on popular music and sound deals with ontology; likewise, critical race, gender, and queer theories that don't name posthumanism or take sound and music as an object of study will inform what happens in this book. In short, I've not only narrowed this study so that I'm focused on a specific strand of posthuman discourse, but I'll also be funneling the theory I use in these pages toward analysis of music and sound—a continued effort "to realign the hegemony of visual media ... by shifting the emphasis to the aural" (Weheliye 2002, 21).

Popular Music and Political Economy

So here's the rub: if vestibular flesh vibrates queerly, illegibly outside the earshot of liberal and neoliberal humanism, outside the flow of power and resources, then how will we hear this in popular music, which is legibly situated firmly within neoliberal flows of capital? Or: hey, Nicki Minaj is super successful and kinda rich; tell me again how this is vestibular flesh?

I have no clue.

No, wait; really I do. The short answer is that popular music can operate on a number of levels all at once. The political idea above? About "containment and resistance" in Hall's terms? Yeah, so the idea is that a single song may resonate with neoliberal humanism and make all kinds of bank that lines the pockets of an artist and every industry exec who's owed a cut *at the very same time* that it vibrates queerly out of range, figuring an existence apart from and/or in opposition to neoliberal humanism. Art and media aren't restricted to meaning or doing only one thing, and we're going to encounter a good deal of tension among the ways different people hear the music I've included in this book. The longer answer is worth some time, as it involves an account of the vestibule—its geography, its residents, its relationality—in the context of popular music's political economy.

So let's start with some observations about the music industry and move to the vestibule from there. Popular music circulates as part of neoliberal hyper-capital. For all the populist clamor over the breakdown of the music industry through file sharing or the circumvention of major labels through venues like Bandcamp, YouTube, and other online platforms, in 2015 roughly two-thirds of the music market belonged to three large corporations: Universal, Sony, and Warner, the three of whom own an even larger chunk of the distribution market (Christman 2016).[4] In fact, online platforms that allow artists to circulate their own music work exactly like neoliberal entrepreneurial self-investment is meant to: use your own time and resources developing your content and "brand," thereby generating profits for Facebook, YouTube, and other social media outlets as well as turn-keying yourself for the record label who eventually signs you. Part of the point is that, even in actions and systems that at first stymie the recording industry—file-sharing technologies, streaming technologies, off-label platforms, broadcasting technologies that can fashion what we used to call "pirate" radio all over the Internet and with high-quality sound—capital eventually finds its way to the biggest corporations. A more important point has to do with the parallel between the way the corporate recording industry profits off of appearing to be anti-corporate and the way multiculturalism works in neoliberalism.

The recording industry doesn't only profit financially by monetizing individual or small-label labor; it also, like neoliberal humanism, profits when it weathers critique. I mentioned at the beginning of the chapter that systems of dominance invite critique from those they oppress because hegemony grows more hegemonic when critiques of it fall short. Mos Def's 2004 "The Rape Over" is a useful example here. Before getting to the anti-Semitic and homophobic core of the song,[5] Mos Def starts by calling out "old white men" and "corporate force" for "runnin this rap shit." It is, linguistically, a simple conceit: the record industry is bullshit and profits on the backs of hard-working artists. It's a conceit that is, in fact, at the heart of independent record labels that often promote and sign artists who want to maintain their autonomy without being sullied by what they see as the corporate greed of major labels. Indeed, Mos Def recorded "The Rape Over" while signed to Rawkus Records, which started as an indie label in the 1990s. By 2004, however, when "The Rape Over" was released, Rawkus was owned and distributed by Geffen Records, which is a division of Universal Music Group, a "corporate force" run by "old white men." Universal not only stands to make money selling Mos Def's song, but it also creates conditions that benefit its public image: if Mos Def can come at the major labels without being blocked by them, how big and bad and powerful can those labels really be? Open critique of the recording industry helps create the illusion that finance and power is not as lopsided as it really is in the industry.

A similar illusion appears in the discussion of market share. As I already mentioned, in 2015, as has been the case for several years, the major labels (until 2012, when they sold to Universal, EMI was the fourth major) controlled about two-thirds of the market. Browsing through a Google search for "2015 record label market share," though, one finds a storyline that praises independent labels for taking the largest share of the market. When grouped, indeed, independent labels accounted for 34.4 percent of the market (Universal was second at 26.7 percent), and Taylor Swift's *1989* had a big year on the indie label Big Machine. But a headline like "Independent Labels Trounce UMG, Sony, and Warner" is misleading, to say the least (Ingham 2015). The majors dwarf any individual indie label and enjoy access to the kind of money, power, and deeply entrenched industry connections that stabilize their existence and leave indies more precarious by comparison (Big Machine *needs* Taylor Swift in a way no major needs any artist).

The major labels use the specter of encroaching indie labels and indie-style anti-corporate sentiment to help maintain the flow of power and resources to the majors in a way that runs parallel to (but doesn't match beat-for-beat) the politics of exception. Recall that exception politics strengthens white supremacy by admitting a select few representatives of minority groups into its ranks while squeezing others further out. The presence of minorities satisfies calls for inclusion without reshuffling the distribution of power and resources too much; neoliberal humanism comes out seeming benevolent and tolerant at a low cost. Similarly, the conditions that make a three-corporation hegemony in the music industry seem like a losing game when compared with all of the independents helps maintain the status quo and keep indie labels permanently precarious and majors dominant.

I draw this parallel to demonstrate that the mechanism that maintains structural inequalities in neoliberal society is the same market logic that governs the structure of the music industry. Mos Def's "The Rape Over" is but one example. "Conscious rap" is held up as evidence of progressive minority inclusion, a black rapper given the voice to speak out against corporate overlords—in a way that lines the pockets of the corporate overlords. Mos Def's "The Rape Over" politics aren't worth dedicating much more space to, but the point about relationality is this: it's complicated. As I outlined regarding vestibular flesh, one's relationship to neoliberal humanism in the vestibule may be one that tries to undermine its power, or one that maps an existence outside of Man's earshot, or both at exactly the same time. When parsing the politics of popular musicians, when analyzing the posthuman content of their music, I work from the assumption that vestibular flesh is not an either/or proposition; rather, music that at once thrives in the capital flows of the music industry may also vibrate queerly out of range.

Returning to the question at the beginning of this section: why popular music? Because of the complex politics of popular media and the recording industry, and because of the relative paucity of work on posthumanism and sound, I find popular music, and specifically rap in my case studies, to be an ideal venue in which to contemplate the posthuman. I'm not claiming that rap music is the best or only way to understand the posthuman, nor that the way I hear the music discussed in this book is the only credible interpretation. Nor am I arguing that sound analysis provides us with a full account of posthumanism. Rather, I am arguing that an account of posthumanism isn't complete without attention to sound, so I offer *Posthuman Rap* as one piece of a broader discourse and hope to intervene in the direction of that discourse by allowing popular music and posthumanism to inform one another throughout the pages of this book.

LISTENING IN THE POSTHUMAN VESTIBULE

Departing as he does from Agamben, Weheliye figures flesh as theoretically similar (though not identical) to "bare life," an existence entirely removed from the lifeblood of liberal or neoliberal society. As I read it, habeas viscus and the vestibule are ways of understanding this removal through, especially, critical race and gender theories, staking out the following sort of logic.:

1. Since the lifeblood of liberal and neoliberal societies is septic, existing apart from it is ultimately ideal if also, because hegemony will try to maintain power at all costs, dangerous. Bare life, flesh, exceptions, pariahs—these all describe violent removals from society. Habeas viscus and vestibular flesh are ways of imagining an existence outside of liberalism or neoliberalism that does not necessitate *further* violent removal. Or, these aren't theories predicated on the necessity of suffering; rather, they are interested in hearing and being and knowing beyond the veil in a way that would ideally require the least amount of harm to groups who have been historically rendered as bare life, flesh, exception, pariah.
2. Short of full removal is the vestibule, the place outside the central narrative of neoliberal humanism, which relies on violent technologies of white supremacy, patriarchy, ableism, cisheteronormativity to define itself against. Black, queer, disabled, feminine: this is the vestibule.
3. From the vestibule, one can tune to the world of neoliberal humanism *as well as* flesh (or bare life or exception). Should one imagine an existence entirely apart from neoliberal humanism that is not just the result of having been violently removed, this is a vantage point from which it might happen. With knowledge of and access to both neoliberal humanism and flesh, the vestibule is where alternative ontologies like (in the immediate interest of this book) posthumanism may flourish. Hence, the return over and again to critical race and gender theory in these pages.

Resonating in multiple registers at once, sounds filtered through the vestibule *may* pass as neoliberal humanist logic at the same time they undulate with alternative ontologies. I stress "may" because this is a description of the way some posthuman popular music works but not all. Passing as neoliberal humanist logic isn't required, but in answer to the question of how an ontology that exists entirely apart from neoliberal humanism may be sounded in a genre that is also financially rewarded by it—or how Nicki Minaj can be so successful in the music industry while also vibrating queerly out of range—I offer this political economic structure: by resonating in multiple registers at once, some posthuman popular music funds the existence of other ontologies by siphoning resources from neoliberal humanism.

The route to the posthuman vestibule in *Posthuman Rap* starts with a critique of the reception of Kendrick Lamar, the politics of which resonate legibly and build not a posthuman vestibule but a black parallel public that pushes others further from power and resources. In the third and fourth chapters of the book, we'll listen to what the exceptions pushed from Kendrick's parallel public sound like, finally arriving in Rae Sremmurd's queerly vibrating club, the posthuman vestibule that leads both into and out of neoliberal humanism's world.

CHAPTER 2

"Cheap and Easy Radicalism"

The Legible Politics of Kendrick Lamar

Kendrick Lamar, by far, realest Negus alive

Kendrick Lamar, "i" (2015)

February 15, 2016, Staples Center, Los Angeles, CA: Stage lights dim, and Kendrick Lamar, silhouetted against a glowing white image of the continent of Africa with "Compton" scrawled across the Sahara, catches his breath. He's just ripped through a six-minute medley of songs from his album *To Pimp a Butterfly*, which would win Best Rap Album that night. The Grammy audience is on their feet. They're cheering a performance that included 1) Kendrick leading a chain gang on stage, 2) singing "The Blacker the Berry" while accompanied by jail cell bandmates, 3) rapping in front of a bonfire while surrounded by backup dancers costumed to signify "Africanness," and 4) finally occupying center stage alone for the finale, which on television included creative cuts that moved his face around the screen as it was pelted with strobe lights. Then that final shot, the glowing continent where Kendrick has planted his Compton flag. Kendrick is fed up with the prison industrial complex and racist policing in the United States and wants to find himself in Africa. The Grammy audience *loves* this idea.

January 21, 2016, BBC Broadcasting House, London, UK: Khalif and Aaquil Brown, the Tupelo-born brothers who perform as the rap duo Rae Sremmurd, declare their love for Major Lazer's "Lean On," then, as Radio 1 DJ Annie Mac dutifully cues it, mangle every lyric as they sing along live on air. They've come to Mac's nightly primetime show as guests for her "party mix" segment, bringing the music they most love to hear when it's time to cut loose. So the bulk of the half hour is spent teaching the Irish-born Mac the finer points of Southern hip hop, like how to swag surf, what it means to unlock one's swag, and the difference between a banger and a slapper. And when do the brothers like to cut loose? Always. Rae Sremmurd's world is a party that never stops.

It's easy to take in these two tableaux and recognize that Kendrick is doing some important work, while Rae Sremmurd are goofing off. Find me a Kendrick track about struggling through addiction or rising above gangbanging or learning to love himself despite the fact that the white supremacist world around him tells him not to, and I'll match it with a Rae Sremmurd song about buying shots for the bar or throwing money at strippers or unlocking their swag. Kendrick's woke is Rae Sremmurd's toke.

But this isn't a chapter that reinforces the importance of Kendrick. It isn't even a chapter about Rae Sremmurd—we'll get to them in Chapter 4 (and you'll like it; it's about the queerly vibrating frequencies of Rae Sremmurd's posthuman vestibule). Instead, it's one where I critique the discourse *surrounding* Kendrick Lamar in order to think through the limits of how we (fans, critics, artists, academics) generally define hip hop politics. This critique sets the table for Chapter 3's analysis of the aesthetics and politics of trap music, a Southern hip hop subgenre whose sounds have permeated pop music even as critical reception of it remains bemused at its kindest. This isn't a thorough account of the history of hip hop politics; rather, it's a snapshot of contemporary hip hop politics that has Kendrick standing at one end of the spectrum and trap at the other. While Kendrick stands in for a completely legible and traditional politics, in trap I hear a different kind of politics, one that isn't immediately recognizable as politics at all, one that echoes Wynter's call for an ontology that doesn't fit mainstream ideas about what it means to be human. To better amplify these echoes, I'll explore the sonic aesthetics of trap in the context of 21st-century state-sanctioned and -protected extermination of black people in the United States. Kendrick (Compton) and trap (mostly an Atlanta sound, but more broadly pulling from the US South) come from opposite sides of the country and operate in different regional milieus, but their music resonates in the same broad social context of (post)racial violence. So this chapter will establish the baseline: the legible politics that permeate the reception of Kendrick and that fit neatly into mainstream ideas about what it means to be human.

Kendrick's music doesn't just read as political; it reads as the paragon of hip hop politics.

> Dan Rys, *XXL* (September 2015): "Any way you cut it, Kendrick Lamar is one of the most important voices in hip-hop today. And his last album, March's *To Pimp A Butterfly*, might just be one of the most poignant socio/political records in recent memory."

> John Noire, *DJ Booth* (2015): "Rarely do we get a rapper in the mainstream that talks about relevant social issues and does it in a way as clever and entertaining as Kendrick."

> Alex Petridis, *Guardian* music blog (March 2016): "Lamar finds himself pressured to push artistic boundaries while selling millions of copies and acting as hip-hop's political conscience, or, as he puts it on *Untitled Unmastered*'s opening track, 'to use my vocals to save mankind for you.'"

> H. Drew Blackburn, *FactMag* (March 2016): "A year after Kendrick Lamar's complicated magnum opus *To Pimp a Butterfly*, its apex and focal point remains 'Alright', a song that reminds me of 'Lift Every Voice' and best represents the robust political and pop cultural force Kendrick has become in the 12 months since its release."

To be sure, framing Kendrick as the center of hip hop politics does not mean everyone *agrees* with his politics. When asked in a *Billboard* interview about the high-profile murders of black men at the hands of police, Kendrick seemed to go full respectability politics: "When we don't have respect for ourselves, how do we expect them to respect us?" The #thinkpieces rolled out, some defending Kendrick's narrow political goals and others calling him out for comments that seemed to completely misunderstand how institutional racism works. But, yeah, agreement isn't the measure here. Rather, the point is that it has become nearly impossible to discuss Kendrick without also talking about his politics: he is primarily legible as a political rapper—being political seems to be his most defining characteristic. Because audiences and critics can easily identify Kendrick as political, the discourse surrounding him tends to mirror mainstream racial politics, which is stacked in favor of whiteness.

In *Stare in the Darkness*, Lester Spence outlines the way rap has "reproduced neoliberalism within the black parallel public" (2011, 54). A parallel public is one outside the mainstream that rises and falls in step with the mainstream and tends to reinforce mainstream norms even as it purports to exist in opposition to that mainstream. Parallel publics could coalesce along a number of axes—gender, class, religion, ability—and Spence is primarily concerned with race. In a white supremacist society like the United States, whiteness is the mainstream, so a black parallel public is one that, on the one hand, exists outside of whiteness and, on the other, reinforces white norms.

> The parallel public allows subjugated groups to address their particular issues and to further develop both a group identity and a group consciousness. However, it does so constrained by societal norms. *The black parallel public operates according to established class, heterosexual, and gender norms, providing a space within which blacks can accommodate, criticize, and generate alternatives to the so-called mainstream public sphere.* In its capacity as an accommodating space, it both inculcates and enforces both at-large and internal norms and values. (9, emphasis mine)

A parallel public operating within a neoliberal society involves a double movement, both inward and outward from the center of power. Spence's account of race within neoliberalism, which I discuss in greater context in Chapter 1, produces three populations: "those perfectly formed according to market logic, those able to be re-formed according to that logic, and the exceptions unable to be re-formed" (15). Spence follows this with a broad but direct observation: "African Americans constitute the exception." Here, market logic, the structuring of society to continuously create and maintain conditions that support the free market, reinforces white supremacy so that whiteness comes out as profitable—"perfectly formed according to market logic"—while blackness is in need of reform. If the black parallel public reinforces norms of the white supremacist mainstream, then it is a movement *into* the population "able to be re-formed according to [market] logic," even as blacks who are not participatory in the parallel public—the exceptions—move even further *from* those populations that can more easily access resources and power. A parallel public, in short, operates according to the notion that, in order to earn their civil rights, it is the responsibility of a marginalized or historically oppressed group to become more like the group who has marginalized or oppressed them.

Spence includes a critique of "crack governmentality" in hip hop, a demonstration of hip hop's parallelism to neoliberal market logic. In response to the depiction of African Americans as "lazy, sexually libidinous, crime prone, and culturally dysfunctional," so-called descriptive realist rappers work from "*within subjected places and populations*" to project themselves as entrepreneurs, experts on how their poor urban neighborhoods work and profiteers of those same locales (15, 27–28). "They use and reproduce contemporary ideas about urban space and about black masculinity and black representation writ large but do so in a way that grants them access and a modicum of political and cultural power" (9). Spence's analysis revolves around a random sample of hip hop lyrics from 1989 to 2004. In what follows in this chapter and Chapter 3, I expand on Spence's study of neoliberal market logic in hip hop parallel publics in three key ways, by considering not just lyrics but also 1) critical reception and 2) sonic aesthetics of artists 3) mostly after 2004 and especially in the mid-2010s.

Back to where I started this section: Kendrick is received as the paragon of hip hop politics, "the most important rapper since Jay-Z," a "rap savior," according to Jessica Hopper (2012). And overwhelmingly, critical reception of Kendrick depicts a politics that does the work of a parallel public, a conscious realism that separates those able to be reformed from those who aren't. The results include a discourse surrounding Kendrick that not only grant him "a modicum of political and cultural power" (Spence 2011, 9) but also use him to define what it is to be a political rapper in the mid-2010s, pushing those who don't follow the same template further from any modicum of political and cultural power. By focusing on the critical reception of Kendrick Lamar, I want to establish not so much what his lyrics convey but how they tend to circulate in the mainstream.

There are two major assumptions built into this. The first is that journalists who write about Kendrick are primarily responding to the lyrical elements of his performance, with music as a secondary or tertiary component of the art that bears his name. Spence's own focus on lyrics and narrative is a common approach to hip hop studies, and by focusing on critical reception, I can extend Spence's work by providing a second-level analysis of the lyrical and narrative content of Kendrick's work. The goal is to achieve a fuller sense of how Kendrick is perceived as a political rapper very much in the space of the black parallel public Spence describes. Unlike the rest of this book, the goal isn't to dive into Kendrick's sound. There, we would find a fuller account of what work his music performs beyond the mainstream critique, and while that would be a study well worth the time and effort, it doesn't fall within the narrower purview of this book. Instead, the purpose of focusing on mainstream critical reception (which tends to default to a mostly lyrical critique) of Kendrick is to show how even a rapper with so much radical political credibility can find his work co-opted into a political discourse designed to maintain white supremacy.

The second assumption is that the pull quotes I've provided above and the article I'll focus the bulk of my time on below are representative of a broader understanding of Kendrick's politics. These articles represent the hits that populate the first few pages of a Google search for "Kendrick Lamar politics"—the Lynch article at the center of the analysis is the top hit for that search—or profiles of Kendrick in widely read periodicals.

Marc Lynch's "The Political Theory of Kendrick Lamar" for the *Washington Post* (March 23, 2015) assembles a set of signifiers that, in marking Lamar as more politician than rapper, point to the kind of post-race performance that solidifies his mainstream legibility. Lynch reads Kendrick's politics as fundamentally black, and he outlines it according to the kind of "established class, heterosexual, and gender norms" that pervade the work of the parallel public (Spence, 9). Lynch also sets up Lamar as a scholar, comparing his guest verses to articles lining his CV, with *To Pimp a Butterfly* standing in as the book that anchors his career. Spence notes the importance of expertise in establishing the black parallel public as capable of being reformed according to market logic, pointing to black social scientists and political and cultural leaders who "depoliticize[d] neoliberal representations of black bodies, spaces, and institutions through their work" (16). Spence tacks toward realist rap because those are the artists who project an authenticity and, well, realism that establishes their own expertise, which they convey through "sentiment and affect" (17). Lynch's characterization of Kendrick as a scholar with a litany of publications further establishes the rapper's parallel public bona fides.

Lynch's article appeared in March 2015 in the immediate aftermath of the release of *To Pimp a Butterfly*, Kendrick's second major label studio album. Lynch, himself a political science professor at George Washington University, doesn't really offer a review of the album, as the arts aren't his beat, but he dropped his political analysis into the ocean of reviews washing perfect scores and breathless accolades onto the Internet's shores. His premise is, loosely, "lemme show you the politics that make this album perfect." Less loosely, it's this: "Kendrick grapples with core political theory questions of power, identity, and the ethics of leadership. He exhibits a challenging ethos of self-critique as a tentative path forward." I'm breaking down Lynch's political read into five key themes that run through his piece: 1) Kendrick's conscious rapper ancestry, 2) the depth and complexity of Kendrick's—and his woke contemporaries'—music and message, 3) the conflation of masculinity and leadership/mastery, 4) Kendrick as scholar, and 5) self-critique as post-race multiracialism. Because Lynch doesn't explicitly organize his analysis along these themes, there's no linear argument that leads from one point to the next; rather, these themes I've identified are interrelated and often dependent on one another (for instance, Kendrick-as-scholar depends heavily on the idea that his music and message are deep and complex, which in turn both feeds and is propped up by the conflation of leadership with masculinity). In the unpacking that follows, I'll connect Lynch's reception of Kendrick with other mainstream pieces on the rapper, and I'll also fold this reception together with Spence's description of the black parallel public.

Kendrick's Conscious Rapper Ancestry

Spence splits political parallelism into spatial and temporal varieties, and Lynch's sprinkling of past rappers and political leaders throughout his analysis demonstrates how temporal parallelism works. "The mirroring of ideas and practices across time," temporal parallelism tracks the way one generation carries on the work of a previous one (Spence, 11). Lynch invokes some of the most recognizable names in realist and conscious rap in his descriptions of Kendrick, including Tupac, Nas, Public Enemy, and the Roots. Tupac, who was killed in 1996, is the only one of those rappers/groups who isn't still active.[1] But these acts are called forth as representatives of "an earlier era of politically committed and musically diverse hip-hop," with Tupac—the only West Coaster in this pantheon—taking the role of "guiding spirit of the album." In Jessica Hopper's 2012 *SPIN* profile, she adds Dr. Dre and Jay Z to the mix, while Josh Eells (2015) and Gavin Edwards (2015) cross genres to summon Miles Davis, Parliament, Marvin Gaye, and Rick James to the pages of *Rolling Stone* and *Billboard*, respectively. Kendrick's ancestry isn't limited to musicians; Lynch quotes or references lyrics in which Kendrick compares himself to Marcus Garvey, Martin Luther King Jr., Nelson Mandela, and Bill Clinton. The problem with temporal parallelism, as Spence argues, is that it is an institutionalization of political strategies that ultimately limits the "political options that elites have at their disposal" (11). Appeal to tradition, to the wisdom of previous generations' leaders, shapes contemporary technique even when the present moment may demand different approaches. Imbuing Kendrick with the spirit of rappers and political leaders past legitimates him within a specific, tightly defined discourse. When Lynch says that "rewriting history is exactly what [Kendrick] wants to do," "rewrite" sounds more like tedious copying than an exercise in editing.

The Conflation of Masculinity with Kendrick's Leadership and Mastery

What's striking (though not at all surprising) about Kendrick's lineage is how cisheteromasculine it is.[2] What holds up Kendrick's reputation? It's straight dudes who were born dudes all the way down. Lynch circles back several times to the idea that Kendrick is primarily concerned with leadership—what to do with the power of being a generational voice—and his rumination on Kendrick as a leader is nestled in a paragraph that juxtaposes him with male political and cultural leaders of the past. Moreover, Lynch sees Kendrick's rise to leadership status as the result of his "mastery of th[e] hip hop game" and his engagement in "intense peer competition." Mastery and competition are the hyper-masculine backbone of the kind of top-down leadership narrative that has, for instance, relegated the women who organized and fueled the Civil Rights and Black Power movements to footnotes or historical curios. Lynch's reception of Kendrick's leadership places him in a public sphere that conforms to the mainstream's gender norms.

The Depth and Complexity of Kendrick and His Woke Contemporaries

The cisheteronormativity of Lynch's reception of Kendrick's work extends into his characterization of it as deep and complex. In addition to his cultural and political ancestry, Kendrick works alongside even more dudes—Killer Mike, El-P, Talib Kweli, J. Cole—who Lynch identifies as producing "artistically ambitious, politically engaged hip hop." In *Fact*, H. Drew Blackburn adds President Obama, who cited "How Much a Dollar Cost" as his favorite song in 2015, to the contemporary mix (2016). Tellingly, the rappers' political engagement—and the president's commentary, too—responds "to the killings of young black men such as Trayvon Martin, Michael Brown, and Eric Garner." Young black *men*. Meanwhile, #sayhername, a movement involved in tracking and fighting police brutality against cis- and transwomen, includes the names of fourteen women killed at the hands of the police in the United States during the same timespan that marks the deaths of Martin, Brown, Garner, and other black men. Here the parallel public turns the same unhearing ear to non-cis-men that the mainstream does, and this narrow political engagement is tied closely to Lynch's assessment of *To Pimp a Butterfly*'s quality. In an establishing shot, Lynch bookends the word "great" with two instances of "politically": "With its politically charged lyrics and jazzy, funky beats, it calls to mind the great albums of an earlier era of politically committed and musically diverse hip hop." Kendrick's access to greatness—only granted through his ancestry, it should be noted—literally hinges on its political work. Elsewhere, Lynch hears *To Pimp* as thematically unified and conceptually ambitious, while his contemporaries, Run the Jewels (the duo consisting of Killer Mike and El-P), are "brilliantly abrasive."

Kendrick as Scholar

Kendrick's depth and complexity ultimately contribute to his status as a scholar. As mentioned above, Lynch's description of Kendrick in academic terms aligns with Spence's description of the importance of expertise in defining the parallel public. Elsewhere, Kendrick's roots in Compton—made famous by the iconic rap group NWA, themselves hagiographized in a 2015 feature film—mark his expertise; he is someone who knows, who has lived the hood he raps about. In both the *SPIN* (2012) and *Rolling Stone* (2013) profiles released as Kendrick hit the public consciousness around the release of his first studio album, *good kid, m.A.A.d. city* (2012), Compton appears in the opening sentence. "He is more reporter than participant," writes Jonah Weiner in *Rolling Stone*, while in *SPIN* Hopper calls the album a "totemic memoir." Lynch carries Kendrick from eyewitness to scholar with a flourish: "Like a great book, 'To Pimp a Butterfly' stands alone, telling a *coherent* story from start to finish in a *unique voice* and making an *important statement* about *big issues*. It is an *organic whole*, a sustained reflection on *complex ideas*, which offers great fun along the way but *makes no compromises* to the format or scope of the 'single'" (emphasis mine). Coherence, organicism, complexity, innovation—these are all descriptions of music Lynch could've cut and pasted from any German nationalist's ~~propaganda~~ writing about Beethoven and Brahms and Wagner in the 19th and early 20th centuries. Here, Lynch blends Kendrick's scholasticism with his uncompromising commitment to making important art until we arrive at an expert of the black parallel public cast very much in the image of the great men of the white supremacist mainstream.

Kendrick's Self-Critique as Post-Race Multiracialism

The reception of Kendrick apparent in Lynch's and other journalists' writings paints a picture that looks like the parallel public Spence describes.

Kendrick is the on-the-ground expert who rises above the excepted population to prove himself and his cohort reformable according to neoliberal market logic. In so doing, he accesses "a modicum of political and cultural power" (all those breathless accolades, the Grammys, the political clout) while reproducing "the established class, heterosexual, and gender norms" of the mainstream (Spence, 9). So what are the politics coming out of this particular parallel public? It's not the crack governmentality that Spence identifies as the neoliberal market logic of late 20th century descriptive realist rap. Instead of the entrepreneurial aspirations of crack governmentality, the parallel public that takes shape in the discourse surrounding Kendrick is formed according to post-race ideology, which affords us the opportunity to think alongside Spence but in terms that better apply to contemporary rap than 90s descriptive realist rap.

Lynch locates Kendrick's political vision in "a deep skepticism about leaders and power," noting he "mistrusts all leaders—including himself." This skepticism marks a virtuous humility in Lynch's assessment: "It takes a remarkable degree of confidence to face up frankly to such limitations and to expose the shortcomings in one's own analysis." Here is where Lynch's reception of Kendrick ties itself into the gnarliest of knots. I reproduce the following two paragraphs, which Lynch uses to launch into his central argument about Kendrick's "auto-critique," in an effort to trace the threads of that argument and discover the underlying assumptions about race that hold it together.

> Kendrick's political vision is deeply shaped by his upbringing in Compton and by a deep skepticism about leaders and power. He is filled with righteous passion, but he refused to glorify violence and mistrusts all leaders – even himself. Years ago, on "The Relevant," he described himself as "militant as Martin Luther King in the penitent." Other rappers play with a violent response to injustice and abuse, whether it is Killer Mike demanding to know "When you n—gon' unite and kill the police?" or The Game musing about going to Ferguson to "murder all the cops/then the cops will probably stop killing" or even Tupac invoking Nat Turner in the album-ending dialogue. Kendrick backs away from such violence. He has seen the human costs of violence in Compton and doesn't want any more dead bodies on his conscience. As he raps in the key track "Hood Politics," "I don't give a f—about no politics in rap, my n—-/My lil homie Stunna Deuce ain't never comin' back."

> That recognition of the limits of solidarity and the futility of violence pushes back against the spirit of today's political age. It is far too easy to spiral into violent polarization between mutually hostile solidarity groups, the dehumanization of rivals and the valorization of the voices offering the most extreme

solutions. Kendrick responds with an ethos of self-criticism, listening to his own arguments with a skeptical ear and finding them wanting: "So don't matter how much I say I like to preach with the Panthers/Or tell Georgia State 'Marcus Garvey got all the answers,'" he raps, only to make clear that he knows that he does not have those answers. (Lynch 2016)

The skepticism, the self-critique, the mistrust of himself as a leader—Lynch *says* repeatedly that Kendrick's critique is turned inward, on himself. But he *shows* critique pointed outward, toward fellow rappers and "hood politics" more broadly. Even the Garvey quote comes from "The Blacker the Berry" (2015), a song Kendrick performs in the first person as a way of packing as many black stereotypes or black cultural maxims into a single person as possible. "The Blacker the Berry" is the song version of Kendrick's thoughts about respectability and the death of Michael Brown. He isn't calling himself a hypocrite; he's standing in for a certain kind of blackness and calling *that* hypocritical. In "The Blacker the Berry" and his comments on Michael Brown, Kendrick does what Spence accuses the expert black social scientists of the parallel public of doing: arguing "that structural factors are not enough to explain concentrated urban poverty; culture has to do at least part of the heavy lifting" (2011, 16).

The process of expertise in the parallel public that Spence describes, though he doesn't put it explicitly in these terms, is the process by which an individual, or a handful of individuals (think of Jesse Jackson or Al Sharpton being invited for commentary on the 24-hour news channels), come to speak for "the black community." Ralina Joseph argues that when "people of color in the media" take up mainstream ideology, their "assertions are used as the authentic voices" (2010, 249). Experts, then, become experts by paralleling the mainstream. Lynch's use of "The Blacker the Berry" is instructive here; he quotes Kendrick's performance of community expert and spokesperson as a way of punctuating his conflation of Kendrick-as-self and Kendrick-as-all-blackness. This isn't a move unique to Lynch at all, and it's common in hip hop criticism. Establishing Kendrick's credentials as a realist rapper in the lineage of Tupac, Public Enemy, and Nas and rooting him in Compton in a way that brings West Coast gangsta rap immediately to mind is a way of authenticating him so that we are more likely to hear his lyrics as an account of the truth, the sort of thing we get from a reporter or the author of a memoir, as Weiner and Hopper underline in their profiles. From here, the shift to authentic voice of all blackness is shamefully simple: Lynch can show us Kendrick being critical of others but tell us he's being critical of himself because Kendrick's hip hop authenticity combines with the process of expertise in the black parallel public to produce a conflation of self and community that works like a familiar racial trope with a twist. Instead of just speaking on behalf of all blackness (as in the Jesse Jackson and Al Sharpton examples above), Kendrick is also perceived to critique himself by critiquing other black rappers and activists. One for all and all-in-one.

Note the beginning of the second paragraph above—Lynch throws "the limits of solidarity" into the mix alongside "futility of violence" as if the previous paragraph had been about both when it was actually only about the futility of violence. This rhetorical sleight of hand, which implies that solidarity leads to violence, is best understood in the context of post-racial ideology. Post-race, as discussed in Chapter 1, encompasses the belief that racial inequality has ended (the Civil Rights Acts are often believed to be the historical endpoint of racism) so that race no longer matters. "Post-racial success," following Joseph, "is one of rising above racism ... to the point where identity categories themselves no longer exist" (2010, 249). Here, racism is an individual problem instead of a set of systemic and institutionalized policies and ideologies. In Joseph's study, it's Tyra Banks, recently called fat in the tabloids, standing in front of a studio audience of women, all of them in red bodysuits with their weights emblazoned on their chests in white numbers, as Banks encourages them to run "around your neighborhood in a bikini screaming 'So What?'" As Joseph notes, such an act is potentially dangerous in a society that polices black women's bodies the way Banks had just experienced; only if body image is an entirely internalized problem can "So what?" work as an effective response (246–48). Banks is the expert in this parallel public, and the contours of her politics are remarkably similar to the received politics of Kendrick Lamar.

In the same way Banks turns the attention from tabloids that would decide what her body should or shouldn't look like, Kendrick's "But when we don't have respect for ourselves, how do we expect them to respect us? It starts from within" individualizes the systemic problem of police violence (Edwards 2015). In each case, Banks and Kendrick feint solidarity that actually just shifts the onus of racism or sexism onto those who experience it. Banks's audience apparently derives group strength from reminding each other to look within to find appreciation of their bodies, while Kendrick's might encourage self-respect that is hopefully literally bulletproof. Meanwhile, the policing of racialized and gendered bodies, from how they live to *if* they live, continues unabated. Tellingly, Lynch nestles the *Billboard* quote about Michael Brown in a paragraph that begins, "This unrelenting ethos of self-critique extends to his own celebration of African-American identity." This is post-race ideology: the celebration of a racial group comes through self-critique, the systemic is individualized.

Since post-race ideology stems from the belief that racism has ended so that race no longer matters, the only acceptable form of racial group solidarity is one that would unravel that same group. Post-race, to borrow Jared Sexton's phrase (loosely—Sexton doesn't explicitly frame multiracialism as post-race, but his description of how multiracialism works resonates with post-race ideology), is a way of "acknowledging racial divisions without acknowledging racial hierarchies;" race *exists*, but it doesn't *matter* (2008, 64–65). Sexton's critique of post-race multiracialism points to its antiblackness and provides a useful rebuttal to Lynch's "limits of solidarity." Multiracialism stands as the goal of post-race ideology, the virtuous mixture of races and ethnicities—the end of racial purity—that would prove race doesn't matter. It's a United Colors of Benetton ad. The problem, as Sexton outlines it, is that because post-race multiracialism proceeds without acknowledging racial hierarchies, then the blending of races can never be virtuous, never de-politicized; instead, "multiracialism . . . is a tendency to neutralize the political antagonism set loose by the critical affirmation of blackness" (65). In other words, racial solidarity—like gun ownership—is something whiteness would prefer to preserve for itself; as soon as blackness claims it, too, racial solidarity becomes a problem. In a multiracial, post-race society, anyone still clinging to a racialized group identity is considered out of step, backwards, antagonistic, racist.

Let's return to Lynch's reception of Kendrick with Sexton's framework in mind. When Lynch, expounding on the "limits of solidarity," says "It is far too easy to spiral into violent polarization between mutually hostile solidarity groups, the dehumanization of rivals and the valorization of the voices offering the most extreme solutions," he is acknowledging racial division (remember, Kendrick's work is a "celebration of African-American identity") without acknowledging racial hierarchies. The police, deployed and legally protected by a white supremacist government, are but a "mutually hostile solidarity group," no more to blame for the deaths of the black citizens whose bodies they leave in the streets than the black citizens themselves, who, but for a little more self-respect, may well not be dead after all. Lynch, having already elided "solidarity" and "violence," suggests that any black solidarity group that isn't self-critically disassembling itself and dispersing into a multiracial public is a danger to itself and others. This is an anti-black account of black solidarity advanced under the guise of diversity. Recalling Lynch's earlier citation of Martin Luther King alongside Kendrick's nonviolence, then pairing it with "the limits of solidarity," we arrive at "an ironic denunciation of black political formations advanced *in the name of* the preeminent modern black political formation [ie, the Civil Rights movement]" (Sexton, 66). What's left is an "ethos of self-critique" that "offers another path towards rebuilding shattered communities and constructing *new* [read: post-racial] *forms* of solidarity" (Lynch, emphasis mine).

KENDRICK'S PARALLEL PUBLIC

Lynch places Kendrick in the position of an expert-leader who is meant to drag black solidarity movements into line with mainstream racial politics, to essentially desegregate them. Lynch doesn't say #alllivesmatter, but he doesn't have to; the intent is clear enough. Lynch, who I think crystallizes a significant strain of Kendrick critique, wants black solidarity movements to work according to the same principles of the parallel public Spence describes in *Stare in the Darkness*. But because Kendrick's immediate milieu isn't the same as the gangsta rap context of the era Spence studies, the mechanics of these parallel publics are different. The black parallel public is a space where African Americans, who are the exception to neoliberal market logic, demonstrate an ability to be reformed according to the neoliberal market, an ability to parallel the mainstream, and Spence's chapter on crack governmentality examines the primary demonstration of the neoliberalization of black communities in realist rap from 1989 to 2004. Neoliberal market logic, like post-race ideology, individualizes systemic problems. By withdrawing Keynesian welfare programs that create public safety nets, neoliberal humanism shifts the onus of income inequality to individuals, who "are forced to develop their human capital and, in effect, to become entrepreneurs, if not corporations of one" (Spence, 38). In late 20th-century descriptive realist rap, those entrepreneurs, those raised up to prove "African Americans [don't] constitute the exception," were drug dealers and gang bangers (15).

Spence's description of the UGK song "Pocket Full of Stones" (1992) makes clear how the drug dealer is "the neoliberal subject, the *homo œconomicus*, is the entrepreneur, the enterprise—the corporation of one, the hustler" (39).

> Bun B details how he took the raw product that a relative sold him, cooked it up, sold it, then put the money back into more product, which he presumably cooked up, then sold again, repeating the process. Soon he had enough to buy a house on the lake, a nice car, and a business he used to launder his money . . . it is clear that rather than being lazy, or shiftless, or lacking in work ethic, Bun B is an extremely hard worker (he cooked the crack himself), is extremely disciplined (disciplined enough not to become addicted to the product he was creating; disciplined enough to produce and reproduce the product over and over again), and is extremely entrepreneurial. (39)

Parallel, indeed. Bun B takes the same work ethic that fuels neoliberal capital and applies it to a shadow business. The money of that shadow business moves through and alongside mainstream capital but never officially. Its product, crack, came to represent blackness during the 1980s' War on Drugs, and from 1992 to 2009, approximately 85 percent of federal crack trafficking prosecutions involved black defendants (Lynch and Omori 2013, 33). The descriptive realist rappers Spence surveys are the experts of their urban communities, and they form a specifically black parallel public by arguing for their communities as entrepreneurial, capable of being reformed according to neoliberal market logic, based on their business in the production and trade of a specifically black drug. The parallel public, importantly, feeds the mainstream in economically viable ways. While the money flowing through and laundered out of the crack trade would circulate unofficially in the mainstream economy, the mainstream also built their own forms of capital—most obviously the prison industrial complex—around crack governmentality, confirming the reformation of an otherwise excepted population according to market logic. In his 1994 study of gangsta rap, Robin Kelley noted some of these market opportunities—"all-male schools, heavier discipline, more policing, censorship, dress codes"—prepared to rush through an open door of gangsta rap critique that would profit off a literal interpretation of gangsta rap violence (225).

The Anti-Drug Abuse Act of 1986 codified a mandatory minimum sentence of five years' imprisonment for possession of certain weights of crack and powder cocaine: five grams of crack, five hundred grams of cocaine. The 1:100 disparity had no pharmacological grounding; in 2007's *Kimbrough v. United States*, Justice Ginsburg wrote in the Supreme Court's majority opinion that "Crack and powder cocaine are two forms of the same drug. . . . The active ingredient in powder and crack cocaine is the same. The two forms of the drug also have the same physiological and psychotropic effects" (II). The disastrous results of the 1:100 ratio, alongside intensified policing of people of color, led to, as Lowney put it in 1994, "a historic over-incarceration of people of color through drug prohibition, an over-incarceration which has increased to epic and unconscionable proportions in the past decade" (167). From 1994 to 2014, the US prison population grew by about 50 percent (from just over 1 million to just over 1.5 million prisoners), and while the rate of black incarceration dropped some over those two decades, by 2014, blacks, who are 12 percent of the US population, were 35.8 percent of the US prison population (Beck and Gilliard 1995, 8; Carson 2015, 15). The "epic and unconscionable proportions" Lowney diagnosed in 1994 somehow managed to become more epic and proved to be perfectly conscionable for the US public at large. Crack governmentality paralleled the mainstream's work ethic and also fed an enterprise—the prison industrial complex—that generated capital within the mainstream. Recall from Chapter 1 that, although neoliberal human- ism claims colorblindness by only making decisions based on an economic bottom line, those bottom lines are produced in a white supremacist soci- ety whose past and present game the system against blackness. So the work ethic Bun B describes in "Pocket Full of Stones" exactly mirrors the entre- preneurialism of the mainstream, where he is welcomed as an economically viable member of society . . . in the form of a prisoner. Neoliberal market logic requires healthy bottom lines, and the white supremacist backdrop of that logic results in a privatized penal system that thrives on black and brown criminality and recidivism.

Compared to the descriptive realist rap Spence studies, the reception of Kendrick Lamar doesn't seem to paint a picture of a particularly entrepre- neurial artist. If he's supposed to be paralleling the market logic of the main- stream, his pushback against the kind of gang-related activity that would include crack governmentality seems counter-productive; he's stepping on the entrepreneurial trope his realist rap predecessors leveraged as evidence of their mainstream work ethic. In fact, Kendrick's stance in relation to crack governmentality is similar to what Spence describes in his analysis of *argumentative* realist rap. Argumentative realists perform, like Kendrick, as experts on the urban communities they come from, but instead of valoriz- ing the drug game as entrepreneurial—instead of participating in it—they, again like Kendrick, critique the systemic problems that lead to the crim- inalization of black men and the unfairness of the US justice system. This critique often incorporates a post-race component (though Spence doesn't use this term) that recommends individual solutions to institutionalized problems (Spence, 46–53). When that post-race component is amplified, as is the case with Lynch's reception of Kendrick, argumentative realist rap- pers like Kendrick, Nas, Public Enemy, and Big Daddy Kane coalesce into a black parallel public that runs counter to crack governmentality.

While Kendrick bears a striking resemblance to the argumentative real- ists in Spence's work, my read of the reception of Kendrick is a critical extension of Spence's work in two related ways. First, Spence leads right up to but doesn't make explicit the connection between post-race ideol- ogy and neoliberal economic viability: "These critiques reproduce neolib- eral narratives by focusing on internal cultural failures—the failures that justify their position in the racial hierarchy, failures that can only be solved by cultural regeneration" (53). By naming this as part of a broader post-race ideology, I arrive at the second extension: while an argumentative realist like Big Daddy Kane marks his reformation in the image of market logic when he "reproduces neoliberalism by emphasizing neoliberal trickle-down economics over politics," Kendrick's economic viability hinges entirely on his post-race politics. The neoliberal argumentative realist of the 2010s operates differently from those of the 1989–2004 era Spence examines. Writing in 2015, Lynch finds no need for Kendrick to offer any particular economic policy or plan like Kane does, noting approvingly that Kendrick "sees power in overcoming the manufactured differences that keep subordinated communities weak, but *refuses to allow any illusions about where such a unified movement might lead*" (emphasis mine). In other words, Kendrick's post-race politics are enough: splintering solidarity groups in order to, as Sexton describes it, neutralize the political energy created "by the critical affirmation of blackness" calls to mind the concept of creative destruction (Sexton, 65).

In "Neoliberalism as Creative Destruction," David Harvey lays out creative destruction in economic terms: "practices that restored class power to capitalist elites in the United States and elsewhere" by gathering the spoils created by the destruction of social safety nets and equity agendas (2007, 35). As Harvey and Spence and other writers on neoliberalism are careful to note, neoliberal policies aren't intended to separate government from the free market or simply repeal welfare policies; "rather, [neoliberalism] is about *continually using the state to create the conditions under which the market can exist*" (Spence, 14). These conditions treat the free market like a wind-up toy; once cranked and set loose, it's just a matter of clearing everything out of the way so it can keep moving. Or, perhaps more appropriately, these conditions treat the free market like Homer Simpson, who, having been told not to eat a pie, says, "All right, pie, I'm just going to do this [chomps mouth repeatedly], and if you get eaten, it's your own fault! [resumes chomping, closes eyes, advances toward pie]" (*The Simpsons* 1994). Harvey argues that neoliberalism is best understood as "a political scheme aimed at reestablishing the conditions for capital accumulation and the restoration of class power," so creative destruction creates capital for elites by winding up its free market toy—or infusing it with Homer Simpson's id, as it were—then wiping out existing economic institutions like welfare and labor unions so that the free market can waddle through and eat everyone's pie (Harvey 2007, 29). Since neoliberalism's conditions are created by the state, creative destruction can often proceed with no firm plan about what will fill the destroyed system; the inexorable forward momentum of the free market will inevitably occupy whatever space it's given.

Lynch's account of Kendrick's post-race work, which would separate black solidarity groups and disperse them into multiracial blocs, creates an isomorphic relationship between Kendrick's politics and neoliberalism's economics. Where Big Daddy Kane offered an economic alternative to crack governmentality, Kendrick is praised for his politics of self-critique—which, as described above, are really group-critique—because they refuse to name what will be created on the other side of destruction. Lynch doesn't name it either, but he admits in the final sentences that Kendrick's politics suggest "another path towards rebuilding shattered communities and constructing new forms of solidarity." How can an unnamed path be suggested? When that path is cleared in the context of neoliberalism, which seeks to fill any void with a set of economic policies that will benefit the elite. The post-race reception of Kendrick takes the same form as neoliberalism's creative destruction; Kendrick's politics parallel neoliberalism's economics.

This deep-dive into the reception of Kendrick Lamar demonstrates that, although he is a rapper with a reputation for challenging the status quo with his socially critical lyrics, Kendrick can be fit "completely [in]side our present conception of what it is to be human," to riff on Wynter. The reception of him as a post-race rapper produces a neoliberal humanist black parallel public that not only re-enforces mainstream norms but also feeds both the multiracial logic that underlines 21st-century white supremacy and the creative destruction that neutralizes black solidarity politics and provides an outsized economic boon to those who have always benefitted from economic boons. If neoliberal humanism—the present conception of what it is to be human—recognizes as human those who are formed according to market logic, then Kendrick is received as decidedly human.

EXCEPTIONS

My focus on reception in this chapter is key: Kendrick circulates in mainstream consciousness as a political artist because listeners can hear the structure and logic of contemporary neoliberal politics in his lyrics. Certainly this isn't an exhaustive reception study of Kendrick. Black Lives Matter activists chanting "We gon' be alright" (from 2015's "Alright") in protests against violent and racist policing certainly hear black solidarity in Kendrick's work, not the splintering of that solidarity. Activists' use of Kendrick's lyrics work as what Hall calls "the dialectic of cultural struggle," as dominant and resistant cultures fight over the meaning of popular art (1998, 447). But even in the case of Black Lives Matter's use of Kendrick, the upshot is that the reception of Kendrick marks him as politically legible within the narrow definition of politics represented in the US mainstream. Returning to a point I made at the beginning of the chapter, I'm not interested here in participating in that struggle. Rather, I want to mark the contours of the reception of Kendrick in order to focus the rest of the book's analysis on politics that don't fit as neatly into the mainstream. Recalling Chapter 1, because Kendrick's politics are legible in the mainstream, then struggling over their meaning requires a politics that squarely faces that which wishes to destroy you and engages on its terms. In that context, it isn't hard to imagine the burning neighborhoods of Ferguson or Baltimore (after the shooting of Freddie Gray in 2015) as the destructive step that clears the way for neoliberal creation, an influx of deluxe condos, perhaps, and some trendy coffee shops and cafes selling locally sourced food stuffs, the creation of neighborhoods that are, to use Sexton's terms, not so much *white* as they are *non-black*.

Spence notes that neoliberalism relies on two technologies: technologies of subjectivity and technologies of subjection. The former describes the induction of "self-animation and self-government in citizens," the tools necessary to cope on a personal level with the problems of institutionalized, structural inequalities (14). Technologies of subjectivity are the province of those who are perfectly formed or capable of being reformed according to market logic—"self-help programs, activities that emphasize entrepreneurialism, and campaigns that encourage and promote healthy living" (14). Technologies of subjection, meanwhile, govern those deemed incapable of reform: prisons, surveillance programs, draconian laws like the Anti-Drug Abuse Act of 1986. Technologies of subjectivity and subjection work together to define who is and isn't human within the framework of neoliberal humanism, ultimately enforcing the boundaries around excepted populations. Those who can't find or remake themselves through technologies of subjectivity are the exceptions to neoliberal market logic, cordoned off and separated from vital resources and power. In crack governmentality, rappers perform an argument for their inclusion in the neoliberal mainstream: they use hip hop as a technology of subjectivity to lobby their way out of the excepted population, which they in turn define. Descriptive realists take on the role of criminals to demonstrate their entrepreneurial wherewithal, leaving snitches, punks, and drug users—those who are too weak to provide for themselves in a competitive marketplace—as the exception that can't be reformed (43–46). Argumentative realists, meanwhile, produce the gangsters and drug dealers—the same roles descriptive realists fill—as exceptions, criminals who aren't able to help themselves to legitimate entrepreneurialism (46–53).

The reception of Kendrick Lamar, similarly, functions as a technology of both subjectivity and subjection. Held up as the would-be gangster who helped himself, the poor inner-city kid whose artistic entrepreneurialism got him over, Kendrick becomes a technology of subjectivity that individualizes systemic ills and provides the role model for how you, too, can overcome. In the same stroke, read as a politically conscious black voice that critiques black solidarity in favor of multiracialism, Kendrick becomes the dividing line that clearly marks those who would preserve black solidarity as those who are incapable of being reformed, as fit for surveillance, prison, punishment, even as his lyrics criticize those same technologies of subjection. This last point distinguishes Kendrick from the descriptive realists in Spence's study. The exceptions produced through the reception of Kendrick include the same gangsters and drug dealers who are targeted by descriptive realists, but they aren't the only targets. The post-race ideology a critic like Lynch finds in Kendrick's politics works so that blackness becomes problematically too pure, a raced existence that is "strictly demarcated" from a more multicultural or diverse society (Sexton, 66). The political upshot of this, as I've noted, is that black solidarity is understood to work at direct odds with a virtuous, post-racial society. White supremacy covers itself in the appearance of multiculturalism in order to render solidarity movements (whether defined by race, gender, sexuality, class) anachronistic and regressive. Aesthetically, this means music that *sounds* black—instead of like a multicultural blending of genres—marks its practitioners as political exceptions. Blackness—and sonic blackness—is relegated to the sidelines of a properly post-racial society.

I've focused primarily here on the reception of Kendrick's *lyrics* because that's the element of his work that shows up most often in discussions of his politics. Returning to Lynch's commentary on the depth and complexity of Kendrick's work, though, brings both lyrics and music to the fore and points to the aesthetics that mark the exceptions produced by post-race neoliberal humanism. Lynch includes three specific comparisons that revolve around the idea that Kendrick's music is smarter than others', and each one relies on self-evident observations that his readers are meant to already agree with. Bourdieu says that this sort of self-evidence marks a public consensus that "goes without saying because it comes without saying," but Lynch says these things anyway, offering the illusion of evidence for statements that assume a willingly agreeable readership (167). I've written elsewhere about Barthes's theory of myth and the way things that go without saying are imbued with ideology (Barthes 1972, 117–18; Burton 2013, 486–88). In this case, I'll look at each of Lynch's comparisons in turn in order to pick up on their self-evidence and the political and aesthetic ideology that crystallizes in their combination.

First, focusing on lyrics, Lynch separates Kendrick from his most financially successful fellow rapper: "where talented contemporaries like Drake rarely venture a thought deeper than 'being rich makes me sad,' Kendrick grapples with core political theory questions of power, identity and the ethics of leadership."[3] Lynch completely misses the mark with Drake. Even if we accept his overly reductive synopsis of Drake's lyrics, there's still the fact that "being rich makes me sad" can be an incredibly acute and effective critique of celebrity, capitalism, gender, race, class, power, identity. Instead, Lynch leans on prevalent strains of Drake critique to render the rapper unserious and tangential—far from the core concerns Kendrick addresses—both because he's sad and because he's sad about the wrong things. Drake has been criticized for practically everything, including the fact that he sings too much, talks about his emotions too much, wears too many sweaters, and is too petty (Roberson 2013). Rappers like Common (on 2011's "Sweet" and then 2012's "Stay Schemin'" bootleg) and writers like Big Ghost (at okayplayer.com) gather these critiques in an effort to challenge Drake's masculinity and seriousness, and the Internet is rife with Drake memes that are unrepentantly silly. Lynch's "being rich makes me sad" jab at Drake is the heart of one of those memes, "Drake the type . . ."[4] This collection of jokes paints Drake as overly sensitive and alternately worried about or delighted by frivolous details:

- Drake the type of nigga that turns down the volume on the TV when his cat falls asleep.
- Drake the type of nigga that sing the alphabet and cry when he gets to X.
- Drake the type of nigga to tilt his head back and open his mouth when it's raining.
- Drake the type of nigga that text his homeboys just to ask how their day is going.
- @drakethetypeofnigga to use a stun gun in gta5 [*Grand Theft Auto 5*] cus he don't wanna kill no one.

By reducing Drake to the gist of a handful of memes, Lynch is able to short-circuit the multivalent performances of Drake that extend beyond his lyrics and also shortchange the potentially meaningful work performed by fans who engage Drake in this extensive meme-ification. Lynch divorces Drake and the fan work that surrounds him from any particular context and judges him politically empty in comparison with Kendrick.

Second, missing "the glory days of hip-hop when leading rappers like Tupac, Nas, Public Enemy and the Roots engaged with big political and social ideas" and training his critical sites on music, Lynch takes a shot at pop: "Instead, brain-dead club thumpers dominate the charts while Killer Mike and El-P's brilliantly abrasive 'Run the Jewels 2' sells only a handful of copies." Lynch's brilliant-versus-brain-dead comparison locks into hip hop's authenticity debate, "attempts to parse out [hip hop's] political potential from its seemingly more sensational and commercialized aspects" (Bogazianos, 58). The authenticity debate reads rappers like Tupac, Nas, Public Enemy, and the Roots as "real" hip hop because (some of) their lyrics are politically engaged, and when their sells are low, it becomes proof that they are committed to a cause—they're "abrasive"—rather than sell-outs. Lynch makes a particularly interesting rhetorical move, shifting from praise for the *lyrics* of the glory day rappers to disdain for the *music* of contemporary hits. The implication is that music made for dancing excludes the possibility of political work; it's brain-dead. Invoking the paragons of authentic hip hop, Lynch can use the shorthand of the authenticity debate to elevate Kendrick above chart-toppers and party music, which are always already brain-dead on arrival.

Finally, Lynch underlines Kendrick's political commitment by separating him not just from other successful rappers like Drake and the club-thumpers, but also from those who pull the strings in the music industry itself: "Emblematically, for the album he transforms his Grammy-winning single "i" into a pseudo-live performance interrupted by crowd noise which he quiets with a heartfelt speech. This would be incomprehensible for the traditional studio executive, but makes brilliant sense in the context of a 79-minute argument." It's hard to fathom what Lynch is even getting at here, as skits and extended versions of songs are such a staple of the hip hop album format that no listener or studio exec would be remotely taken aback by an alternative version of "i" on Kendrick's album. As with Drake and the club-thumpers, Lynch is relying on ideas that go without saying; in this case, it's that studio executives are nefarious and responsible for the commercialization of rap that pulls it from its socially conscious and political roots. Critiques of the recording industry are certainly salient. Recent books by Hugh Barker and Yuval Taylor (2007), Karl Hagstrom-Miller (2010), and Diane Pecknold (editor, 2013) all trace the ways the music industry has defined genre categories according to racial categories more than musical ones. Lynch, though, takes this strain of critique and post-racializes it, mocking *individuals* within the industry as responsible parties rather than recognizing the systemic nature of music industry racism.

These three self-evident observations that Lynch uses to mark Kendrick as smarter, deeper, #woker than other rappers use post-race multiracialism to outline the aesthetics of an excepted population. By triggering the authenticity debate, Lynch sets up Kendrick as authentic and true hip hop, unsullied by the pressures of wealth, club dance floors, and industry executives.

Bogazianos's analysis of the authenticity debate suggests that Lynch isn't just harking back to rappers of the 1980s and 90s but also hip hop academic work of the mid-1990s, which he summarizes as conceiving of rap "primarily as an 'authentic' development of African American cultural expression that had potential for black political voice" (58). In other words, authentic hip hop is authentic black politics, and Lynch has characterized Kendrick's black politics as post-race multiracialism. The purity of Kendrick's black political expression is contingent on his skepticism of black solidarity: the best, most authentic blackness becomes that which is mixed into a diverse pool of races and ethnicities. This is in keeping with what I've argued about the reception of Kendrick in this chapter, but Lynch's comparison with other kinds of hip hop not only defines the ways Kendrick's black politics are able to be reformed according to market logic; the comparison also defines some of the aesthetics and politics of the exceptions—those unable to be reformed according to market logic—without specifically naming a genre. I'm confident we can fit the pieces of the puzzle together, though, and find a genre of music that functions as the exception to Kendrick's post-race multiracialism.

Dirty South Exceptions

In contrast to Kendrick's virtuous diversity, the exception to his post-race multiracialism is music that *sounds* too black. The only real aesthetic description Lynch offers is "club thumpers," music composed and performed for a dance floor. Tying into the Drake example, this music will garner mass appeal, therefore pleasing the nefarious studio executives who would be baffled by Kendrick's principled music. Compared with Kendrick, the music is politically empty, and the musicians who produce and perform it are doing the bidding of racist executives, essentially filling the music with the politics of those executives, who have only their own bottom lines and self-interests at heart. These few clues point toward the Dirty South, a collection of regional aesthetics from cities and ruralities across the US South that have come to dominate hip hop's airwaves for more than a decade. Roni Sarig, in his book on Southern hip hop, notes that "starting in the late '90s and continuing to the present day, Southern rappers, musicians, songwriters, producers, and labels have contributed far more than their share to hip hop's commercial and artistic success—and extending hip hop's hold as pop music's dominant sound by introducing new sounds and fusions" (2007, xiv). When reading Lynch's description of not-Kendrick-enough music as "brain-dead club thumpers," a Southern artist like Lil Jon, with his chant-based lyrics, heavy bass, and misogynist and childish obsessions with sexual organs and acts, springs immediately to mind.

Despite the work of writers like Sarig and Ali Colleen Neff (2009), who take different tacks to a similar argument for hip hop's direct connection to Southern musical genres, the South is ready-made to come up short in the authenticity debate, in part because of its overwhelming focus on dance-ready hits, its revolution around chant-driven lyrics, and its rise to national prominence in time with hip hop's conversion from scrappy subgenre to pop lingua franca in the late 90s and early 00s. Southern hip hop stands as the exception to true hip hop, to the black parallel public Kendrick represents. On its surface, there's often nothing particularly political about Dirty Southern music, which is exactly why I turn my attention to it over the course of the next two chapters. If Kendrick's legible politics function as a black parallel public capable of being reformed according to market logic, then the exceptions it creates—in this case, the Dirty South—may offer an echo of what Wynter points toward, a way of being human that sits outside mainstream definitions of human.

The next two chapters work as the other side of this study of Kendrick reception—a trip to the Dirty South in search of the posthuman. I'll first listen closely to trap, a Southern hip hop subgenre emanating from Atlanta, in order to pinpoint its characteristic stylistic elements—its sonic blackness—and what sorts of politics are embedded in them. Then, I'll turn to Rae Sremmurd, a hip hop duo fluent in but not restricted to trap, to hear how they use parties to resonate black queerness. In each chapter, I'm decidedly disinterested in the kind of politics attached to Kendrick, listening instead for habeas viscus, "relational modes of being in the flesh," that which is "heard, seen, tasted, felt, and lived in the ethereal shadows of Man's world" (Weheliye 2014, 122, 138). Or, more precisely, in the bone-rattling sub-bass of the latest Dirty South production. It's time to pivot from the primarily lyrical analysis of Kendrick, whose "radical self-questioning becomes his vehicle to escape the [black solidarity] traps that have repeatedly led to failure" (Lynch). For the next two chapters, I'll listen closely to the way blackness is sounded in Dirty South subgenres, and I'll start in Chapter 3 by walking right into a trap.

CHAPTER 3

Sonic Blackness and the Illegibility of Trap Irony

A trap gonna be just what it is. It's a trap.
                            Curtis Snow, *Noisey Atlanta* (2015)

Noisey reporter Thomas Morton sits in a dimly lit Atlanta penthouse wearing a mask that says "Free Gucci" across the forehead and that sports an ice cream cone drawing below the right eye. The real Gucci Mane—an Atlanta rap legend—has a real ice cream cone tattoo in the same location. Morton has been chatting with the ATL Twins, identical brothers who experience life as a single person in two bodies and who therefore share everything—house, car, job, romantic and sexual partners—while a guy named The Devil stands in the corner (Nieratko). The Devil, Morton tells us, "made the scariest rap video I've ever seen for the scariest group of rappers I think exist on Earth" (Capper). The video in question is "Bussin" by Trouble, a member of the Duct Tape Army, and it features Trouble and a group of black men standing in front of an apartment complex while holding guns. That's it. They just stand there, occasionally gesturing at the camera as The Devil shoots them from different angles and composites it all into a three-minute video. So what counts as scary for Morton involves unsmiling, armed black men standing around doing . . . nothing.

Nic Cohn opens his book on New Orleans rap with a story about wandering into the Iberville project one afternoon in 2000.

> I headed into the heart of the project. A few strides brought me to a blind corner. When I turned it, the sunlight was shut out. A few more strides, and a group of youth hemmed me in. None of them spoke or touched me, they simply blocked my

path. The brackish smell of bodies was fierce, and I stumbled back against a wall as the youths moved in. Then, just as suddenly as they'd swarmed, they scattered. A city bus had turned the corner and fixed us with its headlamps. I had never known worse fear . . . And what was most shameful of all, I knew my deepest dread had not been of getting robbed or even shot. I'd been afraid of blackness itself. (4)

Cohn mentions shame and presents the tale as a kind of confessional, ultimately proving his progressive relationship with race by experiencing a "faint warmth" spread through him at the sound of bounce music, a sound he is compelled to follow (7). But his telling of the Iberville encounter is telling. The youths he encounters in the project are described as monsters— stinking, swarming, hunting, mob-like creatures who are afraid of the light. "People with no faces," he later remembers (5).

Morton doesn't offer the thick description Cohn does, so we're left to guess as to exactly what it is about "Bussin" that gets his creeps up, but "I'd been afraid of blackness itself" isn't a far-fetched option. The ATL Twins/ Duct Tape Army episode of *Noisey Atlanta* is the fourth in the ten-part series. *Noisey*, a docu-music arm of VICE media, specializes in what VICE specializes in: good, old-fashioned journalistic sensationalism. Specifically, VICE's signature move is sending an intrepid journalist into some closed-off geographic or cultural locale in order to report on how some remote or closely guarded group of people live. Morton's *Balls Deep*, a show on the Viceland television network, is described in exactly this way on its Web site: "To find out what humanity's deal is, Thomas Morton hangs out with different groups of people and gives their lives a try." The first season's episode titles demonstrate some of what Morton explores: "Alaska Natives," "Orgasmic Meditators," "Bears," "Ramadan." The show's audience is meant to find whatever Morton is doing to be bizarre or at least out of the ordinary, and his nebbishness is important to this goal. Morton's brilliant ability to perform the "fish out of water"—or the "nerd's eye view," as another of the show's Web landing pages describes it—helps *Balls Deep*, emblematic of VICE's broader offerings, function as a kind of multicultural primer: if this guy can do it, you can too!

So when Morton wades into the world of Atlanta (known colloquially as ATL) trap, the general ethos of *Noisey* and VICE preps the viewer for an experience of difference, of some culture that operates outside of normal social boundaries. What's different about Atlanta trap? Its sonic blackness. When Morton comments on the "scariest rap video I've ever seen," he is surrounded by more white people—the ATL Twins, The Devil, and the Twins' sexual partner for the night—than at any other moment in the ten-part series. From this vantage point, he admits that "Bussin" scares him, and the juxtaposition of the white space he occupies when he says this and the black space on the screen in front of him parallels the confessional of Cohn: "I'd been scared of blackness itself."

"Bussin," like the music that undergirds and takes center stage for the bulk of *Noisey Atlanta*, is trap music, a subgenre attributed to Atlanta but with sonic roots in broader Southern hip hop. In this chapter, I approach trap as sonic blackness, a term coined by Nina Sun Eidsheim, as a way of considering its posthuman potential. Following the study of Kendrick's reception as a vision of post-race neoliberal humanism, I listen closely to trap in order to hear it as a sonic referent for blackness, which, in the context of neoliberal humanism, is "negatively purified," or not diverse enough (Sexton, 66). This negative purification moves outside mainstream notions of what it is to be human, marking what is posthuman about trap (Scott 2000, 136). By resonating dissonantly with neoliberal humanism's post-race ideology, trap's blackness takes on the sort of monstrousness that frightened Cohn in the Iberville project and Morton in "Bussin"—the kind of monstrousness Nicki Minaj uses to cow the beat in "Monster." Sounding black in a post-racial society is out of step with post-race ideology, provoking responses of fear or dismissal from listeners, and it's at the core of what I term *trap irony*. My sonic analysis of trap starts from a comparison between Desiigner and Future, two rappers—the latter of whom is nearly synonymous with trap—who have been heard as strikingly similar. By paying close attention to how Desiigner and Future sound the same, I'll also note what's different about them and how they sound in relation to other trap artists. This close listening starting at the song level will ultimately map the sonic aesthetics of trap, which I then connect to a broader politics that remains largely illegible in the context of mainstream US politics and that, in its illegibility, I hear as posthuman.

SONIC BLACKNESS

In Loren Kajikawa's study of racialized sounds in rap, he drills down to how it is that, in a genre where "all kinds of people make and listen to rap music," it nonetheless *sounds* black: "Rap has cultivated a mainstream audience and become a multi-million dollar industry by promoting highly visible (and often controversial) representations of black masculine identity ... rap moguls have consistently put their money on black" (2015, 5). Note that the word "representations" is plural; there's no singular performance of blackness that happens in rap, but the genre tends to cohere around notions of blackness all the same. Nina Sun Eidsheim defines sonic blackness, which she says "is *not* the unmediated sound of essential otherness or the sound of a distinct phenotype," in similar terms: "It is not a single phenomenon, but might be a combination of interchangeable self-reproducing modes: a perceptual phantom projected by the listener; a vocal timbre that happens to match current expectations about blackness; or the shaping of vocal tim-. bre to match current ideas about the sound of blackness" (664).

In other words, what we hear as sonic blackness changes from time to time and place to place, and it will include a multiplicity of possibilities at any given moment, but it boils down to "the perceived presence of the black body in a voice" (Eidsheim, 647). Kendrick Lamar, as I argue in the previous chapter, is received as one kind of sonic blackness: post-race blackness that aligns with present conceptions of neoliberal humanist politics. Trap represents something else entirely and, in fact, settles into the excepted population—those "unable to be re-formed [according to neoliberal market logic]"—created by Kendrick's black parallel public (Spence, 15). As such, trap generally reads as apolitical, but in its ironic performance of blackness in a post-race society, it digs in to blackness in a way that undermines post-race ideology without directly addressing it. Blackness itself—that which so frightens Cohn and Morton—becomes posthuman in the sounds of trap.

The opening examples of this chapter, in which Morton and Cohn shudder at blackness, aren't merely or even, perhaps, primarily about sound, and Eidsheim and Kajikawa are both careful to position sound among a variety of social and cultural elements that would mark something as black. Eidsheim describes voices that "match current expectations about blackness" or fulfill "expectations or ideas about blackness" (663–64), suggesting that reception is key to understanding how sonic blackness works. My analysis of trap aesthetics and politics extends the framework of post-race neoliberal humanism laid out in the Kendrick chapter as the backdrop for "expectations or ideas about blackness."

A note about methodology: I follow both Kajikawa's and Eidsheim's work to expound on how trap sounds black, but the term I'm using, "sonic black-ness" is Eidsheim's. Still, Kajikawa's analysis of how race is sounded in rap music includes notions of sonic blackness (and, importantly, sonic white-ness) even if he doesn't employ the exact term. While Eidsheim focuses especially on voice, Kajikawa analyzes music production—the beats—and my approach to trap combines both vocal and instrumental analysis. Finally, Eidsheim hears something positive about upsetting or progressing past the ways we hear blackness. Eidsheim concludes her study of Marian Anderson with an exortation, "Only by educating ourselves about the complex set of practices that constitute listening can we emerge from layers of perception molded by the values, ideologies, fears, and desires carried by our forebears and liberate our hearing from the cultural commodity of blackness" (665). Eidsheim's vision of the future is reminiscent of post-race ideology, where we could hear race in a way that doesn't matter. Kajikawa, meanwhile, places this punctuation on his analysis of Eminem: "Eminem's performance of whiteness in rap music provides a mirror in which numerous tensions and political projects come into focus, a picture of U.S. race relations in which whiteness becomes just another way of being colored" (142). The turn-of-the-century sound of Eminem's whiteness hit the airwaves "when whiteness as a social category was undergoing profound change," and, in fact, the restructuring of whiteness as "just another way of being colored" aligns with multiracialism as Sexton describes it, which includes "a deceptive moral critique of whiteness as something equivalent to the (still unavoidably racialized) *ethnicities* or *cultures* of nonwhite immigrants and American Indians" (Kajikawa, 142; Sexton, 66). My political analysis of multiracialism, as outlined in the Kendrick chapter, follows Sexton's, so while I employ some of the methodology of Eidsheim and Kajikawa in describing *how* sonic blackness works, I'm less concerned with the fact that trap *does* sound black and more interested in how trap artists "match current expectations about blackness" in order to resonate posthumanly, in ways that don't match the dominant idea about what it is to be human.

TRAP VOCAL AESTHETICS

In his remix of Desiigner's "Panda" (2015), Uncle Murda makes a promise and an unrelated observation: "This beat 'bout to get murdered/thought this was Future when I heard it" (2016). Many people, in fact, thought "Panda" was ATL trap god Future when they heard it. In a *Fader* piece titled "11 Experts Weigh In: Is 'Panda' Actually Good?" most of the "experts" note the similarity (Tanzer and Golden 2016). Like Uncle Murda, the first two respondents—DJ Holiday (Streetz 94.5 in Atlanta) and Judnick Mayard (freelance writer and events coordinator for *Fader*)—mention that they registered genuine surprise when they learned the song wasn't Future. Others' reactions go beyond mere surprise. In the same feature, David Drake calls it "creative theft," which he says is totally fine, but the idea of stealing, especially since Judge Kevin Thomas Duffy paternalistically cited the Seventh Commandment in his 1991 ruling against Biz Markie (*Grand Upright Music, Ltd v. Warner Bros. Records, Inc* 780 F. Supp. 182 (SDNY 1991)), isn't a neutral claim to level at hip hop artists, regardless of a commentator's intent.

Drake isn't alone in his skepticism of Desiigner's authenticity. TM88, who produced Future's "Codeine Crazy" (2015), and rapper 50 Cent both question Desiigner's credentials and hear him as a second-rate knock-off of Future (Fu 2016; Mojica 2016). Writing for *Stereogum*, Tom Breihan includes in the opening paragraph the fact that Desiigner, whose first "Panda" verse begins "I got broads in Atlanta," has never even *been* to Atlanta (Breihan 2016). And at the sensationalist end of the spectrum sits Andrew Friedman, clutching his pearls in a piece for *FACT* over the possibility that the entire New York hip hop scene may be inauthentic because of its history of borrowing from other regions. The conspiratorial nature of the title, "Frauds in Atlanta? Why the controversy of Desiigner's 'Panda' goes deeper than you think," is just the jump-off; Friedman capitalizes on a New York exceptionalism ("New York rappers aren't held to the same standards as everyone else") that is chum for clicks in an Internet drowning in "Panda" think pieces.

Along with this concern over Desiigner's authenticity comes a sort of schadenfreude about his ability to notch a higher rated song than Future had ever managed to that point. Indeed, "Panda" reached No. 1 on the Billboard Hot 100, which measures the popularity of all songs regardless of genre, for two weeks in May 2016. For his part, by May 2016 Future had cracked the Billboard Hot 100 top 10 just once, as a featured artist (along with Drake) on Lil Wayne's "Love Me" (2013), and his other appearances in the top 30 were similarly collaborations. So in the same breath that writers note Desiigner's sonic similarity to Future, they often also mention that he's achieved a success Future never has. *GQ*'s Rohan Nadkarni-penned snippet on "Panda" revolves entirely around this idea, from the title, which says Desiigner "now has what Future doesn't," to the penultimate paragraph, which revels in the fact that neither Future, with his "crooning over Metro Boomin beats," nor his *What a Time to Be Alive* (2015) collaborator Drake had ever reached No. 1 (as it turns out, Drake's "One Dance" is the song that would knock "Panda" out of the top spot, and he had twice topped the Hot 100 as a featured artist on Rihanna songs "What's My Name" (2010) and "Work" (2016), the latter of which immediately preceded "Panda" for nine weeks prior to Desiigner's ascension). Breihan, in his *Stereogum* write-up, finds that "Panda"'s success has allowed him to "transcend" Future's success at the same moment he transcended his "fake Future" status.

Of course, as is evidenced by the way listeners immediately associate Desiigner's voice with Future's, Future isn't exactly struggling to be relevant. Though his singles had had middling showings on the Hot 100 when Desiigner struck gold, he's been a Top 20 regular on hip hop and R&B charts since 2011, and all four of his official album releases to that point landed in the top ten of the Billboard 200—the album equivalent of the Hot 100, measuring popularity regardless of genre—including No. 1 showings for 2015's *DS2* and 2016's *EVOL*.[1] This doesn't stop Stephen Horowitz, in responding to the *Fader*'s question about whether "Panda" is actually good (he won't admit that it is), from reiterating that even though Desiigner has "photocop[ied] what came before him," his success "is something Future has yet to accomplish."

This marriage of two strains of "Panda" commentary—1) Desiigner is inauthentic because he sounds like Future, and 2) Desiigner is more successful than Future—sets off my critical alarm bells. Specifically, what I hear in this critique is an ultimate devaluation of trap music that proceeds roughly as follows: Future is synonymous with trap, and Desiigner sounds just like him; if the knock-off—the photocopy—can transcend the original, then the original must not have been very worthwhile to begin with. And it's trap's sonic blackness that, ultimately, makes it a nonstarter in the context of post-race neoliberal humanism. Before unraveling this further, we need to establish how it is that Desiigner sounds like Future and, in so doing, what trap music sounds like.

Though I've found several instances of writers observing that Desiigner sounds like Future, there's usually little or no accompanying detail explaining exactly what the similarity is. Briehan mentions Desiigner's voice but doesn't elaborate, while Reeves describes Desiigner's (and apparently Future's) voice as "husky, nasally." Friedman offers the most: "Desiigner's woozy, subtly Auto-Tuned raps juxtaposed with hype ad libs are the best Future impression imaginable." Some of this is useful but still incredibly broad, so let's start by saying Desiigner's recorded vocals share timbral and affective similarities to some of Future's recorded vocals, then unpack the specific ways that's true.

The phrase "recorded vocals" is intentional; on Desiigner's debut television performance on *The Late Show* (May 11, 2016), it's apparent that his live vocals sound different from what we hear on the "Panda" recording (which is playing as a backing track during his performance). They're much higher and more excited than on the studio version of "Panda."[2] No shade—same goes for Future (and, for that matter, most rappers), whose live performance of "Where Ya At" on a similar stage (*Jimmy Kimmel Live*, November 12, 2015) involves a different, also higher voice than we hear on record. So what I'm comparing when I listen to Desiigner and Future alongside one another involves a combination of their performed voices and some behind-the-glass work from their producers and sound engineers. Future, for his part, doesn't sound the same on every track, and Desiigner doesn't, either; but during the time that "Panda" was his only release, the response to Desiigner was that he was Future's vocal twin. Using listeners' responses to "Panda" as the starting point, this comparison involves sonic sleuthing that locates "Panda"-like vocals in Future's œuvre to hear why this comp is so pervasive. Specifically, I've identified five points of vocal similarity between Desiigner and Future.[3]

Tuning

Desiigner's voice on "Panda" is detuned, resonating slightly off pitch with the instrumental, a technique so common for Future that a listener could cue up any number of his songs and hear him singing only loosely in key; 2011's "Tony Montana," Future's first song to hit the Billboard charts, is a fine place to start. Most mainstream discussions of Future's voice revolve around his use of Auto-Tune (other usual suspects in these conversations include T-Pain, who has told Dave Tompkins that he uses a vocoder, not Auto-Tune, and Kanye West, who employs pitch correction in a good deal of his sung parts), but this greatly simplifies how his vocals are processed (Tompkins 2010, 302).

Auto-Tune is a specific brand of pitch-correcting and vocal processing software distributed by Antares that has become synonymous with a range of vocal processing techniques much the way "Coke" can stand in for all colas in the US South or "Kleenex" means facial tissue. To say Future uses Auto-Tune really amounts to saying that his vocals are processed to sound distinct, and while Auto-Tune can achieve that recognizable sound, so could other vocal processing softwares. The most immediate reference of Auto-Tune has to do with its pitch correction capabilities. Pitch correction software analyzes audio input in relation to a prescribed key, then digitally shifts any input that strays from that key so that it sounds in tune. At its most subtle, pitch correction software can alter a performance in a way that renders the technology unrecognizable; it's an inaudible, hidden technology. Mess with the settings a bit, though? This is the notorious "Auto-Tune" of T-Pain, Kanye, and Future. Here, the pitch correction software is set to recognize and correct input in zero milliseconds, allowing no time for the natural glide of a vocal performance and immediately shifting pitches into the prescribed key. The result is a fairly synthesized and robotic sound similar to what the vocoder produces; it's an audible, obvious technology. Though Auto-Tune is a vocal processing software like many others, capable of both subtle and obvious pitch correction, it has become synonymous with unnatural sounds used by untalented performers who can't actually sing.[4]

Ironically, calling Future's voice Auto-Tuned is actually a way of highlighting its consistently *detuned* nature. While the aggressive pitch correction settings produce the robotic sound, a chain of other effects are necessary to achieve the final product. I have no inside information on the exact settings used to produce Future's voice, and it likely isn't identical on all recordings, but working from standard digital vocal processing effects and the sound of Future's voice, I hear some other broad techniques in play. Future's vocals usually sound doubled or even tripled, so that we're actually hearing more than one vocal track at a time (or the same vocal track split into multiple signals that are then delayed by a few milliseconds each), all pitched slightly differently (this can be achieved by simply setting an entire track to be slightly flat or sharp). The multiple instances of Future's voice are further highlighted with significant reverb and delay, so that the listener hears his vocals echoing after their initial delivery.[5] The effects are likely set so that his vocals also harmonize with themselves, creating multiple pitches from one. Finally, a combination of compression, equalization (EQ), and saturation lends Future's voice the "husky, nasally" quality Reeves perceives. Compression squeezes together the loudest and quietest moments in an audio wave in a way that intensifies the signal (this is the technique used to create television and radio commercials that sound much louder than the rest of what's on the air), while EQ alters the volume of specified frequency ranges. Saturation is a distortion technique that allows the loudest parts of a signal to exceed set limits (i.e., they're too loud to be carried by the equipment) so that their harmonics cut through in the moments the fundamental distorts. Saturation is similar to compression, but instead of squeezing the audio wave together, saturation changes the shape of the wave so that the loudest parts cut out while the rest of the wave remains unchanged. Compression, EQ, and saturation are common effects to use on vocal tracks, regardless of genre or a performer's capabilities; they contribute a sense of space to a recording, defining how different frequency ranges carry in relation to one another. In the case of Future, his vocals tend to carry most in the middle and upper range, suggesting a fair amount of saturation and EQ settings that cut the low end and boost the high end.

All told, the vocal processing settings for a rapper like Future are far more than just pitch correction, and they work together to give his voice a more robotic sound than he would produce without the behind-the-glass tricks. The timbre (i.e., what makes a sound recognizable) of Future's live voice is distinct from the timbre of his produced one, and Desiigner, whose speaking voice isn't far from Future's to begin with, can employ approximate techniques to arrive at a recorded voice listeners could mistake as Future's. Listening to Desiigner's vocals on "Panda," I hear similar approaches to multitracked or delayed vocals, harmony, and detuning, so that each track is slightly out of tune with the others. The compression, EQ, and saturation also tend to emphasize frequency ranges that align with Future's. Desiigner *doesn't* seem to use pitch correction the same way Future does, as his vocals come out less robotic or synthesized than Future's, so the similarities between their voices are more attributable to the vocal processing techniques that aren't synonymous with the notorious Auto-Tune.

Flat Affect

Desiigner delivers his "Panda" vocals with a flat affect, conveying little emotion through inflection. The sections where he repeats the word "panda" demonstrate this (0:33–39, 1:38–46, 2:44–52, 3:51–58). These repetitions precede each verse and then punctuate the end of the song, and rhythmically they signal what should be a turn-up—a run of at least a measure's worth of eighth notes just before the full beat drops. But Desiigner's recitation is emotionless, each instance of the word sounding just like the last. Throughout the rest of the song, if a listener didn't understand the words, it would be hard to guess what Desiigner is rapping about based on any emotive signals. Love? Aggression? Loss? The vocal performance is reportorial, dispassionate.

Future adopts a similar technique in up-tempo songs. His repetition of the words "jumpman" and "noble" in "Jumpman" (2015) and the word "wicked" in "Wicked" (2016) provide parallels to Desiigner's recitation of "panda." And in "Ain't No Time" (2016), Future delivers lines about his clothes and money as casually as he predicts his enemies ending up outlined in chalk; just as in "Panda," a listener who didn't catch the lyrics to "Ain't No Time" wouldn't be able to attach any particular emotional content to the song. This is partly attributable to the vocal processing techniques described above; the more robotic one's voice sounds, the less emotion listeners tend to attach to it. But this is only true to a point. Certainly Kanye West's *808s & Heartbreaks*, an entire album of heavily processed vocals, conveys a depth and variety of emotion that makes that album stand out in his œuvre. At root, the flat affect of Desiigner and Future is performative, enhanced but not defined by the technical production of their vocals.

Say Huh?

Desiigner and Future are both notoriously mushmouths: enunciation is optional. The Internet *loves* this. Whether it's a reporter heading into the streets to ask random passersby what Future is saying in "Where Ya At?" (2015) or a video featuring misheard lyrics from "Honest" (2014) or a hip hop Web site publishing a piece called "What the F**k Is Future Saying (A Very Serious Lyrical Analysis)," Future's indecipherability seems reliable fodder for online clicks (Farese 2016; Totally JK 2013; G 2014). Similarly, the aporetic lyrical content of "Panda" was a running gag at the peak of the song's popularity. The lyrics-centric Web site *Genius* asked Desiigner to slowly recite "Panda"'s lyrics, while BBC Radio 1Xtra chuckled through comedian Kevin Hart's performance of the song as he disbelievingly inter-jected, "Is this really the lyrics to this song? Is this really what he says in this song?" (OPPI 2016; BBC Radio 1Xtra 2016).

Low Registers

Both Desiigner's and Future's performed voices seem to sit low in their registers. As discussed above, the upper end of their vocals tends to be emphasized through compression, EQ, and saturation, but this obser-vation about their low registers is more an embodied one than a matter of production. Desiigner and Future both sound like they produce their vocals by opening the backs of their throats and elongating their vocal cords. While the vocal processing might account for the nasal quality, it's this back-of-the-throat and chest production that Reeves likely hears as "husky."

Flow

The bulk of "Panda"'s verses are in "Migos flow." Migos flow is named for the ATL trap trio Migos, who popularized the style in their song "Versace" (2013). Migos flow is recognizable as a triplet figure that cuts across a beat organized around quarter, eighth, and sixteenth notes, so that a rapper's vocals create a 3:2 or 3:4 cross-rhythm with the instrumental. Beyond rhythm, Migos flow also rises in pitch, starting on the third subdivision of a beat.[6] I show this rising figure in Table 3.1 with Migos's repetition of "Versace" and the second and fourth lines from the opening verse of "Panda" mapped onto it. Each instance of "1" represents a downbeat, but I haven't superimposed this onto any particular meter, as the Migos flow can easily start and end on any beat of a measure.

Future settles into Migos flow regularly too, often delivering entire verses with the figure. Table 3.2 shows two lines from "Digital Dash" (2015), in which Future strings together nearly two full minutes of Migos flow to start the song.

Table 3.1 MIGOS FLOW WITH LYRICS FROM MIGOS'S "VERSACE" AND DESIIGNER'S "PANDA"

	Ver-	sa-	ce	Ver-	sa-	ce	Ver-	sa-	ce	Ver-	sa-	ce	Ver-	sa-	ce	Ver-	sa-	ce
			2			2			2			2			2			2
		1			1			1			1			1			1	
3	3			3			3			3			3			3		
	Twist-	in	dope	Lean	and	the	Fan-	ta	...	Hit-	tin	off	licks	in	the	ban-	do	

Table 3.2 MIGOS FLOW IN FUTURE'S "DIGITAL DASH"

		2			2				2			2			2
	1			1				1			1			1	
3			3			3	3			3			3		
I	did	the	dig-	i-	tal	dash,	I	fucked	that	bitch	in	the	pass-	en-	ger

Other Trappers

So Desiigner's vocals *do* sound like Future's vocals. But that's not all they sound like because these performance and production techniques aren't unique to Future. Adam Krims theorizes dissonance in the mix, like Desiigner's and Future's out-of-tune vocals, as part of the "hip hop sublime" (2000, 73–74). It's an especially popular vocal style among Southern rappers identified with the trap genre. Young Jeezy ("And Then What," 2005), Gucci Mane ("Icy," 2005), and Waka Flocka Flame ("Hard in Da Paint," 2010) all debuted between 2005 and 2010 with vocals multitracked and detuned like Desiigner's and Future's. Lil Yachty, another rapper who popped in 2016 with multitracked and detuned vocals, carries the same flat affect in his first single, "1Night," as is audible in "Panda" and several Future tracks. Yachty, Jeezy, and Flocka all similarly produce the elongated vocal cord, "husky" chest voice we hear in Desiigner and Future.

As for mushmouth rapping, Young Thug's lyrics are as impenetrable as the ones on "Panda" or "Where Ya At," and he's spurred similar Internet fun, including another *DJ Booth* "What the F**k Is He Saying" article and a video of him slowly reading the lyrics to "Best Friend" (2015), this time for *GQ* (G 2014; *GQ* 2016). In that *GQ* feature, Devin Friedman describes Thug as "the most talented lyricist in the world, and his thing is you can't understand what the fuck he's talking about" (2016). Writing for *Wired*, Charley Locke calls Thug's style "warble rap," arguing that he "expresses his feelings more purely through sounds" than lyrics (2015).

Finally, Migos flow, as is obvious from its name, is not Future's proprietary style. In fact, it doesn't belong to Migos, either, though the popularity of "Versace" marked an increase in Migos flow in the mid-2010s. *Complex* posted a video on YouTube in 2014 that begins with "Versace" and several songs released months after it, then progresses backward through time to show other rappers who have employed it, ending on Public Enemy's "Bring the Noise" (1987). In an interview with DJ Vlad on *VladTV*, Gangsta Boo—whose recorded vocals are also multitracked, detuned, and emanating from her lower register—claims that her group, Three 6 Mafia, are the rightful originators of the Migos flow. When pressed, she admits that while she picked up the flow from Triple 6 colleague Lord Infamous and fellow Memphian Skinny Pimp, "Where they got it from? No idea" (DJ Vlad 2014).[7]

As a rhythmic/melodic style that has circulated especially through Southern hip hop for a couple of decades, Migos flow is yet another way that Desiigner sounds like Future but also sounds like so many other rappers, especially those associated with trap music. But focusing just on Future and the Migos flow they both employ obscures the fact that the rest of "Panda" is delivered in a stuttered staccato style very similar to a flow Young Thug often employs. The opening line of "Panda"'s first verse, shown in Table 3.3a, demonstrates this. Note that the first two words, "I got," are grouped in a rapid succession that is then mirrored by the last two syllables of "Atlanta." The line is spread unevenly over the bar in a way that avoids stressing the meter. Table 3.3b visualizes a line from Young Thug's "Stoner" (2011) in which he also groups two syllables in rapid succession and spreads his lyrics unevenly across the bar.[8]

Table 3.3a STUTTERED LINE FROM "PANDA" (THIRTY-SECOND NOTE SUBDIVISION)

	1	2	3	4	5	6	7	8	9	10	11	12	13	14	15	16
Des						I	got		broooads		in	At	lan		ta	

Table 3.3b STUTTERED LINE FROM "STONER" (THIRTY-SECOND NOTE SUBDIVISION)

	1	2	3	4	5	6	7	8	9	10	11	12	13	14	15	16
YT						Hear	My		song			way				

	17	18	19	20	21	22	23	24	25	26	27	28	29	30	31	32
YT	from	the			Y	T		C					R	O		B

Future's vocal similarity to Desiigner makes a quick and easy comparison, but I point to these other vocalists within or closely related to the trap genre who also sound similar to Desiigner in order to make the case that "Desiigner sounds like Future" is really shorthand for "Desiigner sounds like trap music." Though Future stands in as the most prominent trap rapper of 2016, by expanding the scope of analysis to include the fuller genre, we can gather a fuller sense of trap's sound. Using "Panda" as the jumping-off point for the comparison provides a useful filter for hearing trap in 2016 and also tracing the roots of its sound with an ear toward the political work the genre performs.

TRAP INSTRUMENTAL AESTHETICS

The "trap" in trap rap refers to a house used for cooking dope. It has a single entry/exit point so that, once inside, a person is trapped there unless those securing the door allow them to leave. It is, quite literally, a trap. This connection to the production side of the drug game is integral to the spirit of trap, and it also makes nailing down a specific sound quite difficult. Upon the release of his 2003 album, *Trap Muzik*, TI claimed he was making music to be listened to in the context of the drug game, "whether you in the trap selling dope, in the trap buying dope, or in the trap trying to get out" (Patel 2012). TI's explanation, which has become a piece of gospel for both producers of and commentators about trap, narrows the lyrical content of the genre quite a bit, but what the music sounds like? That isn't at all obvious based on TI's description.

A few broad histories of trap exist on the Internet, and like most things on the Internet, there's a good deal of overlapping information, possibly proliferating from a single origin point, even amidst differing opinions about who and what is most important. Across the board, though, TI's *Trap Muzik* is one of a handful of key moments in trap's history that also includes 2010's *Flockaveli* and the 2012 explosion of an electronic dance music (EDM) genre that shared the same name, trap, and a few key sonic markers (Bein 2012; Drake 2012; Hubbell 2013; Patel 2012).[9] Before 2003, the word "trap" shows up occasionally, as in Outkast's "SpottieOttieDopaliscious" (1998), to refer to the trap house and the broader drug game, but the sound of "SpottieOttie," a deep funk cut replete with rising horn line and orgasmic background vocals, is about as far as possible from what trap music sounds like today. *Trap Muzik*, to be sure, featured some of that liquid funk sound that TI's fellow Atlantans Outkast had rapped over for years, but the two lead singles, "Be Easy" and "24's," were DJ Toomp productions, and it's in these two songs that we can hear music production that continues to echo through "Panda."

The easiest way to trace the sound of trap rap from this seminal moment in 2003 to "Panda" in 2016 is to string together some other representative songs along the way. Specifically, I want to listen to TI's "24's" produced by DJ Toomp (2003), OJ Da Juiceman's "Make tha Trap Say Aye" produced by Zaytoven (2008), Waka Flocka Flame's "Hard in Da Paint" produced by Lex Luger (2010), Future's "Turn on the Lights" produced by Mike Will Made-It (2012), and Desiigner's "Panda" produced by Menace (2015). Instead of an in-depth analysis of each song, I will use these as a representative composite of trap over the course of a decade-plus to identify what the core sonic elements of the genre are, noting how, if at all, these core elements have changed over time.

We can start with frequency. Bass is important to trap instrumentals, and it's grown more intense over time. Listening chronologically from "24's" through "Panda," one can hear more and more bass in the mix. "24's" is the only one of this group to use a traditional kick drum and relies primarily on a low synth for resonance in the low frequencies. The other four producers use pitched kick drums that resonate beyond the attack, filling up the space Toomp reserves for the low synth (Luger employs both the pitched kicks and low synths on "Paint" to pack the low frequencies as densely as possible). By the 2010s, the pitched kick drums would be standard in trap rap. Bass, of course, is integral to a variety of Southern hip hop subgenres, including Miami Bass: "the entire genre," David Font-Navarrete suggests, "is arguably a frequency-based fetish" (2015, 490). As I'll focus on in the next chapter, trap music is closely related to music for the club in addition to the trap, and this party vibe makes Miami Bass an easily identifiable influence. Trap's bass also pulls from car-oriented hip hop like Rich Boy's "Throw Some D's" (2007) and the bulk of Big K.R.I.T.'s output—indeed, TI's "24's" revolves around tricked-out cars. The bass produced for cars is different from that produced for the club; the former tends to rely on high-end gear and DIY automobile tinkerers who will amplify low-range frequencies that are absent from the mix without the proper equipment. Club music may also involve some sub-bass, but since its ultimate environment is a party, its bass tends to be more saturated or doubled at higher registers so that listeners can catch the bass even if they're listening on sub-par speakers. In Font-Navarrete's article on the roots of Miami Bass, he notes that many early listeners heard the music over pirate radio stations whose signals couldn't carry the frequency ranges that gave the genre its name, and Wayne Marshall has elsewhere written about listeners' ability to "hear" bass that isn't audibly present when disseminated through audio channels (cell phones, cellular networks, earbuds, computer speakers) poorly equipped to amplify low frequencies (Font-Navarrete, 496–97; Marshall 2014, 58–66).

Trap's bass splits the difference; an amplifier and subwoofer in one's car can uncover bass sounds that are otherwise inaudible, but it kicks hard enough to work for a range of outputs from headphones to club speakers.

It isn't just the bass that is integral to trap, though. Each of these five songs features a common trap intro: high- and mid-range synths with no low-frequency percussion.[10] The introductory synths are usually related or identical to synth motifs that will continue into the full instrumental, and their use in the intro serves to add greater weight to the bass when it finally drops. The low-high frequency spread is common in trap and becomes more pronounced from 2003 to 2015. Listen to "24's" and "Panda" in succession, and the midrange sparseness of later trap is evident. DJ Toomp keeps the midrange synths louder in the mix than the higher piano motif, while Menace achieves the opposite, with the high end of his synths resonating longer and louder than mid- and low-range synths. The evolution of more bass and less midrange over trap's lifetime makes sense from an audio signal perspective: clearing out space in the middle frequencies allows the bass to resonate longer and louder, leading to a genre that tends to favor frequency extremes—quite high and very low.

Timbrally, all of these songs feature bright synths. Bright timbre and high frequency are related but not identical concepts. A bright synthesized sound can be designed in several ways. Brightness can result from setting the higher frequency overtones to sustain long enough to give the sound its primary characteristic. In this way, a low pitch can be bright; the fundamental may be a lower frequency, but its timbre will be characterized by the resonance of its higher frequency overtones. Alternately, a synth patch that uses multiple oscillators, each of which momentarily disrupt the audio signal at different rates, can produce a buzzy or metallic sound that will also register as "bright" with listeners. In trap music, these bright timbres are often combined with higher frequency motifs to further emphasize the frequency spread discussed in the above paragraph. Beyond bright synths, trap instrumentals use low brass and string synths regularly, as can be heard in "24's" and "Paint."[11]

Trap percussion features recognizable timbres, too. I've already noted the growing presence of pitched, sustained kick drums. The other three primary elements in trap percussion—snare, clap, and hi-hat—have remained relatively the same over time. Listening to all five of the examples I've gathered here, the snares, claps, and hi-hats feature the kind of artificiality that has come to be most closely associated with the Roland TR-808 drum machine, the most iconic drum machine in hip hop and dance genres. Most trap producers use digital drum kits modeled on the 808, but even when non-808 elements are introduced, the ethos of the 808's obviously synthesized sounds undergirds the bulk of trap's percussion. Trap snares and hi-hats tend to have quick decays so that the sound is focused almost entirely on the point of attack for a short, staccato-like shape ("Turn On the Lights" features a longer decay—probably heavily reverbed—than the other songs analyzed here; note how the snare takes up more space in the mix after the attack than the snares in the other four). Trap claps have a longer attack and decay, meaning they tend to sound louder in the mix because they hit a few milliseconds after the other percussion and resonate slightly longer.

Before shifting from trap timbres to trap rhythms, a note about the transcriptions that follow. The instrumental of a trap song *sounds* like a downtempo hip hop track, moving around seventy to eighty beats per minute (bpm), with the snare hits falling on the second and fourth beat of each measure at that tempo. In reality, though, the beats are typically composed at twice that speed, around 150 bpm, with the snare hits falling on the third beat of each measure at that tempo. Vocals delivered at 150 bpm would be 16th notes, while vocals delivered at 75 bpm would be 32nd notes, giving the instrumental a half-time feel and the vocals a double-time feel. Here's where theory and performance butt heads: vocalists are probably not thinking in 32nd notes, and producers generally make their tracks at the faster speed, but my music theory interest in the genre's connection to other styles leads me to place the snare hits on the second and fourth beats of a roughly 75 bpm measure because the weak-beat snare is what ties so many genres together. So, when I talk about the first, second, third, and fourth beats of a measure or reference syncopation, I'm working in a half-time feel, even if that's not precisely how the music is composed. This is why my tables are split into consecutive subdivisions of the beat. Instead of marking "1-e-+-a," I use a string of numbers that can more easily be shifted to double-time—if that's what you prefer—as you read the transcription.

Some genres, like Miami Bass, Reggaeton, and bounce, spin out of a basic rhythmic pattern that is repeated or only slightly modified across the genre, and in the case of Reggaeton's "Dembow" beat or bounce's "Triggerman" and "Brown" beats, these are specific samples whose timbral qualities are readily recognizable in addition to their rhythmic components (Marshall 2013; Ellis 2015, 389–90). Trap's rhythmic characteristics are less fixed than Miami Bass or Reggaeton or bounce, but we can observe a few steady principles nonetheless. Claps, which, as I mentioned in the previous paragraph, can sound like loud snares in the mix, aren't required in trap (Mike Will Made-It doesn't use any in "Turn on the Lights," for instance), but when they do appear, they are mostly restricted to the second and fourth beats of a measure; it's rare to hear trap claps anywhere else (I'll discuss an important exception, the booty clap, in the next chapter). Snares also gravitate toward the second and fourth beat of a measure, but trap producers also sometimes syncopate them across the measure at lower volumes than the hits that land on the second and fourth beats. The kick is primarily syncopated, too, landing only on the first beat of the measure, then often catching some combination of upbeats until the next measure begins. Finally, perhaps the most iconic rhythmic element of trap in the 2010s is what happens with the hi-hats, which often bang out steady eighth or sixteenth notes with interludes of inhumanly fast thirty-second, sixty-fourth, or even faster (and also triplet) subdivisions that sound like rattles. These rattles, which are most apparent in the "Paint" and "Lights" examples, can come at unpredictable moments, at varying speeds, and in triple/duple subdivision alternation, so they serve as the least fixed, most lively element in a trap percussion beat. Table 3.4b is a rough percussion composite of the five trap songs included in this sample set, while Table 3.4a traces the backbone of Miami Bass, as illustrated in Font-Navarrete (492).

In Table 3.4b, I've used darker gray to outline the more likely hit points for each instrument, then lighter gray to show possible variants. The hi-hats I've left as straight sixteenth notes, as the rattles can happen at any point. By placing this trap composite next to Miami Bass's basic percussion beat,

Table 3.4a MIAMI BASS FUNDAMENTAL PERCUSSION PATTERN

	1	2	3	4	**5**	6	7	8	**9**	10	11	12	**13**	14	15	16
HH	■		■	■			■	■	■		■		■			
CL					■								■			
SD					■								■			
KD	■						■									

Table 3.4b TRAP COMPOSITE OF FUNDAMENTAL PERCUSSION PATTERN

	1	2	3	4	**5**	6	7	8	**9**	10	11	12	**13**	14	15	16
HH	■	■	■	■	■	■	■	■	■	■	■	■	■	■	■	■
CL		░			■								■			
SD		░			■			░		░			■			
KD	■	░			■		■		░	░	■		░			

Table 3.4c "PANDA" PERCUSSION PATTERN

	1	2	3	4	5	6	7	8	9	10	11	12	13	14	15	16
HH							O								O	
CL					■								■			
SD					■	■	■						■	■	■	
KD	■						■		■				■	■		

I want to highlight the similarities—the claps and snares, the kicks across the first three beats, the relatively busier hi-hats—while also noting that trap percussion tends to heighten the sense of syncopation and becomes more frantic in the latter half of a measure. Saying a genre is related to Miami Bass is almost like saying nothing at all; a good deal of hip hop and dance genres in the 2010s have been influenced by Miami Bass. I find this rhythmic comparison helpful not because a Miami Bass influence is unique but because the rhythmic pulse of Miami Bass is so common that it makes a useful anchor for hearing how a genre like trap recapitulates some of its elements while also forging some new ground. Table 3.4c shows "Panda"'s percussion (the lighter gray on the hi-hats indicates that they only enter for the second half of verses, and the "O" on the seventh and fifteenth hi-hat indicates an open hi-hat).

Combining this percussion with the instrumental timbral and frequency elements common to trap and with Desiigner's vocal similarity to Future reveals why listeners could so easily mistake "Panda" as a Future song. There's one remaining trap element in "Panda" that needs some contextualization in the broader genre: Desiigner's background vocals. But I first want to pause to consider the trap sonic elements I've gathered so far in the framework of sonic blackness, posthuman politics, and what I'm calling *trap irony*.

SONIC BLACKNESS AND TRAP IRONY

Let's return to the recurring double theme in write-ups about "Panda": Desiigner sounds like Future, *and* he has something Future doesn't—a No. 1 single. As I've demonstrated in the trap aesthetics section, to sound like Future is to sound like trap. Calling Desiigner's authenticity into question—he's a kid (he was 19 when "Panda" hit the Internet) from Brooklyn who bought a $200 beat from an unknown producer in the UK—while noting his success in a genre where he doesn't belong is a way of calling that genre into question. If *Desiigner* can do it?

Anybody could. Trap simply isn't taken very seriously—think of the distance between the baseline assumption that Kendrick is always already political and the question "Is 'Panda' Actually Good?"—and critics hold up Desiigner's success as an outsider as evidence that it shouldn't be (Tanzer and Golden 2016).

Steven Horowitz's response to the question is particularly condescending.

> ["Panda"]'s perfectly harmless, but also perfectly plagiaristic. What Desiigner accomplishes is photocopying what came before him—and it's actually incredible that he harnessed that sound and finessed his way to the top of the Hot 100—is something Future has yet to accomplish. Desiigner may have a hit on his hands, but I think a career with longevity is far out of reach. It takes far more than pulling a *Face/Off* to form a solid musical identity.

What Horowitz finds "actually incredible" about "Panda" isn't the song itself or Desiigner's performance, but rather the fact that he achieved an amount of success by plagiarizing a style of music Horowitz clearly doesn't value. Horowitz is the only one to put so fine a point on it, but most of the respondents to the *Fader*'s question are willing to admit that they like the song without committing to the idea that it's actually good; "Panda" functions like a guilty pleasure, something to bang to at the club but not think too hard about the next day.

Or, as Mosi Reeves describes "Panda" in *Rolling Stone*, "it's a momentary sugar rush that evaporates as soon as it ends" (2016). Reeves ostensibly offers an "everybody chill" rebuttal to the kind of anxiety over authenticity evident in Friedman's *FACT* piece, which Reeves says relies on the "patently absurd" notion that anyone can own an idea and that sound-alikes like Desiigner are therefore worthy of disdain. But Reeves's solution to this absurd notion is to say that "Panda" is too worthless to warrant any response: "It's the kind of song you'd never stream in the comfort of your home, but will blissfully lean and dab to when the DJ spins it at the club" (Reeves has obviously never been to my home). And when it's time to make the case that "Panda" isn't worth our time, Reeves relies on two points of attack: the lyrics and the music.

I'll address the lyrical critique first, as it connects directly to the last chapter's discussion of Kendrick Lamar. The line "White X6 look like a panda" refers to a BMW whose white/black grill pattern reminds Desiigner of a panda bear; "In effect, 'Panda' finds a teenage boy lusting over luxury vehicles and 'broads,'" quips Reeves, rendering the song's lyrical content essentially meaningless. This is nothing new for Southern rappers. When Three 6 Mafia (whose crunk style is a progenitor for trap—more on that in the next chapter) were nominated for Best Original Song at the 2006 Academy Awards, Queen Latifah, trying to appear kind and accommodating, compared their "Hard Out Here for a Pimp" with "Chitty Chitty Bang Bang" and "Bippity Boppity Boo," choosing titles literally built from nonsense words as the closest comps to Triple 6. After the group accepted their award, host Jon Stewart spent ten full seconds at the podium just laughing (Oscars 2006). The litany of "What's [Insert Trap Rapper Name Here] Saying??" videos attest to the same devaluation of trap's lyrical content.

In my analysis of the reception of Kendrick Lamar in the previous chapter, I noted that Kendrick's status as a political rapper revolves almost entirely around his lyrics, which are readily legible as "politically engaged." In a write-up like Marc Lynch's for the *Washington Post*, Kendrick's music is deemed worthy primarily because it accompanies what are perceived as deep and meaningful lyrics: "With its politically charged lyrics and jazzy, funky beats, it calls to mind the great albums of an earlier era of politically committed and musically diverse hip-hop" (Lynch 2015). Lyrics lead the way, and the music's virtue simply mirrors the diversity of Kendrick's own post-race parallel public. So meaningful lyrics = meaningful music in Lynch's evaluation of Kendrick, and Reeves makes a similar move in the opposite direction regarding Desiigner, pairing "Desiigner's husky, nasally voice" with "Menace's boilerplate trap beat." Empty lyrics = empty music.

I return to Kendrick not just to point out that he is taken more seriously than Desiigner, Future, and other trappers. I also want to note that the rationale that makes Kendrick politically legible also renders trap *illegible*. Kendrick's worth and trap's worthlessness are not separate or unrelated phenomena but rather, as Spence describes in neoliberal parallel publics, part of the same process whereby some black music is "capable of being re-formed [according to market logic]" while other black music is "not capable of being re-formed" (2011, 15). Trap is the excepted population that doesn't fit into Kendrick's black parallel public. And as I argued in detail in the last chapter, Kendrick's parallel public is built around post-race ideology, where black solidarity is held at a skeptical distance in favor of a diverse alliance that mirrors the United States' increasing reliance on a racial logic that imbues the appearance of diversity with the power and resources that have long accompanied whiteness, then pits that diversity against blackness, which becomes "the source of social crisis . . . the barrier to a postracial future" (Sexton 2008, 65). In this context, sounding black separates one from political legibility and the market logic that defines neoliberal humanism; it's a way of operating beyond the mainstream idea of what it is to be human.

Recall that for Edisheim, sonic blackness is "the perceived presence of the black voice in a body," or, in the case of trap, black voices and bodies in the music (Eidsheim 2011, 647). I'm arguing that the dismissal of trap as unserious and the positioning of it as "scary" stem from the genre's "shaping of vocal timbre"—and, following Kajikawa, I'll add the shaping of music production to this mix—"to match current ideas about the sound of blackness" at a political moment when post-race ideology has made such a virtue of "mixed-ness" that sounding black renders one either apolitical or "the barrier to a postracial future" (Eidsheim, 664; Sexton, 66). Either way, trap's blackness makes its politics inaudible in mainstream political discourse. As Eidsheim and Kajikawa are careful to note, there's nothing clean about the rendering of sonic blackness, as it depends on interweaving, non-monolithic notions of blackness that glom on to or become associated with particular sounds. In the case of trap, I hear its sonic blackness taking shape both by amplifying recent sounds that signify blackness and by operating on a surface level that reads as benignly apolitical, dangerously apolitical, or both. Since post-race politics aims to neutralize black racial solidarity (Sexton, 66), then one way to sound black is to sound apolitical—outside the boundaries of political discourse—and one way to sound apolitical is to sound black.

So, how does trap sound black? The lyrical content and cultural context do a lot of the work. Trap music's relationship with the trap house, the drug game—"whether you in the trap selling dope, in the trap buying dope, or in the trap trying to get out," as TI describes it—operates in a society where decades of unequal policing and imprisonment have marked drug trafficking as a primarily black or brown endeavor. That same policing and imprisonment render the guns Trouble and the Duct Tape Army brandish in "Bussin" primarily a black problem. Misogyny, too. Tricia Rose, in *The Hip-Hop Wars*, notes that conservative critics of hip hop understand it as "a black-created problem that promotes unsafe sex and represents sexual amorality, infects 'our' culture and society, advocates crime and criminality, and reflects black cultural dysfunction and a 'culture of poverty'" (2008, 6). Writing about another Southern rapper, David Banner, Ali Colleen Neff describes the performance of "what looks like cut-and-paste gangsta rap to listeners from dominant groups" as a trickster performance that obscures meaning "from hostile eyes" (2009, 160). Performing negative stereotypes about blackness is an old trick that plays on the mainstream's willingness to invest blackness with all that is wrong in society, and trap deploys that performance alongside specific aesthetic elements that carry the same racialization in their sounds.

To hear this sonic blackness, it's helpful to actually start with Kajikawa's discussion of Eminem's sonic whiteness. Comparing Eminem's debut single, "My Name Is" (1999), with Dr. Dre's "Nuthin' But a 'G' Thang" (1992)

Table 3.5 "MY NAME IS" (KAJIKAWA 2015, 131)

	1	2	3	4	5	6	7	8	9	10	11	12	13	14	15	16
HH	■				■				■				■			
SD					■								■			
KD	■								■							

and Nas's "The World is Yours" (1994), Kajikawa argues that "the majority of rap beats in the 1990s drew upon the generic conventions of funk music, featuring eight- or sixteen-count hi-hats with syncopated snare/kick drum patterns . . . even when the hi-hat does not evenly subdivide the beat, syncopated ostinato patterns in other prominently sounding levels of the groove imply a sixteenth-note subdivision" (2015, 130–31). The beat for "My Name Is," though, doesn't do this. It's an incredibly simplistic beat (Table 3.5).

With kick drum hits on the first and third beats, snares on the second and fourth, and hi-hats without any subdivision, the "My Name Is" beat completely lacks syncopation or drive and sounds "a rhythmic parody of whiteness, toying with the well-known stereotype that white people lack rhythm" (Kajikawa 2015, 132).

Meanwhile, Table 3.4c, a composite beat pulled from the five trap songs I discussed above, demonstrates even greater kick and snare syncopation than Kajikawa observes in 1990s rap, eschewing any kick drum downbeat except the first beat of each measure (by comparison, both "G Thang" and "World" kick on the first and third beat of each measure). This heightened syncopation is then combined with hi-hats that not only drive forward with eighth or sixteenth notes but further subdivide the beat with their thirty-second and sixty-fourth note rattles (these subdivisions include triplet versions of thirty-second and sixty-fourth notes, too). To highlight Eminem's whiteness, Dr. Dre took the sound of 90s black rap and removed syncopation and subdivision. Trap, on the other hand, introduces further syncopation and subdivision to these sounds that have conveyed blackness to the listening public since the 90s.

Trap's use of bass works in similar ways, driving further into blackness. As I mentioned above, bass tends to connote both party and car culture, the former of which I'll develop in detail in the next chapter. Bass frequencies' association with cars has deep roots in hip hop. Dr. Dre described his G-Funk style as being geared toward car listening, and Justin Williams pinpoints compression (which squeezes together the loudest and quietest sounds, making everything seem louder) and "prominent bass frequencies" as two of the main elements of Dre's car-oriented production (2009, 173). Because of the ambient noise of traffic, mixing for automobile spaces requires a good deal of volume, especially at lower frequencies, which are both harder for humans to perceive than higher frequencies and also the dynamic range most likely to be drowned out by other sounds on the road. Kajikawa reads Dr. Dre's music video for "Let Me Ride" (1992) through Robert Farris Thompson's lens of "black quest" (Thompson 1989, 98). Dre's movement through his city in his bass-bumping car, coupled with aerial shots of massive highway interchanges signal "a sense of freedom and mobility" that aligns with Parliament Funkadelic's (G-Funk is a play on P-Funk, and "Let Me Ride" samples from Parliament's "Mothership Connection" (1975)) Afrofuturism to portray an automotive transcendence of one's space.

Transcendence isn't the only thing cars allow, though. Ali Colleen Neff has theorized auto-mobility not only as a vehicle for getting out but as "movement in place" (2013). Adrienne Brown, in her critique of Paul Gilroy and analysis of hip hop cars as "harbor[ing] the specter of commonwealth and collective value . . . galvaniz[ing] types of looking, seeing, and being related to collective forms of ownership," perceives a similar movement in place in hip hop automotivity (2012, 267). Looking at Rich Boy's video for "Throw Some D's," Brown finds "an ambivalent politics at best":

> While the specter of the commons may remain entrenched in the video's auto-motivity, the car's inability to provide any real motion makes the harnessing of this specter harder to actualize or imagine. Rather than providing a means for leaving the space of the block, the cars in the video enact a macro-stance of stasis even amidst their micro-performances of motion, as the circling cars fail to be vehicles of any type of mobility for any of the people filmed crowding their interiors and exteriors. The accessory of spinning rims commonly associated with the excesses of black youth culture, which also features in this video, seems to be an apt metaphor for this demographic's inertia, with the illusion of motion acting as a fiction sustaining enough for its user, even as the vehicle of mobility may be stopped in its tracks. (273)

Far from the transcendence of Afrofuturism that Kajikawa perceives in "Let Me Ride," Brown paints a car culture that doesn't really go anywhere, that can't leave the block.

Trap's use of bass evokes car culture and does so in a way that, if Brown finds Rich Boy's Cadillac to be "ambivalent politics at best," pushes further into the stasis that concerns her. In trap, cars offer neither transcendence nor even "movement in place" in a public commons. Rather, they are one-way trips to a trap, whether the trap house or the imprisonment that follows. Desiigner does little more than mention the two different BMW X6 models that look like a phantom and panda, but his destination is set at the beginning of each verse: Atlanta, home of the trap. Future, in his song "Maybach" (2016), envisions a car used entirely for his criminal activities, choosing to terrorize the block rather than leave it. Probably the most iconic trap song about cars is Ace Hood's "Bugatti" (2013), produced by Mike Will Made-It and featuring Future on the hook: "I woke up in a new Bugatti." This imagery, of waking up in a $2 million car, stalls mobility altogether. In the video, which opens with a shot of Ace Hood asleep in a 2013 Veyron 16.4, which *could* go 0 to 60 in 2.4 seconds, the world's fastest car doesn't move (Zoellter 2012). Instead, it's a static prop for the rappers to lean against, and the opening and closing tableaux feature Ace Hood waking up to find himself surrounded by police, guns drawn. The trap car is programmed to always lead back to the trap and, in "Bugatti," is itself an elaborate and very expensive trap. Just as with its use of heightened syncopation and rattling hi-hats to signify blackness beyond what 90s hip hop sounded, trap's use of bass to evoke car culture amplifies the genre's sonic blackness, digging further into the negative stereotypes—and their consequences—that typify blackness for the "hostile ears" of the mainstream.

Trap's sonic blackness is far from Kendrick's; instead of a post-race multiracialism, trap performs, as Sexton puts it, a "negatively *purified*" blackness. Bogazianos's analysis of rap through the lens of the anti-black drug laws that have disproportionately prosecuted and imprisoned blacks is a useful way to connect with Sexton's negative purification and trap's performance of the drug game. As discussed in the last chapter, the 1986 Anti-Drug Abuse Act imposed mandatory minimum sentences for possession of 5 grams of crack or 500 grams of cocaine, resulting in "a historic over-incarceration of people of color through drug prohibition, an over-incarceration which has increased to epic and unconscionable proportions" (Lowney 1994, 167). In the context of the authenticity debate, Bogazianos overlays the impurities of crack, which is cooked with baking soda and ammonia so that the pure cocaine is diluted, with the "impure, overly explicit" content of rap subgenres that traffic in drugs, violence, and misogyny (Borgazianos 2012, 57). The association between crack and blackness that has been disastrously codified by US drug law and enforcement ensures that what is impure about crack is its blackness, and what is impure about rap that doesn't have a legible politics like Kendrick's is the same: its blackness. Here, Kendrick is some sort of alchemical extraction of what is pure about hip hop, and a genre like trap is what's leftover, the impure blackness that needed to be "purged" (Bogazianos, 57).

I'm cooking Spence, Sexton, and Bogazianos together here to find the overlap in their analyses that also parallel Weheliye's habeas viscus. Each of these authors explores racialization in the US context, tracking how anti-blackness works in a society that is post-racial, multiracial, and neoliberal. And from each author's approach, there is a subset of a previously marginalized or oppressed group that moves closer to power and privilege while the rest of that group is pushed further away. The black parallel public, the US War on Drugs, multiracialism, and the neoliberal politics of exception all mark blackness as problematic and unreformable, then siphon it off from whatever ostensibly virtuous vision of diversity is being offered. As Weheliye theorizes, though, the flesh that is siphoned off—negatively purified, excepted, imprisoned because dangerous, ignored because friv-olous—continues to vibrate out of earshot of the mainstream. Trap, of course, vibrates *loudly* in the mainstream. Future is everywhere; Desiigner has a No. 1 hit; Juicy J features on Katy Perry's No. 1 "Dark Horse" (2014) (strain your ears during Juicy's verse, and you'll even hear a few hi-hats rat-tling in the mix). It's not that the mainstream can't hear trap. Rather, it's that trap, flesh which has been negatively purified into sonic blackness, res-onates beyond just what thumps through mainstream channels. It crackles with a politics illegible, inaudible to post-race neoliberal humanism.

Trap Irony

Trap's sonic blackness is also its politics, what I'm calling *trap irony*. At all turns, trap behaves in unexpected ways. It starts with sounding black in a society that privileges post-race diversity—massaging Eidsheim's formu-lation a bit, I'll describe it as "the shaping of [a musical performance] to match current ideas about the sound of blackness" (664). If post-race ideol-ogy pushes against black racial solidarity, *trap irony* describes the way trap picks up recognizable and negatively stereotyped markers of hip hop black-ness so that its existence becomes an affirmation, an unflinching assertion of blackness in a post-racial milieu (Sexton 2008, 65). It ripples out from there in a series of ironies that envelope its production, circulation, and sonic aesthetics.

Trap music moves through society in ways it shouldn't. Though the image of the trap is a house with only one way in and out, trap aesthet-ics produce a music that seems to constantly find a secret exit, a path not offered, a way around established norms. Materially, the bulk of trap music circulates through and out of Atlanta on mixtapes, beyond the purview of major record labels, depending on word of mouth and the blessings of local radio and strip club DJs to gain traction. In part because trap isn't fully controlled by labels, these mixtapes release at an astonishing rate. From January 2015–February 2016, Future released four mixtapes and two official albums. Young Thug dropped six mixtapes between January and September of 2014, then five more from April 2015 to March 2016. From 2006 to 16, Gucci Mane released twenty-seven albums and forty mixtapes, even though he served multiple jail sentences that added up to around three years behind bars. In fact, trap music moves much like the dope it's associated with, a never-ending supply feeding a ravenous demand.

Trap's supply-and-demand grind recalls the neoliberal entrepreneurialism of the descriptive realist rappers Spence analyzes. The trapper, like the hustler Spence describes, "is *constantly working*, constantly reading the needs of consumers and constantly producing either to meet these needs or even to generate them" (38). Both Spence and Bogazianos drill further down from the hustle to the grind, the latter of which involves endless, tireless labor.

> The hustle is smooth and fast. Grinding, on the other hand, signifies a particular kind of hustling, and it is one that does not retain the same sense of ease. Grinding suggests difficulty—cooking, churning, twisting, pressing. While the hustle represents the swagger of success after it has been realized, the grind suggests all of the many dues paid before that success became reality—the ruthless competition, the social disruption, and the intensified violence that crack-era hustlers had to negotiate. (Bogazianos 2012, 55)

Bogazianos and Spence also both connect the grind of cooking and pushing crack with the grind of the music industry, "the twenty-four-hour, everyday, get-it-done mentality required to be a successful artist and a successful neoliberal subject" (Spence 2011, 41). And there's a goal built into the narrative of these grinds, typified most spectacularly by Jay Z, who has built an entire persona and musical empire around the upward mobility afforded by his grind: you grind to ascend in the drug game, to ascend in the music world, to be your own boss. Trap's drug-related irony is audible in a song like Future's "Move That Dope" (featuring Pusha T and Pharrell) (2014), in which Pusha T, detailing his many years on the grind, asks, "Who doesn't wanna sell dope forever?" Pusha T's indifference to upward mobility is mirrored in Mike Will Made-It's instrumental. Instead of rattling hi-hats, "Dope" features a steady sixteenth note pattern. Its bassline entails a kick drum layered with a bass synthesizer with no decay; each attack is sustained until the next attack, filling the lower register with a relentless signal that, when combined with the evenly distributed hi-hats, feels like it could go on forever, just like Pusha T's dope-dealing days. Trap, then, evokes a grind similar to that of previous eras of rap, but instead of grinding one's way to the top, increasing one's social and political capital as the money piles up, trap stays in the trap—it defies neoliberal market logic by investing in the impurities of criminality, diluted products, and sonic blackness set against a post-race backdrop.

Another drug closely associated with Southern hip hop generally and, especially through the lyrics of artists like Future, trap specifically, is *lean*. Lean is a prescription-drug-based concoction referred to as "syrup," "purple drank," "dirty Sprite," and a variety of other monikers that highlight its basic components: an Actavis-produced cough syrup mixture of codeine and promethazine (it's purple), a sweet drink like Sprite, and candy—often Jolly Ranchers. As with any hard-to-get recreational drug, the ingredients may vary—and since Actavis stopped producing its mixture in 2014, variance is increasingly de rigueur—but the Actavis mixture stands as the exemplary form of lean. Lean is a depressant; Houston's DJ Screw famously built an entire style of hip hop mixing, called "screwed and chopped," around the feeling of lean intoxication. At its most basic, screwed and chopped music slows songs down (with an attendant lowering of pitch) and stutters lyrics, especially at the seams that separate one measure from the next. Kemi Adeyemi, writing for *Sounding Out!*, listens to trap's use of lean "to query how prescription drugs are seen to generate productively intoxicated states that counter the violent realities of a particularly *black* everyday life" (2015).

Productively intoxicated, another trap irony. Adeyemi frames lean within a broader context of black bodies in a neoliberal economy. Rappers like Future and Schoolboy Q slow down the "twenty-four-hour, everyday, get-it-done" grind, the "requirement of black everyday life where maintaining success requires that you work nonstop" (Spence 2011, 41; Adeyemi 2015). Kevin Gates, meanwhile, drinks syrup "because I deal with depression. I don't bother nobody—I don't let my depression bother other people. I just do drugs and record" (Babb 2013). As Adeyemi notes, though, the intersection of 24/7 work and drugs holds a particularly cruel irony: "The slowed pace of lean is also attuned to the national epidemic whereby black people are routinely killed whether they are working or not. The racialized politics of productivity required by neoliberalism are thrown into relief as black people such as Eric Garner are killed *because of* their entrepreneurial efforts." To be productively intoxicated is to be grinding in a society that doesn't need criminality as an excuse to kill you. Adeyemi zooms out from her focus on lean to the "dangerously unintelligible" intersection of black use of pharmaceuticals for "pleasure, physical ailments, mood stabilization," or gender reassignment: "Sandra Bland and Ralkina Jones died while their requirements and requests for the proper prescription meds they

took to remain alive were ignored if not refused outright by the police . . .
The *many* deaths of black transpeople killed in the midst of various stages
of medical reassignment further underscores a need for larger awareness
of the ways that alternative conceptions of reality and consciousness map
onto black life."

Like screwed and chopped production before it, trap also sonifies lean,
a drug associated with blackness not just because of its popularization
among rappers and producers but also, as Adeyemi shows, because of its
ability to intervene in "a particularly *black* everyday life." The barely enun-
ciated lyrics of trap artists like Future, Young Thug, and Rich Homie Quan
perform the woozy, stunted motor skills of a lean-induced stupor. And the
mushmouth delivery of so many trappers adds one more layer of trap irony,
producing a subgenre within hip hop, which for decades has prized witty
lyricists and verbal social/political critiques, that occasionally borders on
indecipherable.

Trap doesn't work like Kendrick. It doesn't engage in a direct politics that is legible to the mainstream, a respectable black parallel public made in the image of neoliberal market logic. Instead, trap taps a
variety of performative and sonic elements that register as scary or
apolitical blackness to the mainstream so that its main work vibrates
outside the proper channels of political discourse. One last piece of
the "Panda" sonic puzzle highlights trap's ill fit within mainstream
politics.

Listen again to the hi-hats in "Panda"—notice anything?

They don't rattle.

Now, as "Move That Dope" has already illustrated, a trap song can exist
without rattling hi-hats. Young Thug's "Best Friend" (2015) similarly
lacks them. But the thing about "Panda" is that it rattles even without
the hi-hats, and it's because of a sonic element of trap that I haven't discussed yet that sits somewhere between vocals and instrumentals: background vocals.

Table 3.4c, which maps the percussion of "Panda," shows that the hi-hat
only enters for the second half of each verse, and when it does, it sounds
very much like the hats on "Move That Dope," pounding out a steady sixteenth pattern (with an open hi-hat—which has a longer decay—on the
seventh and fifteenth hit of each measure) that never rattles. No matter,
Desiigner provides all the rattling necessary. Throughout the track, he adds
a handful of background vocals that trigger at seemingly random points.
Unlike the flat affect of his flow, Desiigner's vocal ad-libs are full of energy,
as if he's egging himself on. One of these vocals is "brrrrrrrrrrrrrrrrah,"
a tongue roll of varying lengths that is meant to produce the sound of a

choppa—a fully automatic firearm—and that replaces the missing hi-hat rattle. Desiigner's background vocals take on the job one of the instruments doesn't do, and in so doing, his choppas highlight the interstitial role of trap background vocals, which are vocal and instrumental all at once and which proliferate in unpredictable and ultimately ironic ways.

A comparison is useful. Los Angeles-based producer DJ Mustard first hit airwaves with his 2011 "Rack City" (performed by Tyga), a song that landed in the Billboard Hot 100 top ten. Mustard called his production style "ratchet," and the song bore several similarities with trap but consolidated into a much tighter soundscape. The percussion is reduced to a kick and snap for the majority of the song, with a syncopated snare used to punctuate ends of phrases and a single open hi-hat hit similarly accenting the beginning of phrases. The only melodic material comes from a two-beat low synth loop. With Mustard pulling the percussion out of the mix altogether rather frequently, several measures include only Tyga's voice for the last two beats. Mustard's ratchet style became his signature sound, and his music flooded the radio dial for the next couple of years. Not everything was quite as minimal as "Rack City," but Mustard consistently favored a sparse texture into which he would interject, without fail, a chorus of men chanting "hey!" on the upbeat. The DJ Mustard "hey" didn't go unnoticed. On July 3, 2014, bigjohnny8383 posted a video to YouTube that was a succession of "eight songs I heard on a single radio station within a day's span which featured this yelling sample."[12] The sample in question was Mustard's "hey," and six of the songs were Mustard productions.

DJ Mustard's ratchet riff on trap helps to highlight the messiness of trap's soundscape. The percussion tends to be busier and more syncopated, the synths multiplied and brighter, and, what draws my attention here, the background vocals unconsolidated and unpredictable. Mustard's "hey" pulls a chorus of black voices into a singular and regimented chant, the sound of a legible and easily locatable black solidarity displaying impeccable rhythm in their syncopation. The DJ Mustard "hey" is the sonification of what Spence calls expertise in the black parallel public. In the same way Al Sharpton or Jesse Jackson became voices speaking for all of blackness on 24-hour news channels, DJ Mustard's "hey" provides the sonic illusion of hearing from everyone at once, in a single, conveniently packaged, and distilled soundbite. They're even positioned right in the middle of the stereo field, sounding equally and evenly from all sides. Trap's background vocals, though? They're everywhere.

"Panda" is a great example of what can happen in the background of a trap song. Desiigner's background vocals move in meter and sometimes lock into a sequence, but he triggers enough different ones at unexpected moments that a listener can't know exactly what sound to expect next, when it will occur, or where it's even coming from. His various sounds come from left and right channels, and some of them start in one ear and finish in the other. Most trap music features these polyphonic background vocals, though there's no singular approach to how to produce the effect. Future's "Turn on the Lights," for instance, uses only a moderate pan and delay to create a slightly exaggerated echo that's barely in the same sonic ballpark as "Panda."[13] On Rich Homie Quan's "Flex (Ooh, Ooh, Ooh)" (2015), a similar echo reverberates in conjunction with more ad-libbed interjections to compound the kind of effect created on "Turn on the Lights." And this combination of echo and ad-libbed interjections is fairly standard in most of Future's output. Desiigner's background vocals, though, sound more like Waka Flocka Flame's or Young Thug's. The vocals on Waka's "Hard in Da Paint" *never stop*, sometimes responding to the main lyrics, sometimes hyping the rapper, sometimes just making those choppa sound effects that would spray across "Panda" years later. They're really loud in the mix, too, creating the sense that whoever's ad-libbing with Waka Flocka is pressed up right against him, a collection of voices working together but not moving as one. Young Thug pushes this to an even greater extreme, creating a conversational interplay between his lyrics and background vocals, as exemplified by his first verse on "Constantly Hating" (2015). Like Desiigner's on "Panda," all of Young Thug's background vocals seem to be produced by Thugger himself, but they range in volume from fairly quiet (the caw during "pulled up on the Birdman") to louder (the car squeal after "hopped in the motherfuckin coupe") than his lead vocals, and they range in content from sound effects (an elongated and very loose choppa after "pulled up on the Birdman") to a questioning repetition of his lead lyrics (a double repetition of "Kanye-condas," first as a question, then, quieter, like a shrugging resolution).

Listen to the background vocals on a trap track, and nothing really fits into a neat space. This last trap irony compounds trap's overarching irony. To sound black in a post-race milieu is to "match current notions of blackness," to be readily recognizable as black when the mainstream is pushing multiracialism. While sonic blackness, as Eidsheim is careful to caution, "is *not* the unmediated sound of essential otherness or the sound of a distinct phenotype," trap trucks in old, worn-out stereotypes that have for so long circulated through the US social, political, and legal systems that it gives the impression that its sonic blackness is, indeed, some kind of essential or distinct phenotypical product (Eidsheim 2011, 647). Trap seems to trap blackness right where the mainstream, where the black parallel public, where post-race neoliberal humanism wants it: in a compromised position, disengaged from political action, waking up from a lean-induced slumber in the driver's seat of a Bugatti paid for with ill-gotten gains, surrounded by police.

But the sonic aesthetics of trap are its politics, too. Instead of a fixed, static blackness that is everything "hostile [ears]" believe it to be, trap offers a plethora of voices sounding from all directions, unable to be hemmed in or pinned down, always finding a way to vibrate and reverberate out of the trap by means other than the single, designated entry/exit point (Neff 2009, 160). Trap uses the performance and sonification of the grind not to argue, as in Spence's conception of crack governmentality, for admittance into the mainstream by way of some entrepreneurial belonging. Rather, trap recycles the losing end of Kendrick's black parallel public in the interest of occupying a sonic and political space that is received as apolitical or even scary, outside the channels of political discourse. In this space exists the possibility of forming what Wynter conceives of as a subjectivity "completely outside our present conception of what it is to be human" (Scott 2000, 136). In this space exists the possibility of a queerly vibrating flesh sounding the posthuman, a possibility Rae Sremmurd enthusiastically fill with a never-ending party.

CHAPTER 4

Party Politics

Rae Sremmurd's Club as Posthuman Vestibule

Shots! Shots! Shots! Shots!

Rae Sremmurd, *"Safe Sex Pay Checks"* (2015)

G rind, hustle, cook, sling: hip hop overflows with words to describe work. If trap irony recycles the losing end of a black parallel public, deploying performances that read as scary or apolitical, it primarily does so by working wrong. The entrepreneurial markers are all there—a 24/7 grind, innovative production techniques, and a bootstrap mentality that allows trappers to achieve financial success against social and political odds—but, unlike the descriptive realist rappers of a bygone era, trap uses that entrepreneurial wherewithal not for upward mobility but to dig further into the trap, moving away from rather than toward legible political discourse (Spence 2011, 37–46). By working wrong, trap opens up a space outside the mainstream that, like the queerly vibrating flesh of Weheliye's habeas viscus, resonates just out of earshot. In this chapter, I'll listen to Rae Sremmurd to hear the way they work wrong. Combining trap and crunk aesthetics with a proclivity to party, the rap duo turn the club into a posthuman vestibule, a space that reconfigures work so that it operates, as Wynter envisions, outside of dominant ideas of what it is to be human, "a stepping stone toward new genres of human" (Scott 2000, 136; Weheliye 2014, 44–45).

In sharp contrast to Kendrick, no one is likely to mistake Swae Lee and Slim Jxmmi, the Tupelo, MS-born brothers who comprise Rae Sremmurd, for a politically engaged duo. The closest they come to electoral matters is the song "Up Like Trump" (2015), released months before being "up like Trump" meant romping through the GOP primary and general elections. In a 2016 South by Southwest performance, when it had become clear that the reality TV star was likely to secure a major party presidential nomination, Swae Lee prefaced "Trump" with a curt denouncement: "Fuck Donald Trump. We're voting for Bernie Sanders" (Mench 2016). It's not much, really. The metaphorical center of their song about partying happened to become a political cartoon villain, so they footnoted the performance with two classic hip hop moves: 1) A fuck you, and 2) The most hip hop thing a person could do in early 2016, <3 Bernie Sanders. Essentially Rae Sremmurd's hand was forced, so they said something about mainstream politics before performing their accidentally kinda political song. Still, it's not as if they pulled a Kendrick and did something as deeply complex and serious as writing "Tupelo" on the Sahara.

The bulk of Rae Sremmurd's output revolves around throwing money at strippers, unlocking swags, drinking, flexing, and drinking while flexing. Building on the concept of trap irony I outlined in the previous chapter, I'll analyze Rae Sremmurd's party music in the context of postwork. After all, what kind of work does a posthuman do? Postwork. If trap is a performance that works wrong, Rae Sremmurd's is a performance that simply doesn't work. Moving from the trap to the club, I'll be primarily theorizing with Lee Edelman's NoFuturity and L.H. Stallings's "black ratchet imagination" in order to hear Rae Sremmurd as "transitional bodies in transitional spaces," the "nook and cranny spaces" of the posthuman vestibule (135–36). Specifically, I'm interested in how Rae Sremmurd produce and reproduce work in queer ways. I'll first offer some background on postwork before zeroing in on Rae Sremmurd's genre, which is a blend of trap and crunk. Finally, I'll listen to Rae Sremmurd's performance of partying as postwork in the context of other crunk and trap party songs in order to hear how the duo construct the sonic contours of a posthuman vestibule that can serve as "a stepping stone toward new genres of human" (Weheliye, 44–45).

POSTWORK

Postwork, like any "post" term, can mean a number of things, depending on who's using it and what their conception of the original term—in this case, work—is. Read the July/August 2015 *Atlantic* article on postwork, and you'll come away with the sense that postwork is the death of human work, the automation and roboticization of jobs (Thompson). In this formula, "work" becomes something to be protected from the machines.

> In the past few years, even as the United States has pulled itself partway out of the jobs hole created by the Great Recession, some economists and technologists have warned that the economy is near a tipping point. When they peer deeply into labor-market data, they see troubling signs, masked for now by a cyclical recovery. And when they look up from their spreadsheets, they see automation high and low—robots in the operating room and behind the fast-food counter. They imagine self-driving cars snaking through the streets and Amazon drones dotting the sky, replacing millions of drivers, warehouse stockers, and retail workers. They observe that the capabilities of machines—already formidable—continue to expand exponentially, while our own remain the same. And they wonder: *Is any job truly safe?* (Thompson)

Thompson sets a spread from the very highest to lowest income jobs, then sprinkles in a task like driving that many readers wouldn't associate with work and rings the alarm to warn of the advancing army of drones and robots coming to take our jobs and turn "the middle class of the 20th century" into "a museum exhibit" (Thompson). Not just protected—work in Thompson's futuristic nostalgia formulation is something to be yearned for.

Stanley Aronowitz et al's 1998 "Post-Work Manifesto," on the other hand, employs a frank, present-day evaluation of what work has wrought as the springboard to reimagining what it can be. To be sure, Aronowitz et al raise the same specter of the grim machine coming to reap all of our jobs, and they do it in terms quite similar to Thompson's (let's call it a pre-echo): "In an era when almost any company can merge with another and machines regularly replace people, can *any* working person honestly say that her or his job is safe?" (36). But that's not the true heart of the manifesto, which is really an appeal to the heart, a reflection on "the kind of life we can and deserve to have in the [21st] century" (38). Aronowitz et al don't approach postwork as something to be feared, like Thompson, but as something to embrace, to speed along. Work isn't something to protect but to argue against, and the manifesto's argument advances by accepting work's promises—financial security, upward mobility, control over one's schedule and environment—but pointing out that work hasn't delivered on those promises. Work is, essentially, a failed politician facing a recall; we want the promises but will vote postwork in to make them realities.

"The Post-Work Manifesto"'s goals align with those of most postwork movements, namely shorter work weeks and guaranteed basic incomes. While a "*no-work* future" strikes Thompson as "hopeless," a "future of *less work* still holds a glint of hope" (Thompson 2015). Aronowitz et al and other postwork advocates generally couch the pitch for less work in the belief that working less time but in more fulfilling ways will result in the same or better productivity than our current work arrangement allows. With "plenty to produce" and "plenty to do," shorter work weeks and guaranteed basic incomes "may lead to a life where we are relatively freed from the oppressiveness of time as we now commonly experience it" (Aronowitz et al. 1998, 33). In an April 2016 *Freakonomics* podcast, economist Evelyn Forget describes something similar: "If you look at the 18th and at the 19th century, some of the great scientific breakthroughs and some of the great cultural breakthroughs were made by people who did not work. These were gentlemen of leisure, right?" (Dubner 2016).

Postwork is modeled on work, and work is not just something people *do* but a factor of who they *are*. Thompson writes about "the intrinsic fulfillment of work itself" or "the sanctity and preeminence of work" that undergirds US society; unsurprisingly, joblessness is the destruction of "cultural cohesion," and a universal basic income could not "prevent the civic ruin of a country built on a handful of workers permanently subsidizing the idleness of tens of millions of people" (Thompson 2015). On the *Freakonomics* podcast, venture capitalist Sam Altman allows that a guaranteed basic income would mean that "maybe 90% of people will go smoke pot and play video games" (Dubner 2016). In each case, and in Aronowitz et al's vision of "the future we can and deserve to have in the [21st] century," whether or not one works goes a long way in determining a person's worth. In a neoliberal humanist society, nothing less than the conflation of economic viability and human worth is exactly to be expected.

Kathi Weeks, in her *The Problem with Work* (2011), follows a Marxist feminist postwork path that is similar in her advocation for shorter work weeks and a guaranteed basic income but that ultimately settles into a more complex futurity. Here, work is necessary to function in the neoliberal present, but demands for shorter work weeks and guaranteed basic incomes open the possibility for radically reconfiguring what we imagine work to be and, in so doing, hint at a future without work as we know it.

> There are advantages, I claim, to more partial visions of alternatives, fragments or glimpses of something different that do not presume to add up to a blueprint of an already named future with a preconceived content. I will use the label "postwork society" not to anticipate an alternative so much as to point toward a horizon of utopian possibility, as it seems preferable to hold the space of a different future open with the term "post" than to presume to be able to name it as "socialist." (Weeks 2011, 30)

The fundamental problem with Weeks's utopian vision is that it works best for white heteronormativity, which is part of the problem postwork is supposed to solve. In this way, her "different future" also recreates the fundamental nature of work that it purports to replace. Like posthumanism that takes liberal and neoliberal humanism as the only kinds of humanism, Weeks's postwork future is premised on heternormative logic, so that guaranteed basic incomes, for instance, are "not for the common production of value, but the common reproduction of life . . . income to sustain the social worlds necessary for, among other things, production" (230). I suspect Weeks wants to use "reproduction" metaphorically, but even metaphor is incredibly problematic when the result of it is the sustenance of existing social worlds: the heteronormative reproduction metaphor becomes incredibly tone deaf, a double down on white supremacist patriarchy that, like the social worlds she wants to preserve, continues to push queer and black populations further from resources and power. Weeks's postwork is just another kind of politics of exception, finding room for joblessness but only in a liberal "family values" style of framework. Still, even if Weeks teases out this utopian vision with troubling details, her underlying notion of using the "post" in postwork to hold open an undefined space of possibility produces sympathetic resonance with something like a posthuman vestibule, where new ways of being human can be imagined in full knowledge of but with separation from Man. If Weeks offers an antiproductive but pro-reproductive utopian demand, as she claims, I think listening to Rae Sremmurd can expand this to a queerly antireproductive futurity. But before I can make that expansion, we need to establish Rae Sremmurd's aesthetics.

CRUNK + TRAP (BECAUSE "TRUNK" AND "CRAP" ARE LOUSY BLENDS)

Rae Sremmurd isn't exactly trap. They aren't exactly not trap, either. To best hear their aesthetics, it's helpful to expand the genre conventions we're working with to include trap's most immediate ancestor, crunk. Where trap revolves around the drug game, crunk lives in the club, with lyrics that "usually include a strong emphasis on sex, violence, and intoxication" (Miller 2008). An outgrowth of Miami and Atlanta bass genres, crunk rose to popularity in the 90s and crested in mainstream consciousness with a series of releases especially from Lil Jon & The Eastside Boyz, the Ying Yang Twins, and Three 6 Mafia in the mid-00s. Crunk performs a sonic blackness not by recycling the discarded bits of crack governmentality like trap does but by projecting black hyper-masculinity in leisure rather than work set-tings. When Three 6 Mafia released "Tear da Club Up" in 1995 (they would re-record the song for a 1997 release, too), it landed in a hip hop context dominated by gangsta rap with a few party hits occasionally rising to the top. Billboard's rap chart in 1995 featured Tupac and Notorious B.I.G. jock-eying for the No. 1 spot from January to August, then was anchored by two huge hits from Coolio and LL Cool J in the fall. Before Pac and Biggie duked it out for coastal dominance, it was the 69 Boyz's barely euphemistic Miami Bass track "Tootsee Roll" enjoying the end of a five-week run that had started in December 1994. "Tear da Club Up" splits the lyrical differ-ence between the gangstas and partiers, as Triple 6 is dedicated to the club but in the most violent terms possible.

Importantly, the crunk club isn't a place to do business. Whereas trappers always trap, crunk rappers, whatever their business may be, come to the club to party. The violence in the club, then, is typically about claiming territory or simply being violent as a form of release akin to dance. In fact, dance moves associated with crunk have been described as "rough and chaotic" and are sim-ilar to the kind of moshing that happens at punk concerts. The video for Lil Jon and the Eastside Boyz's "What U Gon Do?" (2004) feature the performers posturing at imagined adversaries, while Bonecrusher romps through town like a Godzilla after being denied entrance to the club in the video accompany-ing his "Never Scared" (2003). Crunk's performance of the party on the edge of destruction aligns with New Orleans's bounce's use of dance and public space to overwhelm its confines and proliferate unbounded.[1]

> The music is itself in some ways radically confining—overwhelmingly loud, threatening the body, making its integrity feel in flux, pressing you up against sound waves that feel both hard edged and viscous. But the music also releases the listener and the dancer from that confinement that it evokes. The very repe-tition of the form enables embodied release. (Ellis 2015, 399)

The lyrics and bodily movements of crunk invest in a violence bounce does-n't, but each seeks a release from confinement in the space of a party. Where bounce is more readily queer (more on crunk's queerness soon!), crunk reads on the surface as a hyper-masculine pursuit. As such, it is, as we saw with trap in the previous chapter, *so scary*! In a *Washington Post* review of Lil Jon's 2004 *Crunk Juice*, Andy Battaglia says it outright: "The Atlanta native epito-mizes the Dirty South at its dirtiest. And it's scariest, too." Rappers "bark grave orders," beats "stomp like soldiers marching over a bridge groaning under their weight," and the "aura of doom" is capped with "horror-movie strings" (Battaglia 2004). Reviewing the same album for *Rolling Stone*, Jon

Caramanica joins the chorus of frightened critics by starting with "Crunk is war, and Lil Jon is its Alexander" (Caramanica 2004). While trap is able to sound a sonic blackness that resonates as apolitical by recycling tired stereotypes of crack governmentality, crunk reverberated in a context where descriptive realists were still building a parallel public out of crack governmentality's entrepreneurialism. By divorcing violence from business and pulling it into the club, crunk was able to perform a combination of entrepreneurial and moral abandon that read as apolitical for the 1990s.

Crunk splits the difference between gangsta and party rap, lyrically, and its music tends to do the same. Listen to early crunk songs like Three 6 Mafia's "Tear da Club Up" (1995 and 1997) and "Gette'm Crunk" (1996), and Lil Jon and the Eastside Boyz's "Who U Wit?" (1997), and "I Like Dem Girlz" (2000), and you can hear the bass music elements rattling alongside some especially West Coast gangsta elements. Table 4.1 outlines the kick drum hits from these four songs. In each case, the percussion is rounded out with snare/clap hits on the second and fourth beat and eighths or sixteenths in the hi-hats that occasionally rattle up to thirty-second speeds.

Crunk's kick drum is far less predictable than trap's but maintains a commitment to syncopation that allows us to hear a through line from Miami Bass to crunk to trap. While crunk doesn't composite as easily as trap does, note that all four of these songs hit on the downbeat of one and the upbeat of two, and they also find a sixteenth note syncopation within the first beat. The downbeats of two and four are left entirely open for the snare/clap, and the latter half of the measure is generally less rhythmically complicated than the first. Percussively, crunk is a close cousin of southern bass music, as East Coast and West Coast hip hop still tended to lay the kick on the downbeat of the first and third beats of a measure.[2]

But remember those "horror-movie strings" Battaglia mentioned? Crunk tends to include some high-pitched, dissonant tremolo strings that linger in the background of a mix or staccato strings that pulse over top of a mix

Table 4.1 KICK DRUM PATTERNS FOR "TEAR DA CLUB UP" (95), "GETTE'M CRUNK" (96), "WHO U WIT" (97), AND "I LIKE DEM GIRLZ" (00)

	1	2	3	4	**5**	6	7	8	**9**	10	11	12	**13**	14	15	16
95	■	■		■	■		■	■	■		■				■	
96			■	■			■	■	■		■		■			
97	■	■		■	■		■		■							
00	■			■	■		■									

and, after decades of horror movie conditioning, connote a sense of dread or, in fact, horror. Dr. Dre's G-Funk sound incorporates this horror movie string sound regularly, usually as an element that isn't static in the mix but rather appears occasionally throughout a beat; the persistent strings in "The Day the Niggaz Took Over" (1992), though, sounds quite similar to the ongoing string backgrounds that would be common especially in Three 6 Mafia's œuvre (Lil Jon in this era was less wed to the strings but would often incorporate them, like Dre, at least as a recurring sonic element or would replace them with a high-pitched whistle or pan flute sound).

At the center of crunk's sound, though, is call-and-response. Like Miami Bass and New Orleans bounce, the participatory nature of crunk does as much as anything else to locate it in a club. The performance of crunk *sounds* like you're at a party, and "Who U Wit" stands as the prototypical crunk chant song, in this respect. The track contains no recognizable verse, just a back-and-forth among partiers. Most early crunk songs involve some level of call-and-response within the lyrics of the song, even if it's only implied at the hook level.

Crunk's recession from the mainstream in the mid-00s dovetails with trap's rise, and it's easy to hear the connections. As I outlined in the previous chapter, trap dives further into bass than crunk does, and while it is music played at clubs, its content leads inevitably back to the drug game and the trap house, with the club-based call-and-response of crunk diffusing into a less orchestrated group of background voices scattered about the trap. Rae Sremmurd's aesthetics parlay the two genres, as their music gravitates toward trap (the bulk of their 2015 debut album, *SremmLife*, is produced by trap stalwart Mike Will Made-It) but their lyrical content is always already a party. Rae Sremmurd's club doesn't carry the overt violence of the crunk club, but I find crunk a better party rap comparison for the duo's work than Miami or Atlanta bass specifically because their music often still manages to evoke a sense of dread reminiscent of crunk, regardless of lyrics. Rapping at the intersection of crunk and trap, Rae Sremmurd's sound is situated within the neoliberal humanist context of the mid 2010s. While crunk pivoted away from crack governmentality in the mid-90s to combine violence and partying in a thoroughly nonentrepreneurial performance and trap recycles those old crack governmentality stereotypes as a way of outmoding itself to appear apolitical, Rae Sremmurd find a different tack. The duo employ the sonic elements of crunk that encoded violence in the soundscape alongside the current apolitical sonic elements of trap, then queer all of it. In so doing, they tap into a party scene that reads on the surface as disengaged and frivolous but that vibrates queerly out of earshot of neoliberal humanism. By moving their club outside the

discourse of mainstream politics, Rae Sremmurd map a posthuman vestibule. From this vantage point, we hear the violence that besieges it emanating not from inside but from outside its walls. Before listening closely
to Rae Sremmurd's sound, especially in their song "Safe Sex Pay Checks,"
I want to pull together partying and work in the interstices of crunk and
trap to see how leisure and labor are often the same endeavor. From there,
I'll argue that Rae Sremmurd's posthuman club is a place for postwork,
where they "hold the space of a different future open" as a "stepping stone
to new genres of human" (Weeks 2011, 30; Weheliye 2014, 44–45).

PARTY, WORK, AND THE BLACK RATCHET IMAGINATION

Partying, enjoying yourself, when the world intends you to suffer can be a
powerful political activity. This is perhaps as central to hip hop as anything
else. The genre's emergence on commercial airwaves coincides with a sharp
neoliberal turn in the United States and West, a turn that has included the
cordoning off—including in prisons—of populations deemed unhealthy,
separating them from social services and other state and federal resources.
Race, gender, sex—these are never the explicit rationale for this severance,
but in a country with centuries of violently institutionalized power differentials, the scales are programmed to tip away from black, feminine, and queer
bodies. Time and again, some subgenre of hip hop can be heard at these
sites of severance. Just thinking of public planning projects that razed and
choked off neighborhoods highlights this point. In *Black Noise*, Tricia Rose's
social history of hip hop centers Robert Moses's Cross-Bronx Expressway,
which plowed through the Bronx in the 1960s, left thousands searching for
housing, accelerated the post-industrial decline of the borough, and "devas-
tated kin networks and neighborhood services" (Rose 1994, 31). In David
Font-Navarrete's genealogy of Miami Bass, it's the construction of I-95 and
I-395—also in the 60s—that "effectively strangl[ed] the neighborhood [of
Overtown] geographically and economically" and turned both Overtown and
Liberty City into what "might as well be a foreign country" (Font-Navarette
494). Nadia Ellis roots her theorization of bounce's boundless repetition in
yet another 1960s highway project, as New Orleans's I-10 expansion blazed
through the Treme and Seventh Ward, "cutting through the community and
creating a gaping swathe that violated the vibrant space that had been created by African Americans along the famed Claiborne Avenue" (Ellis 2015,
391). In each case, a highway designed to expedite movement through—
not within—neighborhoods populated by people without the political or
economic clout to reroute the construction projects elsewhere left those

populations further from resources and power. And the music that arose from these areas? Breakbeats, bass, bounce: music for dancing, for cutting loose when you've been cut off. Music that is a refusal to do the physical and emotional labor of suffering that has been tasked to you.

But for neoliberal humanism, where the goal is for life to mirror the free market so that a person's worth accrues beyond just the hours they work, partying goes hand-in-hand with labor. On the one hand, leisure refreshes the worker to do more and better labor. This is the crux of the postwork advocates' argument for shorter work weeks—with more time to spend doing what we like, we will show up to work fitter, happier, more productive. An artist like Kevin Gates uses the hyped, maximalist sounds of trap to push him through the six jobs and two phones that exhaust him ("I Don't Get Tired" (2014) and "Two Phones" (2015)); he doesn't have time to rest, but he can use the sonic elements of other people's party music to fuel his labor. On the other hand, partying is its own work. In a *Guardian* profile of Lil Jon, Hattie Collins pinpoints the King of Crunk's extension of his performance outside the recording studio:

> "I have two sides. Lil Jon be wild, pouring tequila down everybody's throats whereas the regular me, I'm just quiet. I don't like to say nothing," he confesses. "People expect me to be crazy and wild all the time but sometimes I go to the club and I might be tired. Everybody wants me to get the party started. But why can't they get the fucking party started? I always get the party started," he grumps. (Collins 2006)

Lil Jon's job *is* partying, so a realm of leisure becomes his labor. Lil Jon, of course, doesn't have to get the party started every time, but even if he isn't directly making money on a public appearance (and he's a shrewd business-person, so he probably is), the proliferation of his persona in live settings helps sell his recordings and concert tickets and other professional endeavors like the energy drink Crunk Juice that shares a name with his first solo album.

Partying for Lil Jon isn't so much about accruing capital as it is about financializing his performance. Randy Martin's *The Financialization of Daily Life* captures this process.

> Finance is not only the question of what to do with the money one has worked for, but a way of working that money over, and ultimately, a way of working over oneself. With the new model of financial self-management, making money does not stop with wages garnered from employment. Money must be spent to live, certainly, but now daily life embraces an aspiration to make money as well. (Martin 2002, 16–17)

Lil Jon's method of "working over oneself" involves a nonstop, full throttle party. And while Lil Jon has tons more money than most to work over through an ongoing performance of his persona, such financialization through leisure practices is common in the 21st century. Facebook tends to stand as the paragon of financialized leisure. In her analysis of the 2016 introduction of the Web site's expanded range of emotional responses (before this, users could only "like" something), Jenny Davis notes that even the "negative" responses like anger and sadness are so cartoonish as to fit neatly into Facebook's long established "happiness paradigm." "Advertisers post there, and it wouldn't do to have users who openly dissent against those who paid for ad space" (Davis 2016). Social media Web sites are places where users spend their leisure time "working over [themselves]," sometimes for direct profit, as in the case of businesses that interact with customers, but often in a less tangible arena of social capital, which is not far off from what Lil Jon does. But *everyone* on Facebook puts Facebook's advertisers' money to work: "Keeping things cheerful keeps users coming back, which keeps eyeballs for sale and ad space more valuable" (Davis 2016). In a society where leisure time isn't leisure, where partying is work, how might music at the intersection of crunk and trap sonify this?

Kevin Gates's moody trap aesthetics do some of this work. Despite the title of his 2014 hit, "I Don't Get Tired," Gates gets *so tired*. The fourth and eighth measures of his eight-measure chorus is built around the line "Get it get fly, I got six jobs, I don't get tired." The first two words of each of the three phrases ("Get it," "I got," and "I don't") are delivered in rapid staccato thirty-second notes, while the final two words of each are eighths. The effect, similar to the flow Desiigner and Young Thug have in common, is of contraction and expansion, an engine misfiring before turning over and running smoothly through the more metrical parts of the chorus and verses that follow. There's a manic nature to Gates's sound that gives the listener the impression that Gates is always right at the edge of what he's capable of doing.

Contrast this to Atlanta oddball ILoveMakonnen, whose "Tuesday" is a weary account of partying when one is too overworked and tired to party. Makonnen and guest artist Drake sing of running drugs and performing shows—a marriage of the crack game and music industry akin to Bogazianos's and Spence's accounts detailed in Chapter 3—then partying on a Tuesday. Why do Makonnen and featured guest Drake have the club going up on a Tuesday? Because they "ain't got no motherfuckin time to party on the weekend," that's why. Like Lil Jon, it behooves Makonnen and Drake to step into the club, to move the party along in a way that works over their selves, so Makonnen and Co. clock in to the job, but, as Robin James notes in a 2014 analysis, they don't really do the emotional labor expected of them. Everything about the track is tired, from the synth loop that barely manages to crank itself over each bar line to the lyrics that decline to dance or even take Xanax to Makonnen's constrained vocals that begin to crack in the final minute as he waits for it all to end. "Tuesday" is a track about working through your leisure time when your work time has expanded so much that it cuts your leisure time to practically nil, and the weariness of the proceedings means it's hardly a banger.

The "Tuesday" instrumental is a collaboration between veteran trap producers Sonny Digital and Metro Boomin, and it uses recognizable trap sounds in uncommon ways. Instead of hyped background vocals, "Tuesday"'s vocal soundscape is empty but for the echoes of Makonnen's leads. The hi-hats are there, but they pound out straight sixteenth notes with nary a rattle to be heard. And as opposed to the rising synths that help fuel Gates's 24/7 grind, the "Tuesday" deep bass synth nosedives. If Mike Will Made-It's production on "Move That Dope" presents an entirely mundane and static soundtrack for the drug game, "Tuesday" mirrors that in the club when all the wage-earning work is done. Like the rappers who don't have the energy to dance, the instrumental just manages to hold itself together and never bothers to do more than it has to. Lil Jon, in a moment of candor, may complain about always having to get the party started; "Tuesday" ratchets that complaint into a glum occupation of the space that's supposed to be turnt. In the same way "Move That Dope" frustrates notions of the upwardly mobile dope boy, "Tuesday" sits at the intersection of crunk and trap—party music with a hardened criminal shell—and shrugs off the financializing work of partying. Though its lyrics are entirely about working and working to party, its sonic aesthetics are staunchly *anti*productive.

But this boils down, really, to a critique of work not unlike what we've already seen from the postwork advocates. It isn't hard to imagine that Makonnen and Drake and Gates might all rally behind legislation for shorter work weeks and guaranteed basic incomes. What I want to listen for in Rae Sremmurd's music, though, is something that resonates more with Weeks's notion of a space held open for the purpose of imagining a completely different future, one that isn't reliant on present conceptions of what it is to work or what it is to be human, and certainly one that doesn't revolve around reproduction, as Weeks imagines it. To hear the antireproductive nature of Rae Sremmurd's music, I want to call in L.H. Stallings's "black ratchet imagination" and turn an ear to how crunk and trap clubs are always already queer.

Following L.H. Stallings into the hip hop strip club opens up a space very different from what it appears to be on the surface.

Wait, actually, let's talk about imagination for a moment. Stallings's use of "imagination" as part of her theoretical framework parallels Adrienne Brown's approach to cars in "Drive Slow" (2012). In each case, the call for imagination is a call to move past what appears—or vibrates—on the surface so that we can find the delightful possibilities underneath. Iton refers to this as "pushing back the frame" (2008, 289). Iton's black fantastic is the product of imagination, which brings "into the field of play those potentials we have forgotten, or did not believe accessible or feasible" (290). Brown's account of hip hop cars shifts our focus from the automobile as marker of autonomy to creator of commonwealth, and her analysis requires imagination because we must step outside of the easiest, most politically legible interpretation to access this different kind of hip hop car. If politics, as Manchard puts it, "creates it's own set of structural limitations," then it's no surprise that Iton situates the black fantastic in relation to but out of step with political discourse, as being "in search of the black fantastic" means operating beyond the boundaries of mainstream discourse (Manchard 2006, 11). That's where we'll find the "minor-key sensibilities generated from the experiences of the underground, the vagabond, and those constituencies marked as deviant" (16).

Deviant is kind of a big deal here. Stallings works from a queer theoretical framework, where *queer*ing something means taking it outside of normative contexts. Queerness most directly signifies sexuality, but—especially if we employ an intersectional approach that helps us understand how things like sexuality, gender, race, and class are all linked—queerness can describe the deviation from a number of norms. The queerness we're about to find in Rae Sremmurd's club deviates from sexual norms, to be sure, but it's closely related to the deviance I outlined in the previous chapter, where trap maps a politics that doesn't situate itself inside mainstream discourse. Trap is massively popular, so we're not dealing with the underground or vagabond here. Rather, trap is a deviant kind of black fantastic, circulating in a mainstream that, if it isn't using its imagination, will miss all that's happening—all that's deviant and queer and deeply if unexpectedly political—when we "push back the frame."

So, here: drink this. It's Sprite mixed with imagination and a Jolly Rancher. Ready?

Following L.H. Stallings into the hip hop strip club opens up a space very different from what it appears to be on the surface. Strip clubs are typically discursively confined to a misogynistic corner of capital, where the male gaze becomes a transaction, the exchange of dollars for sightings. Stallings, framing her analysis in terms of "antiwork efforts and postwork imagination" that functions outside of political discourse and that, "in Sylvia Wynter's parlance … unmakes … the order of knowledge," calls attention to the ways gender is undone, queered, transed in the hip hop strip club (Stallings 2015, 177; Stallings 2013, 135). Like trap, which seems more interested in downward mobility and a performance that moves away from a respectable black parallel public, the hip hop strip club trucks in sex work that is "a radical reading and position against the current order of work society" (Stallings 2015, 21). Stallings's primary strip club focus in *Funk the Erotic* is on the trans-aesthetics of women dancers and patrons and the range of genders they perform together. In "Hip Hop and the Black Ratchet Imagination," Stallings lingers on the male gaze that takes in these varied gender performances and the "new performances of black masculinity" opened through that gaze (138). Here, I join Juicy J in the club in order to expand Stallings's analysis from visual to aural, listening to the ways Juicy J's strip club maps not a fixed structure, either of a building or of a performance of gender, but "the nook and cranny spaces of transitional bodies in transitional spaces" (Stallings 2013, 135). From there, we'll better hear the queerness of Rae Sremmurd's performance of clubs and strip clubs.

Juicy J, the Three 6 Mafia member most likely to be known by casual hip hop and pop fans, is a heel. Issa Rae, on an episode of her YouTube series "Ratchetpiece Theatre," captures this fact with a flourish. Describing Juicy J as having a "homeschool doctorate in ratchetology," Rae lampoons him as misogynist fool—"obviously the kid in middle school who couldn't read yet always volunteered to"—whose inability to pronounce words matters very little, as his music boils down to the imperative to "just dance for those bands of money, ho" (Rae 2012). Indeed, Juicy J's appearances as a featured artist on other musicians' songs always involve recognizable markers of sonic blackness. On Katy Perry's 2013 "Dark Horse," it's in Juicy J's verse that the hi-hats begin to rattle and the chorus of DJ Mustard "hey"s sneak into the mix (both are much quieter than usual, though). Similarly, on the official remix of Rihanna's "Pour It Up" (2013), Juicy J's verse is the only one to include those same choruses of Mustard "hey"s, as well as his signature ad-lib looping in the background, "yeah, ho!" On Usher's "I Don't Mind" (2014), Juicy J first calls into existence the deep 808 trap kick drum, then spends the entire track taking up more and more space in the mix, adding background vocals and then an entire guest verse that swerves into an explicit territory Usher doesn't dare go. Finally, on Usher's most emotionally confessional R&B melisma in the final measures of the track,

Juicy J punctuates the singer's soulfulness with a simple "woot woot" that seems to underline the distance between Usher's earnestness and Juicy J's flippant misogyny.[3] Juicy J carries the markers of sonic blackness that delineate him from the kind of black parallel public Kendrick or, for that matter, Usher represents. He is, in Spence's terms, the exception who can't be reformed. In Iton's, the deviant. In Rae's and Stallings's, the ratchet.

While Juicy J brings sonic blackness onto a variety of tracks, perhaps his most notorious is "Bandz a Make Her Dance" (2012). This is the subject of Issa Rae's *Ratchetpiece* analysis, and it's also the sonic fabric of Rihanna's "Pour It Up." Both songs are produced by Mike Will Made-It, so the similarity between the undulating synth lines in each song is no accident.[4] When Rihanna steps into the club and starts raining money on strippers, she's performing *as* Juicy J; when Rihanna needs a recognizably problematic figure of black masculinity to undo through her own gender performance, Juicy J is the persona she chooses. The transitional gender performance of "Pour It Up" signals that all is not as it seems with Juicy J, and Stallings's black ratchet imagination provides the possibility to hear him differently, not as an apolitical misogynist rehearsing heteronormative transactions at the strip club, but as the queer vibrations of a transitional body in a transitional space.

"Bandz"'s instrumental bears the markers of sonic blackness that are common in trap and that I outline in Chapter 3. In addition, and what helps situate "Bandz" in the sonic space of the strip club, the second repetition of each hook includes a "booty clap," where the percussive clap sound migrates from its usual place on the second and fourth beat to a pattern of steady eighth notes across the measure, a sonic rendering of a dancer's glutes when bounced during a twerk move.[5] The booty clap is the sound of misogyny turned up in the mix; lyrics aside, the booty clap is an instrumental element that signals heteronormative hyper-masculinity. As I argued in the trap irony chapter, trap's sonic blackness works to recycle tired stereotypes about drugs, violence, and misogyny in hip hop so that the genre reads as scary or apolitical in comparison with the post-race politics ascribed to Kendrick Lamar. Juicy J trots out the figure of the rapacious black man in his performance of hyper-masculinity, and, as with trap, there's more happening in this performance than a surface-level evaluation would suggest.

Stallings notes that the strip club draws on and allows a broad spectrum of gender performances on the stage, including butch and trans femininity that exist somewhere other than firmly within a gender binary: "This is what rappers get caught up in—the fantasy of woman whose origin is in the female dancers' undoing of woman" (Stallings 2013, 138). Juicy J's performance of hyper-masculinity occurs in an arena where being hyper-masculine means getting "caught up in" something that can't firmly hold together as simply masculine. Stallings points out that, "when woman is undone in this way, we note the potential for such undoing to temporarily queer men" (138). Or, in Spillers's terms, the strip club opens the possibility for Juicy J to experience "the power of 'yes' to the 'female' within" (1987, 80). The trap irony of Juicy J's misogyny is that his hyper-masculine sonic blackness sounds like a straightforward hetero-masculine transaction when, in fact, no player in that transaction is stably situated: he is destined to be hyper-undone in his masculinity. The video delivers the visuals that complement Stallings's black ratchet imagination.

In the video for "Bandz," there are strippers, and there are strip club patrons, but the relationship among them—who is performing for whom—remains ill-defined at best. Though Juicy J and guest rappers Lil Wayne and 2 Chainz are ostensibly there to ogle dancers, none of the three of them are ever shown actually looking at a stripper. Instead, the camera is positioned between stage and audience so that no firm connection is established between the co-ed group sitting on a leather couch and the dancers working the pole. We only see them in separate shots interspersed with Juicy J, Wayne, and 2 Chainz rapping from different vantage points. Moreover, all three rappers themselves appear to be on stage as well as in the audience. In one recurring shot, Juicy J makes money rain from his hands as a dancer bounces behind him; instead of raining the money on her, Juicy J occupies the same performance space as the stripper, and the money flows from them toward the audience. Here, the strip club stage holds a dual performance of femininity and masculinity collapsed into one, and the transactional nature of audience/dancer is reversed. In another scene, 2 Chainz stands amid what looks like catwalk scaffolding, framed by two poles that appear at first glance to be the same poles the dancers move up and down on. Through the filter of trap irony and the lens of the black ratchet imagination, the video comes into focus: the flat performance of hyper-masculinity undertaken by Juicy J, Lil Wayne, and 2 Chainz is as constructed and tenuous as the flat performance of femininity (wrongly) assumed to be contained in the strippers' moves. Everyone in this video is werking so that gender and sexuality can't work the way it's assumed to.

Following Spence's biopolitical formulation, the excepted populations Juicy J and other crunk and trap rappers perform through hyper-masculine sonic blackness are meant to be pushed far from money and power. Far enough, in fact, that they are likely to be shot in the street or killed in a jail cell by state-sanctioned and -protected police violence. But in the always already queer space of the club, a different logic, one operating, as Wynter puts it, "completely outside of our present conception of what it is to be human," takes hold. Juicy J dismantles respectability, performs a queered and transed masculinity, and reverses the flow of money. Here is a black, queer postwork futurity: rooted in the Dirty South club, sounded through trap and crunk aesthetics, we tap into Stallings's black ratchet imagination, where everything that should be, isn't. In terms of work, this involves money ending up where it shouldn't. As I turn my attention to Rae Sremmurd, these are the pieces of postwork analysis I will use: a queer futurity that ties trap and crunk aesthetics to improbable flows of capital.

RAE SREMMURD'S POSTHUMAN VESTIBULE: THE QUEER CLUB

Did I mention Rae Sremmurd party? Because they do. And when they're done partying, they party some more. When they're not partying? Look closer; they're actually still partying. As outlined above, partying when the world intends you to suffer—intends you to work at the emotional and physical labor of suffering—can be its own form of resistance or refusal. Part of what Rae Sremmurd do is party in exactly this way, as a refusal to work. They look and sound like kids (Swae Lee, the younger brother, was 18 when their first single dropped), which matters in a specific way in the context of increasing national attention to the deaths of black men and boys at the hands or by the sanction of the state.[6] Rae Sremmurd, like all black bodies in the United States, are marked for death, and they juxtapose this un-naïvely in "Safe Sex Pay Checks." If Sonny Digital's and Metro Boomin's "Tuesday" instrumental sounds exhausted, Mike Will Made-It's "Safe Sex" beat is besieged. The synth line sounds like it's being cranked out of a music box, glitchy and always on the edge of falling silent. Rae Sremmurd's high-pitched, cracking voices sound insistent, stretched, and stressed as they party on with danger closing in around them. In this context, the section that revolves around the double-entendre call "Shots! Shots! Shots! Shots!" with its attendant response, "Now let's fuckin party" becomes a spectacular performance of not being dead, of not doing the work of death. We've watched government-sponsored murder of black men and women play out in ways that work for the powers that already be, whether by serving as the catalyst for creatively destroying neighborhoods that will be reborn in the splendor of neoliberal consumption or the justification for further militarizing police forces with body armor, chemical weapons, and free reign to enforce whatever their idea of peace may be. As long as they party, as long as they live in the spectacular excess of not being dead, Rae Sremmurd defiantly don't do that kind of work.

As noted in the previous section, though, partying is increasingly another kind of work—an articulation of one's brand and a windfall for leisure services and social media. If the goal of postwork is to hold open a future beyond work as we know it, just partying doesn't really do the trick anymore. This is where Stallings's black ratchet imagination comes into play. By queering the site of the club, the hip hop party swerves away from healthy respectability, complicates the performance of race and gender, taps into the irony of trap's sonic aesthetics, and opens the postwork possibility of funneling money toward queer of color populations that are otherwise meant to be cordoned off from resources.

"Throw Sum Mo"

I'll come back to "Safe Sex Pay Checks," but an ideal entry point for Rae Sremmurd's postwork club returns us to the strip club, where Nicki Minaj greets us. Now, Nicki Minaj can rap. She can and has rapped circles around Rae Sremmurd, both in her remix of the duo's first single "No Flex Zone" and in "Black Barbies," a full-length reimagining of Rae Sremmurd's "Black Beatles" (2016). In "No Flex Zone," she launches into her verse with "Hell nah, you can't use my lip gloss" and takes up all the lyrical space in the song, reducing the duo's role to only Swae Lee singing the hook as a bookend to her extended verse. Taking up space and reconfiguring male rappers' roles is a standard Minaj move. She kings on rappers at every turn, gleefully undermining their hetero-masculinity, with the likes of Jay Z, Kanye West, Big Sean, Drake, and Lil Wayne on her trophy wall. Savannah Shange, analyzing Minaj as "strategically queer," legible as neither straight nor gay, watches how Minaj moves in relation to Usher in "Lil Freak" and 2 Chainz in "Beez in the Trap." In each instance, she upends the heteronormative role assigned to her, siphoning off women to target for her own sexual pleasure instead of hooking them up directly with Usher, and "danc[ing] alongside 2 Chainz but never *with* him," maintaining a distance that "establish[es] them as platonic peers" (Shange 2014, 37). Rae Sremmurd didn't stand a chance when she jumped on "No Flex Zone" and "Black Barbies," and she literally annihilates them as rappers, leaving Swae Lee to perform the role of hook girl around her displays of verbal prowess on "Flex" and preserving only background moans on "Barbies." Minaj's presence on a track tends to throw all hetero-norms into disarray, her gender undoing, following Stallings, queering both her and the men she shares sonic space with. Shange reads her sexuality in much the same way: "She *appears* to perform 'straight' or 'queer,' but upon closer examination, she refuses both" (30).

I say all that about Minaj to say this: when the first words on Rae Sremmurd's strip club anthem, "Throw Sum Mo," spill from *Nicki*'s mouth? It's a clear signal that not everything will be as it seems. For instance, though she can rap Rae Sremmurd under the table, on "Throw Sum Mo" she takes on the role she delegated to Swae Lee in "Flex": the hook girl. Her contribution to "Throw" is to repeat the same refrain four times over the course of the song, a standard task often assigned to women in hip hop. As always with Minaj, though, she performs a seemingly simple and gendered role with some complexity. A hallmark of Minaj's vocal style is her ability to rapidly switch inflection and to produce a variety of sound effects. Listen to a handful of her songs, and you'll hear growls, trills, foreign accents, and a range of gender-fluid inflections. But she sings the "Throw Sum Mo" hook robotically, dispassionately. Minaj's narrow, staid vocal performance draws attention to the subservient but sonically integral role of the hook girl in hip hop and undermines the heteronormativity of the proceedings. In the same way Makonnen clocks in but does little else to fuel "Tuesday"'s party, Minaj withholds her emotional labor, leaving the masculine prowess of Rae Sremmurd, who can't get Minaj to behave right, in question.

The duo's other guest on "Throw" is Young Thug, whose aesthetics I touched on in the trap irony chapter. Thug's performance of his gender and sexuality has been the source of Internet rumors and homophobia for years. For what it's worth, Thug—and here it's hard to tell the difference between the performer and the person—seems much less concerned with defining his sexuality than others are and prefers women's clothes because "they fit like they're supposed to. Like a rock star" (Hairston 2015). His lyrics are rife with the same kind of misogyny one would find on a Juicy J or run-of-the-mill trap track, and he's also comfortable being photographed in a dress or tutu and calls men he is close to "bae," "hubby," and "my love" (Sandberg 2015; Abiola 2014). In language that recalls Shange's description of Minaj's sexuality, *Guardian* writer Sam Wolfson, without attributing it as a direct quote and possibly just shrugging off the question of Thug's sexuality as a useless pursuit, notes that "Thug says he is neither gay nor straight" (Wolfson 2015). If Rae Sremmurd tapped Minaj and Thugger as guests in the interest of presenting some uncomplicated hyper-hetero-masculinity, well, they're doing it wrong: the presence of their two guests involves a performance of gender and sexuality that's a "syncopated two step between 'maybe' and 'no' that dances away from the 'yes' that would proclaim" anything fixed (Shange 42). The video bears this out.

Set in a roller-rink-*cum*-strip-club, "Throw" is chock full of the shots "Bandz" denies: male audience members directly engaged with female dancers. Swae Lee and Slim Jxmmi (with Mike Will Made-It in tow) are shown in a variety of locations, from the dressing room to the stage, touching, dancing with, and raining money on dancers at every turn. These visuals are what Stallings calls "dominant theories of a Western gaze" that employ ocularity in a way that covers or misses other ways of sensing and feeling (2015, 178). This is also Wynter's critique of discourses; the familiarity of Mulvey's theory of the gaze pulls the viewer's attention to the more spectacularly audacious scenes of "Throw" and, I suspect, fill in the gaps in Juicy J's "Bandz," making each an easy heteronormative transactional narrative. Young Thug, though, positions himself differently in relation to the dancers. His verse and appearances are split between a parking lot scene and shots of him alongside Rae Sremmurd, Mike Will Made-It, and Minaj. In both sets, dancers abound, but in the parking lot, Thug sits atop a van rapping directly to the camera while women dance on the ground below him. In the club, his movements recall Shange's description of Minaj and 2 Chainz in "Beez": he "dances alongside [the dancers] but never *with* [them]" (2014, 37). Especially compared to Swae Lee and Slim Jxmmi, Young Thug, like Juicy J in "Bandz," performs next to the dancers in a way that "establishes them as platonic peers," multiple parts of a set piece rather than members in a sexual transaction with one another.

Minaj's turn in the video proves particularly disruptive. Seemingly relegated to the role of hook girl, the "Throw" video reveals that Minaj is actually running the show, with all the money in the club routing through her. Her power can actually be heard on the track. In the introduction to this book, I observed Minaj scaring off pieces of the instrumental to Kanye West's "Monster," and in "Throw Sum Mo," her voice similarly alters the accompanying track. At each hook, Mike Will Made-It's beat routes through a high pass filter so that the lower frequencies are removed from the mix. The effect is magnetic, like the beat is pulled upward toward Minaj's voice, the instrumental recognizing and responding to her authority. During the second hook (which comes after the first verse), Minaj offers a visual reminder of her power over the instrumental track by reminding us what's missing: the booty clap. As she sings the words "bad bitches," Minaj claps her hands (see Figure 4.1) together in a complex overlay of audiovisual signification: we see her hands meet and can respond by supplying an imaginary synth patch that has migrated in the space of the hip hop strip club from a sound that conjures clapping hands to one that stands in for clapping asses. Minaj runs this club, controls this space, and, as she demonstrates in her mimed performance, holds or withholds the booty clap. Though she appears femme, more visually linked to the dancers than anyone else in the video, Minaj performs in a dominant role. Her "refusal to cede to any regime of recognition confound the multiple common senses—hip hop/

Figure 4.1 Minaj mimes the booty clap with her hands in "Throw Sum Mo."

Figure 4.2 Minaj receives money from a dancer during the second hook of "Throw Sum Mo."

patriarchy/ homonormativity—that seek to produce her as a compliant subject" (Shange 2014, 42).

Also in the second hook, we see Minaj seated at a counter, flanked by bodyguards, receiving cash from a dancer (Figure 4.2). Remarkably, moments later, Minaj hands a stack of cash to a patron entering the club (Figure 4.3).[7] The latter sequence, where Minaj gives the club's earnings to a guest, is repeated several times throughout the video, revealing that the money that rains down in the club is part of a liquid cash cycle where it collects on the floor and in dancers' clothes, evaporates into Minaj's puffy fur coat, then condenses in patron hands before precipitating again.

This liquidity of money in "Throw" short-circuits the work that otherwise *appears* to be happening. If the strip club in "Throw" isn't a place of business, a place where performers dance for money and audiences pay for titillation, then what is it? Playing on the famous Atlanta strip club Magic City, Stallings theorizes black strip clubs as "magic cities" by shifting emphasis

Figure 4.3 Minaj hands cash to a patron of the club in "Throw Sum Mo."

away from discourses that "revolve around men as patrons and consumers" and toward black women performing "the particular practices of black dance" (2015, 189). Rooting her analysis in traditions of black orgy and public ritual, Stallings finds "cultural practices that merge the rituals embedded in orgy with those of carnival so that party fulfills the exterior needs of social advancement and the interior needs of individual transcendence" (180). "Throw Sum Mo," in its severance of transactional capital, creates a magic city, a party that allows its participants to slide along various performances of gender and sexuality that place sex, like the money in the club, in a nonreproductive role, bringing it into focus as pleasure rather than work.

Minaj and Young Thug, responding to the trans-aesthetics rooted in the dancers' performances, perform an undoing of gender, which is audible in the filtered hook instrumental and Minaj's removal of the booty clap from the mix, and which is visible in the flow of cash in the club and the gender role reversal that slots Thug in performance with the dancers and Minaj as club king. Minaj and Thug "sustain fluid androgyny so as to undo fixed binaries of gender that uphold work society's divisions of sexual labor" (Stallings 2015, 177). In undoing gender, "Throw" also undoes the transactional nature of all those Franklins raining everywhere: there are cash bandz, and there are strippers, but the link between them is broken. "Throw Sum Mo" is queer capital, a postwork imaginary full of transitional bodies in a transitional space, where werking and sex isn't sex work.

"Safe Sex Pay Checks"

So, Rae Sremmurd are certainly, as Stallings reads men in the hip hop strip club, queered by association. But they aren't just bystanders, and I want to return to "Safe Sex Pay Checks" and think Stallings's notion of "transitional bodies in transitional spaces" with Lee Edelman's critique of reproductive futurism to hear the queerness in their performance. Let's start back at an observation I made previously: Rae Sremmurd sound like kids. Their voices, which don't receive the usual multitrack detuning of trappers, are relatively high, and their vocal performances usually include reaches to the upper limits of their register so that we can hear the crack in their breaks, a sonic moment akin to a boy in the midst of puberty. To further mark the highness of their voices, the duo often feign gravitas with the kind of growling lower register a kid might use to approximate a deeper voice. All of this is apparent in Slim Jxmmi's verse from "No Flex Zone." His first two lines, "young niggas gotta get to the money" and "five chains so they look at me funny" each rise in pitch in the second half—on "get to the" and "look at me." Jxmmi produces this rise by squeezing off his vocal cords so that the words sound pinched, and his voice cracks especially on "the" and "at." Later in his verse, he growls out the lines "four five six seven chains on/just stay in your lane, son" in a way that adds distortion to the edge of his voice but very little of the depth in pitch that such growling would often produce.

It's Swae Lee who performs the cracking voice in the hook of "Safe Sex Pay Checks." The very first word, "safe," sounds as if he's straining his vocal cords to reach over his break, and he cracks again, this time with the help of pitch correction processing, on the final syllable of the phrase "don't forget about." That pitch correction moment is a technological mimicking of the crack on the word "safe," and it also creates a melisma effect—a ratchet moment where the usually soulful, respectable melisma (think back to Usher) is achieved via nobody's favorite vocal effect, the auto-tuner. The performance of this refrain highlights Rae Sremmurd's transitional bodies: they sound like boys, with their high, cracking voices but are men, sexually active and financially viable.

Mike Will Made-It's instrumental provides the transitional space. I called this beat "besieged," and beyond the political context of partying while young and black, Mike Will Made-It achieves this sonic affect through four specific techniques. First, the synth that carries the looping melodic motif has a heavy glissando (gliss), so moving from one pitch to the next means sweeping through every pitch in between. The experience of this gliss is the sensation that the song is constantly having to wind itself up, a hand-crank propulsion that could give way any moment. This pairs with the second technique, the periodic cutting of the instrumental's signal mid-phrase. The synth's recurring disappearance destabilizes its presence in the song, and the gliss adds to the wind-up effect whenever the signal is restored. The gliss and recurring cuts together make the instrumental sound like it's in a stupor, stumbling around in a vulnerable daze. I think of these first two techniques working together to sonify the internal state of the instrumental, what one feels like—a bit woozy, intoxicated—in Rae Sremmurd's club.

The third and fourth techniques, meanwhile, similarly work together but as elements external to the club, and these are filtered percussion and sidechained synths. In the opening measures of the track and at each iteration of the hook, beat one of every measure includes a heavily filtered percussion hit. A filter removes a good deal of frequency range from a musical event, and in this case—which sounds like a band-pass filter, the removal of both high and low frequencies so only a ghostly mid-range remains—the result is a sound that seems to be coming from the distance, perhaps outside the club. The short, percussive nature suggests moments of aggression, perhaps the ramming of a door or a gunshot. More prominent in the mix are other filtered percussion: the snare hits on the second beat of every measure in the verses, the scatter shots sprayed through the refrain. The velocity (i.e., how hard the attack is and therefore how loud the beginning of the sound is) and filter settings on each of these makes them nearer or farther away in the soundscape, a sense of danger approaching unpredictably. Finally, the synth includes a sidechain compression effect for the final measure of each refrain. Sidechain compression causes a reduction in gain/volume for one track when another track is playing. This can be used to create a little bit of space in the mix, or, in this case, it can be set for a dramatically excessive ducking effect. Each beat of the final measure of the refrains seems to be sidechained to a heavy percussive moment that is muted in the final mix. So, each time that percussive moment happens, the synth line is compressed out of the mix to make room for a sound we never hear.[8] Combined with the stupefied nature of the synth line and the gunshots around the edges of the club, the sidechain is a violent and structurally crucial moment: each refrain feels like it may be the last, like the song may drop to the ground unable to move on.

These techniques—cuts, glisses, filters, and sidechains—are not unique to "Safe Sex Pay Checks," and they operate in a broader context of trap and crunk aesthetics. My contention here is that they combine with Rae Sremmurd's vocal performances to map out a party that doesn't work the way it's supposed to. Like crunk parties, violence is imminent, but instead of coming from inside the club, a hyper-masculine male posturing that equates cutting loose with aggressive altercation, "SSPC"'s violence encroaches from outside, the echo of government terrorism whose work is to reap black bodies whether they are working or partying. It's a party, on the one hand, that performs not-being-dead, refusing the work appointed to young black bodies. And, on the other, it's also a party that, by veering so close to being dead, fails to replenish its participants, existing instead in the transitional space between excessive life and encroaching death. Transitional bodies in transitional spaces.

Swae Lee's and Slim Jxmmi's performance of youth in "Safe Sex Pay Checks" is a queer postwork futurity that, like "Bandz" and "Throw Sum Mo," queers capital. Lee Edelman, in *No Future*, figures queerness as a death drive aimed squarely at reproductive futurism, the what-goes-without-saying in US politics that lends any "won't someone please think of the children?!" political platform immediate credence. The Child, Edelman argues, "remains the perpetual horizon of every acknowledged politics, the fantasmatic beneficiary of every political intervention" (3). Well, sorta. The White Child, sure, but the Black Child? The Black Child is tasked to labor in death not as beneficiary but *for the benefit of* the state. Rae Sremmurd's transitional bodies, between boys and men, perform, with their youth, a kind of shadow Child, the unacknowledged life taken in exchange for the Child of "every acknowledged politics." Their exuberant performance of not-being-dead prevents money from moving the way it should; their non-death won't fuel 24-hour news cycles, won't pay overtime to instigating police forces in riot gear armed with tear gas, won't create ad space on Web sites performing the ritual hand-wringing that accompanies police violence each time, won't light fire under servers managing death traffic on social media, won't lay another brick on another prison built to hold another black body whose very existence, often in the moment of peaceful repose or compliance, is perceived as a threat to be contained or exterminated.

But Rae Sremmurd, as sexually active hetero-men, perform another, a queer instance of the Child: the refusal to reproduce. Stallings notes the queerness of black ratchet sexuality that is "just fucking"—sex as pleasure rather than as the work of reproduction, sex that isn't mediated "through a public sphere created and maintained by the authors of sex as knowledge, terror, or violence" (2015, 178). Similarly, Edelman's death drive revolves around queerness as nonreproductive, imagining a future without the Child. Edelman argues that the Child's symbolic positioning as representative of an innocent, unmarred, better future "marks the fetishistic fixation of het-eronormativity: an erotically charged investment in the rigid sameness of identity that is central to the compulsory narrative of reproductive futurism" (2004, 21). Heteronormativity, in other words, is cooked into the fabric of society and politics; without the Child and the heteronormativity required to reproduce the Child, there is no future, no way to imagine what comes next. Instead of focusing on the politics of gay adoption and gay marriage, Edelman argues that queerness will never have a space in the national imaginary without dismantling the centrality of the Child. His notion of death drive is one that kills off the Child so that we might reconfigure "the figural relations in which social identities are always inscribed" (17). Edelman, working within a Lacanian framework, figures the Child and the death drive that would take it out within the order of the Symbolic, the organizing structures of meaning and being in the world. The death drive, in other words, isn't anti-child or a call for those who identify as queer to refuse children or families; rather, it is a strategic disturbance or queering of all the Child represents, "recognizing and refusing the consequences of grounding reality in denial of the drive" (17). It's building a new concept of reality through strategically queer means; it's no future *that has been imagined yet.*

Rae Sremmurd's call in the middle of "Safe Sex Pay Checks," "safe sex, no babies!" and their interest in condoms and birth control in general—Slim Jxmmi relays an interaction in his "Flex" verse, "She said, 'Why you got so many condoms witcha?' I said, 'I'm a player to be honest witcha' "—function in a less figurative way. As children, Rae Sremmurd party as a way of not-being-dead; as not-dead men, they party without reproducing more shadow Children whose lives would be under constant threat and whose deaths would feed the economy of black suffering that besieges Rae Sremmurd's club. The constant threat of extermination at the hands of the government injects a jarring and necessary bit of critical race into Edelman's theory. The safe sex Rae Sremmurd propagate isn't a personal but political choice. Under the cover of a sonic blackness that reads as apolitical and profligate, Rae Sremmurd respond to the reality of the world around them by refusing to produce their labor for an economy of black death or reproduce children to contribute to that same economy.

The cruel irony in Rae Sremmurd's voluntary birth control is that it plays out as a parallel to the population control of the eugenics movement enacted under official state sanctioning across the 20th century. As Angela Davis accounts in *Women, Race, & Class*, the intersection of birth control and eugenics is a lethal one for people of color. Tracing the history of compulsory sterilization alongside arguments for birth control according to Margaret Sanger's position, "more children from the fit, less from the unfit," Davis details the tragic results of the sweeping definition of "unfit," which would include "morons, mental defectives, epileptics, illiterates, paupers, unemployables, criminals, prostitutes, and dope fiends" (Davis 1983, 213–15; Gordon 1977, 281; Corea 1977, 149). One might even use the word deviant. A cursory look at the list of descriptors for "unfit" people reveals a number of overlaps with what, exactly, sonic blackness references in trap and crunk music. It's no wonder, then, that "Guy Irving Birch, director of the American Eugenics Society . . . advocated birth control as a weapon to 'prevent the American people from being replaced by alien or Negro stock, whether it is

by immigration or by overly high birth rates among others in this country'"
(Davis, 214; Gordon, 283). The result was widespread and deceptive sterilization disproportionately performed on women of color. Rae Sremmurd,
partying in their queer club, refusing to produce and reproduce, to work the
way they're supposed to, arrive at an antireproductive postwork futurity
that finds itself facing a problematic history where state-sanctioned death
at the hands of the police is just another form of population control.

The Posthuman Vestibule

The intersection of birth control—safe sex—and sterilization abuse points
to a tension in Rae Sremmurd's party. "Just fucking," in Stallings's terms,
may be about "reorganiz[ing] the senses to detect sacred energies of others
in relation to the self so as to produce a new metaphysics of political struggle," but as long as the club is besieged, as long as the black bodies inside
are marked for death outside, "just fucking" will always be threatened by
"a public sphere created and maintained by the authors of sex as knowledge, terror, or violence" (2015, 178). The romantic notion of clubs is that
they have always provided safe spaces, especially for queer of color groups.
Realistically, this can only ever be true to a point, as these spaces are always
threatened, always under siege.

The final iteration of the refrain in "Safe Sex Pay Checks" segues into the
outro, featuring Swae Lee singing "oh oh" over and over. Eventually his vocals
fade as the instrumental swells in his place. The dying moments of the song,
which are also the end of the album, are that sidechained bar, slightly fading
in volume and then abruptly ending on the upbeat of 4, no downbeat to follow. There will be no firm resolution here, and Mike Will Made-It leaves us
suspended in the tension of Rae Sremmurd's queer club. Was the club over-
run? Did the song end when the partiers fell to the floor, unmoving?

Having listened to postwork in a queer of color context, Weeks's notion
of the utopian nature of postwork resonates with much greater possibility: "alternatives, fragments, or glimpses of something different that do not
presume to add up to a blueprint of an already named future" (30). The bind
that Rae Sremmurd find themselves in, the knot formed by the cinching of
birth control and population control, is one that can only be temporarily
wriggled out of in mainstream political discourse. As long as one operates
in the arena of neoliberal humanism, argues or responds to or tries to specifically resist its terms, neoliberal humanism can entrench and retrench.
In a society that recreates everything in the image of the market, putting
black death to work may be primarily a matter of compulsory sterilization

one day, racist drug policies the next, and police violence the day after that. If Rae Sremmurd directly resist police violence and craft a parallel public that voices black critique in legible terms, they may find themselves gaining ground on one front even as the politics of exception push other queer of color people further from resources, extending to and including the resource of having a right to one's life. It is from this vantage point that something like liberal humanism or neoliberal humanism can seem totalizing.

What the posthuman vestibule offers, however, is more varied relationality. Spillers's notion of vestibular flesh takes shape in a way that looks and sounds very much like Rae Sremmurd's club, a room attached to neoliberal humanism's world but not entirely inside it, filled with flesh—those unable to be formed or reformed according to liberal or neoliberal humanism— that *may* turn right back into neoliberal humanism's world, that *may* exit the club and face down the advancing terror, or that may vibrate its way all the way out of that world's reach, out of its earshot. The vestibule leads in, but it leads out, too.

Remembering the two-pronged approach of embattled humanism, which I've adopted as the strategy of the posthuman in response to neoliberal humanism, I hear Rae Sremmurd's "Safe Sex Pay Checks" as the construction of a posthuman vestibule from which postwork partiers can frustrate the market logic of black death, can neither produce nor reproduce for that economy, can queer money so that it, like the bills raining in Juicy J's and Minaj's clubs, can flow where it shouldn't, can cycle through excepted populations despite the best efforts of the mainstream and parallel publics to control it. This is a direct relationship with neoliberal humanism that seeks to dissolve it so that it can't choke off other ways of being human. At the same moment, in the accrual of funds and resources, in the engagement in sex as pleasure instead of work, in the viscous performances of gender and androgyny, in the joy of life that all happen in Rae Sremmurd's club, it is a posthuman vestibule that is aware of but has no relationship with neoliberal humanism. In this context, "safe sex, no babies!" is shorthand for "safe sex, no babies *for you*," a denial to reproduce for the neoliberal market. The club as posthuman vestibule that leads out, away from the mainstream? As Stallings imagines it, it's neither reproductive nor antiproductive but, rather, *a*productive, a postwork, posthuman imaginary that neither mandates nor prevents production or reproduction.

Rae Sremmurd's queer sonic blackness constructs the posthuman vestibule from which they vibrate their way out of earshot and into some unnamed future we have no blueprint for.

Epilogue

Posthuman Sub-Bass

I done cut up my bang, and I shook up the stars
——Big K.R.I.T., *"My Sub (Part 2)"* (2012)

B ig K.R.I.T. likes his subwoofer. To date, he's written three songs about
it (all called "My Sub"), spread across two albums and a mixtape. In the
first installment of "My Sub," K.R.I.T. maps his movements around town by
the collateral effects of his system, which is "quakin, shakin, wakin up the
folk" in his neighborhood. Later, in "My Sub Part 3," he reminisces on these
earlier subwoofer exploits, "Now this is how it all started way back/Your
neighbor neighbor neighbor neighbor hate that," plotting the radial limits
of his disruptive frequencies: four houses down, they can feel his trunk
quake. There's a trajectory across the three tracks that pumps more and
more bass from his speakers, intensified vibrations achieved through endless tinkering—K.R.I.T. notes that it took him more than a year to calibrate
his sub. The third installment also finds K.R.I.T. detailing the destruction
his amplified sub-bass frequencies cause around town.

It's a narrative trajectory that invites Steve Goodman's sonic warfare
filter. Describing sound system culture, Goodman paints a scene of musical
competition: "bass rig against bass rig, sound 'bwoy' against sound 'bwoy,'
dubplate against dubplate, DJ against DJ in a spiraling logic of hype esca-
lation, intensification, and mobilization of the dance" (2010, 28). Through
this filter, K.R.I.T. would be engaged in a one-sided clash, "destroy[ing]
the whole hood" with a mobile sound system whose amped lower frequencies disseminate unmatched. In Goodman's terms, K.R.I.T. builds a bass
materialism that spreads "a sonic ecology of dread" across the Mississippi

countryside where he lives and works (29). Zandria Robinson describes K.R.I.T.'s country existence as one "rooted in dirt and power, and the ability to survive and maneuver through a world that would rather [him] not" (2014). Survival, in Goodman's terms, involves an all-out vibrational offensive, squarely facing and attacking that which wishes you harm.

What I hope to have traced in the pages of *Posthuman Rap* are ways of listening that tune to sounds that are just out of earshot, that involve posthuman strategies that, on the one hand, may dissolve neoliberal humanism, as K.R.I.T.'s subwoofer does when heard through a filter like Goodman's, but that, on the other hand, map out ways to exist beyond its reach. Mixing together Kendrick, trap and crunk aesthetics, and the ironic and queer strategies sounded in those aesthetics, I've plotted one kind of posthuman vestibule—Rae Sremmurd's club—but the contours of vestibules may be different from one place to the next. With that in mind, I want to use the epilogue of this book to listen past the combative surface of K.R.I.T.'s "My Sub" series to hear what shape other posthuman vestibules could take. How does K.R.I.T. use sub-bass as a "stepping stone toward new genres of human" (Weheliye 2014, 44–45)?

The refrain on "My Sub (Pt. 2: The Jackin')" is a line ripped from Dallas rapper Big Tuck's "Southside da Realest": "I done cut up my bang, and I shook up the stars."[1] Bang, here, is the subwoofer, and Tuck and K.R.I.T each suggest that the power of their subs can jostle celestial bodies light years away. Because . . . how, exactly? The most immediate answer has less to do with the stars themselves and more to do with the frame through which K.R.I.T. views them. If his subwoofer can shake the foundation of houses all the way down the block, then his car must be palpitating but good. It's not the stars themselves that are shook up but the windshield, the filterlens through which he views the universe. The glass ripples, light distorts, stars shake.

Robinson's grounding of K.R.I.T. in the country is crucial. To sit in K.R.I.T.'s car is to sit in the country, a place relegated to the sidelines of the hip hop urban imaginary—Robinson notes that "'country' is oft-times a pejorative term meant to denote someone's greenness, lack of sophistication, or backwardness"—and a place embedded in the mix of each instance of "My Sub." K.R.I.T.'s ruminations on his car's sound system all include crickets chirping in the musical background, processed to resonate and echo across the entire stereo field so that the soundscape feels as boundless as a countryside. This marks a wide-open space, one where starlight cruises past unfiltered by ambient city lights, where the amplified low end can resonate unfettered by the sounds and skyscrapers of a metropolis. Here, in the country, we can see and hear closer to the extremities of bandwidths, extremities that would be swallowed up somewhere else.

Sub-bass, in fact, is about listening past those extremities. Sub-bass moves to the edge of frequencies perceptible to the human ear and amplifies them until they can be heard. When K.R.I.T. goes on and on about the power of his subwoofer and the destruction that it causes around town, he isn't engaged in an assault on his neighborhood; rather, he's detailing the side effects of an ongoing effort to push farther and farther past that edge, into a space that exists out of earshot. "My Sub Pt 3" is subtitled, "Big Bang," a reference to the size of K.R.I.T.'s woofer as well as the worlds it can call into being. The sub-bass frequencies that K.R.I.T. follows emanate from the reverberant space of a posthuman vestibule on the other side of perception, a space that makes audible "potentials . . . we did not believe accessible or feasible" (Iton 2008, 290).

K.R.I.T. performs his own existence at the edge in parallel with the extremities of aural bandwidths, the edges that mark off what humans can hear. As K.R.I.T. lies on the ground at the end of "My Sub (Pt. 2)," suffering from a gunshot wound, the sub-bass is absent from the mix, out of earshot as K.R.I.T. seems ready to tip over the edge into death. But this isn't the end. Rather, it's a moment of uncanny remix, accompanied by some deft cutting and splicing of the Indeep lyrics "Last night a DJ saved my life." K.R.I.T. emerges, undead, in "My Sub Pt. 3," where he's learned to use his subwoofer to create new worlds, big bangs. K.R.I.T. performs his death and undead-ness across "My Sub" as a kind of embattled posthumanism, with one foot in neoliberal humanism's world, rattling windows and knocking pictures off the wall, and the other out of earshot, past the edge of human perception, where he crosses the event horizon of perceptible low-range frequencies and emerges, monstrously undead, "completely outside the present conception of what it is to be human" (Scott 2000, 136).

From one perspective or the other, K.R.I.T. is either engaged in sonic warfare with neoliberal humanism or else taking off to antihumanist, Afrofuturist abodes. By theorizing the posthuman as vestibular flesh, able to lead back to or away from neoliberal humanism, I'm suggesting that there's more for us to hear, whether it's metaphorically past the edge of our human perception in a black hole of sub-bass or on the other side of the orthodox body of political discourse in the rattle of inhumanly fast hi-hats. That past the boundaries of what we perceive to be human are the queerly vibrating frequencies of other ways to exist.

NOTES

INTRODUCTION

1. A note on terminology: I'll refer to musicians throughout this book by their performing names or the informal nicknames fans apply to them. So, Nicki Minaj is Nicki Minaj or Minaj or Nicki but not Onika Tanya Maraj, and Young Thug is Young Thug or Thug or Thugger but not Jeffrey Lamar Williams. By maintaining an engagement with these performers' personas, I intentionally distance them from whatever person embodies that persona. Because of the public and popular nature of these personas, they are much more knowable than the people who perform them and almost exclusively the only iteration of those performers that fans ever interact with. Millions of listeners, for instance, know a great deal about Nicki Minaj; very few people know much about Onika Tanya Maraj.

2. Clavé rhythm is a one-measure pattern especially prevalent in musical genres found throughout sub-Saharan Africa, the Caribbean, and American popular music. The basic pattern unfolds as a 3 + 2 figure as demonstrated in Table I.4a.

   Posthuman Rap is not an in-depth study of clavé rhythm, which is the subject of a rich body of literature in disciplines ranging from music theory to musicology to ethnomusicology to cultural studies subdisciplines concerned with the Americas, Caribbean, and sub-Saharan Africa (David Peñalosa's *The Clavé Matrix* (2012) is a particularly helpful entry point to this discourse). But because of its prevalence in US popular music and much of the hip hop that I'll discuss in this book, it's worth a moment to mark its pattern. The *tresillo* rhythm is a simplified version of clavé that is a 3 + 3 figure (so, the first eight units of Table I.4a would also become the last eight units of the measure) and is the one we'll hear most often in the examples I discuss. The kick drum pattern in "Monster" that I describe as "modified clavé" is shown in contrast to the standard clavé rhythm in Table I.4b. So, by "modified clavé," I mean that the measure opens in a way that sonically references a standard clavé rhythm, then departs for the last half of the measure.

3. I'm using the timing from the video posted at https://vimeo.com/24789963. The video has been banned from many Web sites, including YouTube, but this Vimeo post has been live since 2011 and seems the most stable place to listen/view online for free.

4. The echoing mid-range percussion sounds like a beat repeat effect applied to a rim shot (the striking of a drum stick on the edge of a snare drum), where the initial attack of an instrument can be programmed to be repeated—in this case, at a lower volume—at prescribed intervals.

5. I use "financializable" (which isn't really a word) as distinct from "capitalizable." To capitalize on something or someone suggests a straightforward transaction— money for service or money for person. To be able to financialize something or someone (including oneself) is a more nebulous endeavor. Financialization is an ongoing process that makes one capable of bringing in capital in ways that don't always involve a direct transaction. If Facebook gets paid because I clicked on an advertisement on their site, that's capitalization—a direct transaction— and I'm capitalizable. If Facebook gets paid by an advertiser because I use Facebook (whether I click on any particular advertisement or not), that's financialization—an indirect transaction—and I'm financializable.

CHAPTER 1

1. Thanks to the anonymous peer reviewers who encouraged me in this direction at the proposal stage.
2. In "After Humanism" (1984), Wynter speaks of entire areas of study revolving around race, gender, ethnicity becoming "entrapped" in an educational system that could only tolerate them as exceptions to the norm and that used these studies as a way of ultimately reinforcing those norms, "to exempt," for instance, "English departments from having to alter their existing definition of American literature" (38). In a wide-ranging interview with David Scott, Wynter describes the limits of colonial education in more individual terms: "We weren't even taught Caribbean geography in the schools. The geography we were taught was that of England, the history that was taught was English history" (2000, 129).
3. Jenny Davis calls this "compulsory happiness." Reflecting on the cruelty that resulted from Facebook's 2014 "year in review" videos, compiled by an algorithm that seemed to assume Facebook was a place to simply perform happiness but sometimes ended up reviewing a year of grief and trauma, Davis points out that the Web site has an "insistent structure of compulsory happiness. This insistence is reflected in a "Like" button, without any other one-click emotive options; it is reflected in goofy emoticons through which sadness and illness are expressed with cartoon-like faces in cheerful colors; it is reflected in relationship status changes that announce themselves to one's network. And as users, we largely comply. We share the happy moments, the funny quips, the accomplishments and #humblebrags, while hiding, ignoring, or unFriending those with the audacity to mope; to clog our newsfeeds with negativity" (Davis 2014).
4. Independent record labels often strike deals with major labels to distribute their physical albums. Indies seem to find it more profitable to give majors a cut of album sales in exchange for distribution rather than create their own networks of distribution.
5. For those of you who read "anti-Semitic and homophobic" and thought, "but I thought Mos Def was a conscious rapper?!" Uh huh. We need to talk about "conscious rap," but that's another book.

CHAPTER 2

1. Well, mostly. Tupac has had a lively posthumous career, releasing as many studio albums after his death as before and jumping onto a slew of singles as guest vocalist. It's a tailor-made case study for Stanyek and Piekut's theory of deadness (2010). Tupac also famously showed up at Coachella 2012 in Computer Graphics Interface (CGI) form to rap alongside Snoop and Dre. Conspiracy theorists who

believe Pac is still alive can direct their comments to the Internet, where I'll be sure to read them.

2. Lynch does finally cite some non-cismen in the final paragraph. If I weren't feeling charitable, I'd chalk up the citation to an editor asking Lynch if he can think of any women to include anywhere at all in the piece.

3. In *Forbes*'s annual list of the wealthiest rappers, Drake clocked in at No. 5 in 2016, behind usual suspects Birdman, Diddy, Dr. Dre, and Jay Z, all of whom began amassing their fortunes a decade or more before Drake's career kicked off (Greenberg).

4. The examples listed here can be found on @drakethetype's Twitter timeline. Memes circulate so quickly and widely that it is difficult to track down who first posted each of these.

CHAPTER 3

1. Even 2015's collaboration with Drake, *What a Time to Be Alive*, hit No. 1 in Billboard 200 sales, despite the fact that it was technically a mixtape, not an official album release.

2. Hey, reader, I like you. I want you to be happy. So please go watch that ebullient Desiigner performance from *The Late Show*.

3. Timestamps for "Panda" refer to the official music video posted at https://www.youtube.com/watch?v=E5ONTXHS2mM.

4. A June 2016 kerfuffle underlines this use of the term "Auto-Tune." In an interview with *The Sun*, David Bowie producer and bassist Tony Visconti decried the state of contemporary radio: "You turn the radio on and it's fluff, you are listening to 90 percent computerized voices. We know Adele has a great voice but it's even questionable if that is actually her voice or how much has been manipulated" (Nelson 2016). Reporting on Adele's retort ("Dude, suck my dick"), *HipHopWired* used the headline "Adele Accused of Using Autotune," even though neither Visconti nor Adele ever mentioned the software.

5. In contemporary digital audio workstations (DAWs)—composition software like Ableton Live, ProTools, or Logic Pro—there are multiple ways to achieve similar effects, which is why my description of vocal processing is somewhat speculative. Detuned and delayed vocals could be produced using a variety of plug-ins or on-board effects or simply by employing some general mixing techniques that mimic hardware-based processing. If Future's vocal multiplicity is produced by delaying one of the differently tuned vocal tracks so that it is triggered a few milliseconds after the original, this is the same general technique used to produce the famous "slapback" sound in Elvis Presley's early music ("Blue Moon of Kentucky" is exemplary here, and Mark Katz dissects it in detail in *Capturing Sound*) (Katz 2010, 48–49). Decreasing the amount of time that lapses between the initial and secondary vocal tracks results in a more subtle echo than one hears in early Presley.

6. This is what I'd call "standard" Migos flow, but there are variations that play with the pitch movement across the hemiola rhythm.

7. Indeed, on an early collaboration with future Three 6 Mafia member DJ Paul, Lord Infamous drops Migos flow in the second verse of "Where Is Da Bud?" (1993).

8. I mark these vocals as thirty-second-note subdivision, but, as explained in the trap rhythm section later in this chapter, trap features a double-time/half-time flux that means I could realistically set these as sixteenth or thirty-second notes.

Because I choose the half-time (roughly seventy-five bpm) transcription for the instrumentals, I maintain that for the vocals, meaning these are rendered as thirty-second notes even though most vocalists probably aren't thinking in thirty-second notes.

9. In fact, the bulk of the writing dedicated to defining trap shows up in the midst of the confusion between EDM trap and trap rap.

10. The intro to "24s" is eight measures. Zaytoven similarly uses eight measures of synths-only, then another eight measures of synths plus snare/hi-hat in "Aye." Luger's low synths actually carry the intro of "Paint" for 20 measures—the last four of which are only OJ's voice—with 808 hi-hats emphasizing every fourth measure. Mike Will Made-It uses a filter sweep to open up a high, bright register over the first eight measures of "Turn on the Lights." And Menace stretches his intro for "Panda" to twenty-four measures, using claps as the only percussion and a pitch riser to wipe out all but Desiigner's voice and some sustained synths for the final eight count.

11. Lex Luger's huge brass and string sounds would be incredibly influential on EDM trap.

12. None of the songs in the video was Katy Perry's "Dark Horse," but in January 2014, her song went to No. 1 in part on the back of competing "hey" samples: the first sounding very much like the chorus form indie band the Lumineers' 2012 "Ho Hey," and the second a pitched-down Mustard "hey" quietly sneaking into the mix (along with the aforementioned rattling hi-hats) during Juicy J's verse. Perry's "Dark Horse" is the textbook white-led version of the post-race multiracialism I analyzed in detail from the perspective of Kendrick Lamar reception in the previous chapter.

13. "Lights" is about looking for someone you can't find; the loneliness implied by the absent background vocals is almost certainly intentional. In other words, even when trap's background vocals are missing, they're present as context.

CHAPTER 4

1. Seven years later, Big Freedia's video for "Y'all Get Back Now" would feature an oversized version of her, like Bonecrusher, stomping through her city.

2. No. 1 songs from 1995 bear this out: Notorious B.I.G.'s "Big Poppa," Tupac's "Dear Mama," Dr. Dre's "Keep Their Heads Ringing," Coolio's "Gangsta's Paradise," and LL Cool J's "Hey Lover." Exceptions to this rule include Method Man's "I'll Be There for You" and Notorious B.I.G.'s "One More Chance," both of which feature more kick drum syncopation.

3. Regina Bradley and Robin James have used Stallings to listen to "Pour It Up" and "I Don't Mind," respectively, and James has also discussed "Pour It Up" at length in *Resilience & Melancholy* (2015). Both writers make mention of Juicy J and reference his performance of what I've termed the heel, but neither use Stallings to open up any space for the queerness I'm theorizing here; he remains a stock misogynist in their work (Bradley 2014; James 2016).

4. Bradley (2014) hears "Pour It Up" as a sample of "Bandz," but I don't think that's the case. Rather, I hear two incredibly similar but ultimately different instrumentals composed on the same producer's laptop.

5. As far as I can tell, Pitbull's "Culo" (2004), produced by Lil Jon, is the first entry of the booty clap in rap, though Chicago's ghetto house genre had long combined an obsession with posteriors with music that employed the percussive clap in this same figuration.

6. I mention black men and boys not to exclude black women and girls, who also die at the hands and by the sanction of the state, but to name what national attention is primarily drawn to.

7. The first three patrons to enter the club and receive money from Minaj are Quavo, Takeoff, and Offset, the three members of the Atlanta-based trap trio Migos. It isn't clear where the money in "Throw Sum Mo" originates (which is part of the point), but an interesting possible read of this first handoff of cash is that Minaj or Rae Sremmurd are claiming a degree of success that funds other rappers' careers.

8. I call this a sidechain compression *effect* because I'm not positive the sound is achieved through sidechaining. It's possible to create a similar sonic effect by manually cutting a signal's audio and then quickly tapering the volume back in. Mike Will Made-It may well have achieved this effect manually instead of sidechaining the synth to a percussive event, as I describe in the text, but the *effect* recalls sidechain compression regardless of the technique used to achieve it.

EPILOGUE

1. The Big Tuck line is actually "I can't starve, I drive fast cars/Cut up my bang, I done shook up the stars."

BIBLIOGRAPHY

Abiola, Jordan. "Is Rapper Young Thug Admitting He Is Gay On Twitter?" *360Nobs. com*, December 20, 2014. Accessed July 7, 2016. https://www.360nobs.com/ 2014/12/is-rapper-young-thug-admitting-he-is-gay-on-twitter/.

Adeyemi, Kemi. "Straight Leanin': Sounding Black Life at the Intersection of Hip-Hop and Big Pharma." *Sounding Out!* September 21, 2015. Accessed March 4, 2017. https://soundstudiesblog.com/2015/09/21/hip-hop-and-big-pharma/.

Adorno, Theodor W. *Philosophy of New Music.* Edited by Robert Hullot-Kentor. Minneapolis, MN: University of Minnesota Press, 2006.

Anderson, Bob. "Lisa On Ice." *The Simpsons.* Fox, November 13, 1994.

Appiah, Kwame Anthony. "Is the Post- in Postmodernism the Post- in Postcolonial?" *Critical Inquiry* 17, no. 2 (1991): 336–57.

Aronowitz, Stanley, and Jonathan Cutler. *Post-Work: The Wages of Cybernation.* New York: Routledge, 1998.

Auner, Joseph. "'Sing It for Me': Posthuman Ventriloquism in Recent Popular Music." *Journal of the Royal Musical Association* 128, no. 1 (2003): 98–122.

Babb, Fletcher. "Lean On Me: Emoji Death Threats and Instagram's Codeine Kingpin." *NOISEY*, October 24, 2013. Accessed July 7, 2016. http://noisey.vice.com/blog/ lean-on-me.

Barker, Hugh, and Yuval Taylor. *Faking It: The Quest for Authenticity in Popular Music.* New York: W.W. Norton, 2007.

Barthes, Roland. *Mythologies.* Translated by Annette Lavers. New York: Hill and Wang, 1972.

Battaglia, Andy. "Hip-Hop's Dirty Martini: In Lil Jon's 'Crunk Juice,' A Triple Shot of Venom." *Washington Post*, November 17, 2004. Accessed July 7, 2016. http:// www.washingtonpost.com/wp-co/hotcontent/index.html?section=print/style/ inside.

BBC Radio 1Xtra. *Snowball (aka Kevin Hart) Covers Desiigner's Panda*, 2016. Accessed July 7, 2016. https://www.youtube.com/watch?time_ continue=87&v=QbUHtWWvoWo.

Beck, Allen J., and Gilliard. "Bureau of Justice Statistics (BJS) - Prisoners in 1994." August 17, 1995. Accessed June 9, 2016. http://www.bjs.gov/index. cfm?ty=pbdetail&iid=1280.

Bein, Kat. "It's a Trap! An 11-Part History of Trap Music, From DJ Screw to Gucci Mane to Flosstradamus." *Miami New Times*, July 25, 2012. Accessed July 7, 2016. http://www.miaminewtimes.com/music/its-a-trap-an-11-part-history- of-trap-music-from-dj-screw-to-gucci-mane-to-flosstradamus-6475986.

Beltran, Mary C. "The New Hollywood Racelessness: Only the Fast, Furious, (and Multiracial) Will Survive." *Cinema Journal* 44, no. 2 (2005): 50–67.

bigjohnny8383. *Excited Dudes Love Yelling on Hip-Hop Songs*, 2014. Accessed July 7, 2016. https://www.youtube.com/watch?v=ES03SQyU_2o.

Blackburn, H. Drew. "To Pimp A Butterfly One Year on: How Kendrick Lamar Scorched a Hole in American Politics." *FACT*, March 20, 2016. Accessed July 7, 2016. http://www.factmag.com/2016/03/20/to-pimp-a-butterfly-one-year-on-kendrick-lamar-american-politics/.

Bogazianos, Dimitri. *5 Grams: Crack Cocaine, Rap Music, and the War on Drugs*. New York: New York University Press, 2012.

Bourdieu, Pierre. *Outline of a Theory of Practice*. Translated by Richard Nice. Cambridge Studies in Social Anthropology; 16. Cambridge; New York: Cambridge University Press, 1977.

Bradley, Regina N. "Fear of a Black (In The) Suburb." *Sounding Out!*, February 17, 2014. Accessed July 7, 2016. https://soundstudiesblog.com/2014/02/17/fear-of-a-black-in-the-suburb/.

———. "The (Magic) Upper Room: Sonic Pleasure Politics in Southern Hip Hop." *Sounding Out!*, June 16, 2014. Accessed July 7, 2016. https://soundstudiesblog.com/2014/06/16/the-magic-upper-room-sonic-pleasure-politics-in-southern-hip-hop/.

Braidotti, Rosi. *The Posthuman*. Malden, MA: Polity Press, 2013.

Breihan, Tom. "Desiigner's 'Panda' Is The Future Ripoff That Transcended Its Future-Ripoff Status." *Stereogum*, April 20, 2016. Accessed July 7, 2016. http://www.stereogum.com/1872404/desiigners-panda-is-the-future-ripoff-that-transcended-its-future-ripoff-status/franchises/status-aint-hood/.

Brown, Adrienne, (Author). "Drive Slow: Rehearsing Hip Hop Automotivity." *Journal of Popular Music Studies* 24, no. 3 (2012): 265–75.

Burton, Justin. "Azealia Banks, Seapunk, and Atlantis: An Embattled Humanist Mixtape." *Shima* 10, no. 2 (2016): 81–93.

———."From Barthes to Bart: The Simpsons vs. Amadeus." *Journal of Popular Culture* 46, no. 3 (June 2013): 481–500.

———. "The Roots, Undun. Def Jam 001628202, 2011. Kanye West and Jay-Z, Watch the Throne. Roc-A-Fella/Roc Nation/Def Jam 001542602, 2011." *Journal of the Society for American Music* 7, no. 3 (August 2013): 343.

———. "Tomahawk Chopped and Screwed: The Indeterminacy of Listening." *Sounding Out!*, February 20, 2014. Accessed November 18, 2016, https://soundstudiesblog.com/2014/02/20/tomahawk-chopped-and-screwed-the-indeterminacy-of-listening/.

———. "Topologies: The Popular Music Survey and the Posthumanities." *Journal of Music History Pedagogy* 5; no. 1 (2014): 125–32.

Capper, Andy. *Noisey Atlanta*. VICE Media, 2015.

Caramanica, Jon. "Lil Jon: Crunk Juice." *Rolling Stone*, December 15, 2004. Accessed July 7, 2016. https://web.archive.org/web/20071014221204if_/http://ad.doubleclick.net/adi/rollingstoneonline.com/rs60artistsalbums;pageurl=/artists/liljon/albums/album/6627334/review/6660782/crunk_juice;sz=1x1;tile=7;ord=16959;contentid=6627334;cat=artists;subcat=albums;artist=65314;genre=Hitmakers;.

Carson, E. Ann. "Bureau of Justice Statistics (BJS) - Prisoners in 2014." September 17, 2014. Accessed June 9, 2016. http://www.bjs.gov/index.cfm?ty=pbdetail&iid=5387.

Christman, Ed. "U.S. Recording Industry 2015: Streams Double, Adele Dominates." *Billboard*, January 5, 2016. Accessed July 7, 2016. http://www.billboard.com/articles/business/6835216/us-recording-industry-2015-streams-double-adele-dominates-nielsen-music.

Cohn, Nik. *Triksta: Life and Death and New Orleans Rap*. New York: Vintage Books, 2007.

Collins, Hattie. "Hattie Collins Meets the One-Man Brand That Is Lil Jon." *The Guardian*, August 5, 2006. Accessed July 7, 2016. http://www.theguardian.com/music/2006/aug/05/urban.popandrock1.

Complex. "Tracing the Lineage of the Migos Flow." *Complex*, 2014. Accessed July 7, 2016. https://www.youtube.com/watch?v=A8QVVFilrEc.

Corea, Gena. *The Hidden Malpractice*. New York: A Jove/HBJ Book, 1977.

David, Marlo. "Afrofuturism and Post-Soul Possibility in Black Popular Music." *African American Review* 41, no. 4 (2007): 695–707.

Davis, Angela Y. *Women, Race & Class*. New York: Vintage Books, 1983.

Davis, Jenny. "Facebook Reactions and the Happiness Paradigm." *Cyborgology*, March 1, 2016. Accessed July 7, 2016. https://thesocietypages.org/cyborgology/2016/03/01/facebook-reactions-and-the-happiness-paradigm/.

———. "Facebook's Structure of Compulsory Happiness." *Cyborgology*, December 30, 2014. Accessed March 3, 2017. https://thesocietypages.org/cyborgology/2014/12/30/facebooks-structure-of-compulsory-happiness/.

Dery, Mark. "Black to the Future: Interviews with Samuel R. Delany, Greg Tate, and Tricia Rose." *South Atlantic Quarterly* 92 (1993): 735–78.

Diep, Eric. "How Desiigner's 'Panda' Ended Up on Kanye West's 'The Life of Pablo.'" *Genius*, February 16, 2016. Accessed July 7, 2016. http://genius.com/a/how-desiigners-panda-ended-up-on-kanye-wests-the-life-of-pablo.

DJ Vlad. *Gangsta Boo: Lord Infamous Created "Migos Flow,"* 2014. Accessed July 7, 2016. https://www.youtube.com/watch?v=8rcHucFh_lg.

Drake, David. "Real Trap Sh*t? The Commodification of Southern Rap's Drug-Fueled Subgenre." *Complex*, October 9, 2012. Accessed July 7, 2016. http://www.complex.com/music/2012/10/real-trap-sht-the-commodification-of-southern-raps-drug-fueled-subgenre.

Dubner, Stephen J., and Greg Rosalsky. *Is the World Ready for a Guaranteed Basic Income?* Freakonomics, April 13, 2016. Accessed July 8, 2016. http://freakonomics.com/podcast/mincome/.

Edelman, Lee. *No Future: Queer Theory and the Death Drive*. Series Q. Durham: Duke University Press, 2004.

Edwards, Gavin. "Billboard Cover: Kendrick Lamar on Ferguson, Leaving Iggy Azalea Alone and Why 'We're in the Last Days.'" *Billboard*, January 9, 2015. Accessed June 7, 2016. http://www.billboard.com/articles/news/6436268/kendrick-lamar-billboard-cover-story-on-new-album-iggy-azalea-police-violence-the-rapture.

Eells, Josh. "The Trials of Kendrick Lamar." *Rolling Stone*, June 22, 2015. Accessed July 7, 2016. http://www.rollingstone.com/music/features/the-trials-of-kendrick-lamar-cover-story-20150622.

Eidsheim, Nina Sun. "Marian Anderson and 'Sonic Blackness.'" *American Opera* 63, no. 3 (September 2011): 641–71.

Ellis, Nadia. "New Orleans and Kingston: A Beginning, A Recurrence." *Journal of Popular Music Studies* 27, no. 4 (December 2015): 387.

Farese, Dave. *No One Really Knows What Future Is Saying*, 2016. Accessed July 7, 2016. https://www.youtube.com/watch?v=1NgpV5NZpMw.

Font-Navarette, David. "Bass 101: Miami, Rio, and the Global Music South1." *Journal of Popular Music Studies* 27, no. 4 (December 2015): 488.

Fraser, Nancy. "Behind Marx's Hidden Abode." *New Left Review* 86 (April 3, 2014): 55–72.

Friedman. "Frauds in Atlanta? Why the Controversy over Desiigner's 'Panda' Goes Deeper than You Think." *FACT Magazine: Music News, New Music*, April 26, 2016. Accessed June 22, 2016. http://www.factmag.com/2016/04/26/panda-desiigner-future-new-york-rap/.

Friedman, Devin. "What Planet Is Young Thug From?" *GQ*, February 16, 2016. Accessed July 7, 2016. http://www.gq.com/story/young-thug-best-rapper-alive-interview.

Fu, Eddie. "This Is The Rapper Everyone's Talking About On Kanye West's New Album." *UPROXX*, February 15, 2016. Accessed July 7, 2016. http://uproxx.com/smokingsection/who-is-desiigner-kanye-new-album-good-music/.

Ganz, Caryn. "The Curious Case of Nicki Minaj." *Out Magazine*, December 19, 2010. Accessed July 7, 2016. http://www.out.com/entertainment/music/2010/09/12/curious-case-nicki-minaj.

G, Lucas. "What the F**k Is Future Saying? (A Very Serious Lyrical Analysis)." *DJBooth.net*. June 23, 2016. Accessed July 7, 2016. http://djbooth.net/news/entry/what-the-fk-is-future-saying-a-very-serious-lyrical-analysis.

———. "What the F**k Is Young Thug Saying? (A Very Serious Lyrical Analysis)." *DJBooth.net*, 2014. Accessed July 7, 2016. http://djbooth.net/news/entry/what-the-fuk-is-young-thug-saying.

Gilroy, Paul. *Against Race: Imagining Political Culture Beyond the Color Line*. Cambridge, MA: Harvard University Press, 2000.

Ginsburg, Ruth Bader. *Kimbrough v. United States* (Justice Ginsburg, Opinion of the Court, U.S. Supreme Court 2007).

Goodman, Steve. *Sonic Warfare: Sound, Affect, and the Ecology of Fear*. Cambridge, MA: MIT Press, 2010.

Gopinath, Sumanth, and Jason Stanyek, eds. *The Oxford Handbook of Mobile Music Studies, Volume 2*. New York: Oxford University Press, 2014.

Gordon, Linda. *Woman's Body, Woman's Right: A Social History of Birth Control in America*. New York: Penguin Books, 1977.

Goveia, Elsa V. "New Shibboleths for Old." *Caribbean Quarterly* 10, no. 2 (1964): 48–54.

GQ Editors. "Watch A Video of Young Thug Reading His Lyrics So That You Can (Kind Of) Understand Them." *GQ*, February 17, 2016. Accessed July 7, 2016. http://www.gq.com/story/young-thug-reads-lyrics-best-friend.

Greenberg, Zack O'Malley. "The Forbes Five." *Forbes*, March 3, 2016. Accessed June 20, 2016. http://www.forbes.com/forbesfive/.

Hairston, Tahirah. "Why Rapper Young Thug Wears Women's Clothing." *Fusion*, September 29, 2015. Accessed July 7, 2016. http://fusion.net/story/204840/why-rapper-young-thug-wears-womens-clothing/.

Hall, Stuart. "Media Power: The Double Bind." *Journal of Communication* 24 (1974): 19–26.

———. "Notes on Deconstructing the Popular." In *Cultural Theory and Popular Culture: A Reader*. Edited by John Storey, 2nd ed., 442–53. New York: Pearson/Prentice Hall, 1998.

Haraway, Donna Jeanne. *Simians, Cyborgs, and Women: The Reinvention of Nature*. New York: Routledge, 1991.

Harvey, David. *A Brief History of Neoliberalism*. New York: Oxford University Press, 2005.

———. "Neoliberalism as Creative Destruction." *The Annals of the American Academy of Political and Social Science* 610 (2007): 22–44.

Hofer, Sonya. "I Am They: Technological Mediation, Shifting Conceptions of Identity and Techno Music." *Convergence: The Journal of Research into New Media Technologies* 12, no. 3 (August 2006): 307–24.

Hopper, Jessica. "Kendrick Lamar: Not Your Average Everyday Rap Savior." *Spin*, October 9, 2012. Accessed July 7, 2016. http://www.spin.com/2012/10/kendrick-lamar-not-your-average-everyday-rap-savior/2/.

Hubbell, Noah. "From UGK to Chief Keef: A Look at the History of Trap in Rap and Its Subsequent Influence on Drill." *Westword*, October 23, 2013. Accessed July 7, 2016. http://www.westword.com/music/from-ugk-to-chief-keef-a-look-at-the-history-of-trap-in-rap-and-its-subsequent-influence-on-drill-5687320.

Ingham, Tim. "Independent Labels Trounce UMG, Sony and Warner in US Market Shares." *Music Business Worldwide*, July 29, 2015. Accessed July 7, 2016. http://www.musicbusinessworldwide.com/independent-label-us-market-share-trounces-universal-sony-warner/.

Iton, Richard. *In Search of the Black Fantastic: Politics and Popular Culture in the Post-Civil Rights Era*. New York: Oxford University Press, 2008.

James, Robin. "Club Goin Up On A Tuesday, Or, No 48 Hours for 48 Thrills." *It's Her Factory*, December 3, 2014. Accessed July 7, 2016. http://www.its-her-factory.com/2014/12/club-goin-up-on-a-tuesday-or-no-48-hours-for-48-thrills/.

———. "Listening to Sounds in Post-Feminist Pop Music." *Sounding Out!*, February 15, 2016. Accessed July 7, 2016. https://soundstudiesblog.com/2016/02/15/listening-to-sounds-in-post-feminist-pop-music/.

———. "'Robo-Diva R&B': Aesthetics, Politics, and Black Female Robots in Contemporary Popular Music." *Journal of Popular Music Studies* 20, no. 4 (January 1, 2008): 402–23.

Joseph, Ralina L. "'Tyra Banks Is Fat': Reading (Post-)Racism and (Post-)Feminism in the New Millennium." *Critical Studies in Media Communication* 26, no. 3 (August 2009): 237–54.

Kajikawa, Loren. *Sounding Race in Rap Songs*. Berkeley: University of California Press, 2015.

Katz, Mark. *Capturing Sound: How Technology Has Changed Music*. 2nd ed. Berkeley, CA: University of California Press, 2010.

Kelley, Robin D.G. *Race Rebels: Culture, Politics, and the Black Working Class*. New York: The Free Press, 1994.

Krims, Adam. *Rap Music and the Poetics of Identity*. New York: Cambridge University Press, 2000.

Spence, Lester K. *Stare in the Darkness: The Limits of Hip-Hop and Black Politics*. Minneapolis: University of Minnesota Press, 2011.

Locke, Charley. "Young Thug Isn't Rapping Gibberish, He's Evolving Language." *WIRED*, October 15, 2015. Accessed July 7, 2016. http://www.wired.com/2015/10/young-thug-evolution-of-language/.

Lowney, Knoll D. "Smoked Not Snorted: Is Racism Inherent in Our Crack Cocaine Laws?" *Washington University Journal of Urban & Contemporary Law* 45 (January 15, 1994): 121–71.

Lynch, Marc. "The Political Theory of Kendrick Lamar." *Washington Post*, March 23, 2015. Accessed July 7, 2016. https://www.washingtonpost.com/blogs/monkey-cage/wp/2015/03/23/the-political-theory-of-kendrick-lamar/.

Lynch, Mona, and Marisa Omori. *Legal Change and Sentencing Norms in Federal Court: An Examination of the Impact of the Booker, Gall, and Kimbrough Decisions.* Irvine, CA: U.S. Department of Justice, Office of Justice Programs, National Institute of Justice, 2013. Accessed July 7, 2016. https://www.ncjrs.gov/pdffiles1/nij/grants/243254.pdf.

Manchard, Michael. *Party/Politics: Horizons in Black Political Thought.* New York: Oxford University Press, 2006.

Marshall, Wayne. "Dembow: A Loop History | Red Bull Music Academy Daily." *Red Bull Music Academy Daily*, July 2, 2013. Accessed July 7, 2016. http://daily.redbullmusicacademy.com/2013/07/dembow-a-loop-history.

———. "Treble Culture." *The Oxford Handbook of Mobile Music Studies, Volume 2.* Edited by Sumanth Gopinath and Jason Stanyek. New York: Oxford University Press, 2014: 43–76.

Martin, Randy. *Financialization of Daily Life.* Philadelphia: Temple University Press, 2002.

Mench, Chris. "Rae Sremmurd Denounces Donald Trump At SXSW." *Complex*, March 17, 2016. Accessed July 7, 2016. http://www.complex.com/music/2016/03/rae-sremmurd-denounces-donald-trump-at-sxsw.

Middleton, Richard. "'Last Night a DJ Saved My Life': Avians, Cyborgs and Siren Bodies in the Era of Phonographic Technology." *Radical Musicology* 1 (January 1, 2006). Accessed July 7, 2016. http://www.radical-musicology.org.uk/2006/Middleton.htm.

Miller, Karl Hagstrom. *Segregating Sound: Inventing Folk and Pop Music in the Age of Jim Crow.* Durham, NC: Duke University Press, 2010.

Miller, Matt. "Dirty Decade: Rap Music and the US South, 1997–2007." *Southern Spaces*, June 10, 2008. Accessed July 7, 2016. http://southernspaces.org/2008/dirty-decade-rap-music-and-us-south-1997%E2%80%932007.

Mojica, Nicholas. "50 Cent Doubts 'Panda' Rapper Desiigner's Future, Not Sure He Can Make Another Hit." *Design & Trend*, February 22, 2016. Accessed July 7, 2016. http://www.designntrend.com/articles/70679/20160222/50-cent-doubts-panda-rapper-desiigner-future-not-sure-he-can-make-another-hit.htm.

Nadkarni, Rohan. "Desiigner, the Rapper Who Sounds Like Future, Has Now Achieved What Future Hasn't." *GQ*, April 26, 2016. Accessed July 7, 2016. http://www.gq.com/story/desiigner-panda-no-1.

Neff, Ali Colleen. "Auto-Mobility: A Cultural Studies Approach to the World of Black Music." presented at *Black Music in America*, Rider University, April 4, 2013.

———. *Let the World Listen Right: The Mississippi Delta Hip-Hop Story.* American Made Music. Jackson: University Press of Mississippi, 2009.

Nelson, Patrice. "Adele Accused Of Using Autotune, Tells Critic 'Dude, Suck My D*ck.'" *Hip-Hop Wired*, June 13, 2016. Accessed July 7, 2016. http://hiphopwired.com/2016/06/13/adele-accused-of-using-autotune-tells-david-bowie-suck-my-dick-video/.

Nieratko, Chris. "Meet the Nieratkos - The Twins of Atlanta." *VICE*. Accessed June 21, 2016. https://www.vice.com/read/meet-the-nieratkos-the-twins-of-atlanta.

Nishime, LeiLani. "The Mulatto Cyborg: Imagining a Multiracial Future." *Cinema Journal* 44, no. 2 (2005): 34–49.

Noire, John. "The Blacker The Berry: Respecting Kendrick Lamar's Respectability Politics." *DJBooth.net*, 2015. Accessed July 7, 2016. http://djbooth.net/news/entry/kendrick-lamar-respectability-politics.

OPPI. "Desiigner Reads All The Lyrics To 'Panda.'" *Genius*, May 17, 2016. Accessed July 7, 2016. http://genius.com/a/desiigner-reads-all-the-lyrics-to-panda.

Oscars. *"It's Hard Out Here for a Pimp" Wins Original Song: 2006 Oscars*, 2006. Accessed July 7, 2016. https://www.youtube.com/watch?v=du_01sqzsck.

Patel, Puja. "From T.I. To TNGHT: A Look At Trap Rave." *Stereogum*, August 6, 2012. Accessed July 7, 2016. http://www.stereogum.com/1115091/from-t-i-to-tnght-a-look-at-trap-rave/top-stories/.

Pecknold, Diane, ed. *Hidden in the Mix: The African American Presence in Country Music.* Durham, NC: Duke University Press, 2013.

Peñalosa, David. *The Clavé Matrix: Afro-Cuban Rhythm: Its Principles and African Origins.* Redway, CA: Bembe Books, 2012.

Petridis, Alexis. "Kendrick Lamar's Untitled Unmastered: 'The Work of Someone Who's in It for the Long Haul.'" *The Guardian*, March 4, 2016. Accessed July 7, 2016. https://www.theguardian.com/music/musicblog/2016/mar/04/kendrick-lamar-untitled-unmastered-first-listen-review-alexis-petridis.

Rae, Issa. "[Ep. 4] | Juicy J (Dr. Ratchet)." *RATCHETPIECE Theatre*, 2012. Accessed July 7, 2016. https://www.youtube.com/watch?v=0PmxNHqshVQ.

Roberson, Justin. "The 10 Dumbest Reasons to Hate Drake." *Complex*, August 9, 2013. Accessed March 3, 2017. http://www.complex.com/music/2013/08/why-do-people-hate-drake/.

Robinson, Zandria. "Mississippi Prometheus: Big K.R.I.T. and The Southern Black/Rap Snapback." *New South Negress*, May 21, 2014. Accessed July 7, 2016. http://newsouthnegress.com/mississippiprometheus/.

Rose, Tricia. *Black Noise: Rap Music and Black Culture in Contemporary America.* Middletown, CT: Wesleyan University Press, 1994.

———. *The Hip Hop Wars: What We Talk About When We Talk About Hip Hop-And Why It Matters.* New York: Basic Civitas Books, 2008.

Rucker, Philip. "Mitt Romney Says 'Corporations Are People.'" *Washington Post*, August 11, 2011. Accessed July 7, 2016. https://www.washingtonpost.com/politics/mitt-romney-says-corporations-are-people/2011/08/11/gIQABwZ38I_story.html.

Rys, Dan. "Kendrick Lamar's Most Political Lyrics." *XXL Mag*, September 10, 2015. Accessed July 7, 2016. http://www.xxlmag.com/news/2015/09/kendrick-lamar-political-lyrics/.

Sandberg, Patrik. "Inside the Eccentric World of Young Thug." *Dazed*, August 11, 2015. Accessed July 7, 2016. http://www.dazeddigital.com/music/article/25802/1/young-thug-eccentric-in-chief.

Sarig, Roni. *Third Coast: OutKast, Timbaland, and How Hip-Hop Became a Southern Thing.* Cambridge, MA: Da Capo Press, 2007.

Sartre, Jean-Paul. *Existentialism Is a Humanism.* Translated by Carol Macomber. New Haven, CT: Yale University Press, 2007.

Scott, David. "The Re-Enchantment of Humanism: An Interview with Sylvia Wynter." *Small Axe: A Caribbean Journal of Criticism* 4, no. 2 (September 2000): 118–208.

Sedgwick, Eve Kosofsky. "Paranoid Reading and Reparative Reading, Or, You're So Paranoid, You Probably Think This Introduction Is about You." In *Novel Gazing: Queer Readings in Fiction.* Edited by Eve Kosofsky Sedgwick. Durham, NC: Duke University Press, 1997: 1–37.

Sexton, Jared. *Amalgamation Schemes: Antiblackness and the Critique of Multiracialism.* Minneapolis: University of Minnesota Press, 2008.

Shange, Savannah. "A King Named Nicki: Strategic Queerness and the Black Femmecee." *Women & Performance* 24, no. 1 (March 2014): 29–45.

Shaviro, Steven. "Supa-Dupa Fly: Black Women as Cyborgs in HipHop Videos." *Quarterly Review of Film & Video* 22, no. 2 (2005): 169–79.

Sheth, Falguni. *Toward a Political Philosophy of Race*. Albany: State University of New York, 2009.

Sinker, Mark. "Loving the Alien—Black Science Fiction." *The Wire*, February 1992.

Spillers, Hortense J. "Mama's Baby, Papa's Maybe: An American Grammar Book." *Diacritics* 17, no. 2 (1987): 65–81.

Stallings, L.H. *Funk the Erotic: Transaesthetics and Black Sexual Cultures*. Urbana: University of Illinois Press, 2015.

———. "Hip Hop and the Black Ratchet Imagination." *Palimpsest: A Journal of Women, Gender, and the Black International* 2, no. 2 (2013): 135–39.

Stanyek, Jason, and Benjamin Piekut. "Deadness: Technologies of the Intermundane." *TDR: The Drama Review* 54, no. 1 (2010): 14–38.

Tanzer, Myles, and Zara Golden. "11 Experts Weigh In: Is 'Panda' Actually Good?" *The FADER*, April 28, 2016. Accessed July 7, 2016. http://www.thefader.com/2016/04/28/desiigner-panda.

Taylor, Chris. "The Civil War and Farcical Politics." *Of C.L.R. James*, June 23, 2015. Accessed July 7, 2016. http://clrjames.blogspot.com/2015/06/the-civil-war-and-farcical-politics.html.

"The 10 Dumbest Reasons to Hate Drake." *Complex*. Accessed June 20, 2016. Accessed July 7, 2016. http://www.complex.com/music/2013/08/why-do-people-hate-drake/.

Thompson, Derek. "A World Without Work." *The Atlantic*, August 2015. Accessed July 7, 2016. http://www.theatlantic.com/magazine/archive/2015/07/world-without-work/395294/.

Thompson, Robert Farris. "The Song that Names the Land." In *Black Art: Ancestral Legacy: The African Impulse in African American Art*. Edited by Robert V. Rozelle, Alvia Wardlaw, and Maureen A. McKenna. Dallas: Dallas Museum of Art, 1989.

Tompkins, Dave. *How to Wreck a Nice Beach: The Vocoder from World War II to Hip-hop—The Machine Speaks*. Brooklyn: Melville House, 2010.

Totally JK. *Future - "Onions,"* 2013. Accessed July 7, 2016. https://www.youtube.com/watch?v=O7TdO_UEc0g.

Weeks, Kathi. *The Problem with Work: Feminism, Marxism, Antiwork Politics, and Postwork Imaginaries*. Durham, NC: Duke University Press, 2011.

Weheliye, Alexander G. "'Feenin': Posthuman Voices in Contemporary Black Popular Music." *Social Text* 20, no. 2 (2002): 21–48.

———. *Habeas Viscus: Racializing Assemblages, Biopolitics, and Black Feminist Theories of the Human*. Durham, NC: Duke University Press, 2014.

Weiner, Jonah. "Kendrick Lamar, New Kid on the Block." *Rolling Stone*, February 27, 2013. Accessed July 7, 2016. http://www.rollingstone.com/music/news/kendrick-lamar-new-kid-on-the-block-20130227.

Williams, Justin A. "'You Never Been on a Ride like This Befo'': Los Angeles, Automotive Listening, and Dr. Dre's G-Funk." *Popular Music History* 4, no. 2 (August 2009): 160–76.

Wolfson, Sam. "Young Thug: 'I like Everything People Say about Me – You Gay, You a Punk, You Can't Rap, You're the Hardest'." *The Guardian*, October 8, 2015. Accessed July 7, 2016. http://www.theguardian.com/music/2015/oct/08/young-thug-hits-bring-money-lil-wayne.

Wynter, Sylvia. "Beyond the World of Man: Glissant and the New Discourse of the Antilles." *World Literature Today* 63, no. 4 (1989): 637–48.

———. "No Humans Involved—An Open Letter to My Colleagues." *Forum NHI: Knowledge for the 21st Century* 1, no. 1 (1994): 42–73.

———. "The Ceremony Must be Found: After Humanism." *boundary 2* 12, no. 3 (1984): 19–70.

———. "Unsettling the Coloniality of Being/Power/Truth/Freedom: Towards the Human, After Man, Its Overrepresentation—An Argument." *CR: The New Centennial Review* 3, no. 3 (2003): 257–337.

Zoellter, Juergen. "Bugatti Veyron - Car and Driver." April 2012. Accessed July 7, 2016. http://www.caranddriver.com/bugatti/veyron.

DISCOGRAPHY

69 Boyz. "Tootsee Roll." Single. Rip-It, 1994.

Ace Hood featuring Future and Rick Ross. "Bugatti." Single. We the Best Music Group, Cash Money Records, Republic Records, Universal Records, 2013.

Big K.R.I.T. "My Sub." *Return of 4Eva*. Song, Mixtape. Cinematic Music Group, 2011.

———. "My Sub (Pt. 2: The Jackin')." *Live from the Underground*. Song, Album. Cinematic Music Group, Def Jam, 2012.

———. "My Sub Pt. 3 (Big Bang)." *Cadillactica*. Cinematic Music Group, Def Jam, 2014.

Bonecrusher featuring Killer Mike and TI. "Never Scared." Single. So So Def, Arista, 2003.

Desiigner. "Panda." Single. GOOD, Def Jam, 2015.

Drake. "One Dance." Single. OVO Sound, Cash Money Records, Young Money Entertainment, 2016.

———. "Jumpman." Single. Young Money Entertainment, Cash Money Records, Epic Records, Republic Records, OVO Sound, Freebandz, 2015.

Drake and Future. *What a Time to Be Alive*. Album. Young Money Entertainment, Cash Money Records, Epic Records, Republic Records, OVO Sound, Freebandz, 2015.

Dr Dre featuring Snoop Dogg. "Nuthin' but a 'G' Thang." Single. Death Row, 1992.

Dr Dre featuring Snoop Dogg, RBX, and Dat Nigga Daz. "The Day the Niggaz Took Over." *The Chronic*. Song, Album. Death Row, Interscope, Priority, 1992.

Eminem. "My Name Is." Single. Aftermath, Interscope, 1999.

Future. "Ain't No Time." *EVOL*. Song, Album. A1, Freebandz, Epic, 2016.

———. "Codeine Crazy." *Monster*. Song, Mixtape. Freebandz, 2014.

———. "Honest." Single. A1, Freebandz, Epic, 2013.

———. "Turn on the Lights." Single. A1, Freebandz, Epic, 2012.

———. "Wicked." Single. A1, Freebandz, Epic, 2016.

Future featuring Drake. "Tony Montana." *Pluto*. Song, Album. A1, Freebandz, Epic, 2012.

———. "Where Ya At." Single. Freebandz, A1, 2015.

Future featuring Pharrell, Pusha T, and Casino. "Move That Dope." Single. A1, Freebandz, Epic, 2014.

Gucci Mane. "Icy." Single. Tommy Boy, 2005.

ILoveMakonnen featuring Drake. "Tuesday." Single. OVO Sound, Warner Bros, 2014.

Indeep. "Last Night a D.J. Saved My Life." Single. Sound of New York, Becket Records, 1982.

Juicy J featuring Lil Wayne and 2 Chainz. "Bandz a Maker Her Dance." Single. Taylor Gang, Kemosabe, Columbia, 2012.

Kanye West. *808s & Heartbreak*. Album. Roc-A-Fella, Def Jam, 2008.

Kanye West featuring Jay Z, Nicki Minaj, Rick Ross, and Bon Iver. "Monster." Single. Roc-A-Fella, Def Jam, 2010.

Kanye West featuring Rihanna. "All of the Lights." Single. Roc-A-Fella, Def Jam, 2010.

Kanye West and Jay Z. *Watch the Throne*. Album. Roc-A-Fella, Roc Nation, Def Jam, 2011.

Katy Perry featuring Juicy J. "Dark Horse." Single. Capitol Records, 2013.

Kendrick Lamar. *good kid, m.A.A.d. city*. Album. Top Dawg, Aftermath, Interscope, 2012.

———. *To Pimp a Butterfly*. Album. Top Dawg, Aftermath, Interscope, 2015.

Kevin Gates. "2 Phones." Single. BWA, Atlantic, 2015.

Kevin Gates featuring August Alsina. "I Don't Get Tired." Single. Atlantic, RCA, 2014.

Lil Jon & the Eastside Boyz. *Crunk Juice*. Album. BME Recordings, 2004.

———. "What U Gon' Do." Single. BME Recordings, 2004.

———. "Who U Wit?" *Get Crunk, Who U Wit: Da Album*. Song, Album. Mirror Image, 1997.

Lil Jon & the Eastside Boyz featuring Jazzy Phe. "I Like dem Girlz." *We Still Crunk!!* Song, Album. BME Recordings, 2000.

Migos. "Versace." Single. Quality Control, 2013.

Mos Def. "The Rape Over." *The New Danger*. Song, Album. Rawkus Records, Geffen, 2004.

Nas. "The World Is Yours." Single. Columbia, 1994.

Nicki Minaj. "Come on a Cone." *Pink Friday: Roman Reloaded*. Song, Album. Young Money, Cash Money Records, Universal Republic, 2012.

———. "Stupid Hoe." Single. Cash Money Records, 2011.

Nicki Minaj featuring 2 Chainz. "Beez in the Trap." Single. Young Money Entertainment, Cash Money Records, Universal Republic, 2012.

Nicki Minaj and Mike Will Made-It. "Black Barbies." Remix Single. EarDrummers, Interscope, 2016.

OJ da Juiceman. "Make tha Trap Say Aye." Single. So Icey Entertainment, Mizay, Asylum, 2007.

Outkast. "SpottieOttieDopaliscious." *Aquemini*. Song, Album. LaFace, 1998.

Public Enemy. "Bring the Noise." Single. Def Jam, 1987.

Rae Sremmurd. "No Flex Zone." Single. EarDrummers, Interscope, 2014.

———. "Safe Sex Pay Checks." *SremmLife*. Song, Album. EarDrummers, Interscope, 2015.

———. "Up Like Trump." *SremmLife*. Song, Album. EarDrummers, Interscope, 2015.

Rae Sremmurd featuring Gucci Mane. "Black Beatles." Single. EarDrummers, Interscope, 2016.

Rae Sremmurd featuring Nicki Minaj. "No Flex Zone (Official Remix)." Remix Single. EarDrummers, Interscope, 2014.

Rae Sremmurd featuring Nicki Minaj and Young Thug. "Throw Some Mo." Single. EarDrummers, Interscope, 2014.

Rich Boy. "Throw Some D's." Single. Interscope, 2006.

Rich Homie Quan. "Flex (Ooh, Ooh, Ooh)." Single. TIG Entertainment, Empire, 2015.

Rihanna. "Pour It Up." Single. Def Jam, Roc Nation, SRP, 2013.

Rihanna featuring Drake. "What's My Name?" Single. Def Jam, SRP, 2010.

———. "Work." Single. Rock Nation, Westbury Road, 2016.

Three 6 Mafia. "Gett'em Crunk." *Chapter 1: The End*. Song, Album. Prophet, 1996.

———. "It's Hard out Here for a Pimp." Single. Grand Hustle, Atlantic, 2005.

———. "Tear da Club Up (Da Real)." *Mystic Stylez*. Song, Album. Prophet Records, 1995.

———. "Tear da Club Up '97." *Chapter 2: World Domination*. Song, Album. Relativity Records, 1997.

TI. "24's." Single. Grand Hustle, Atlantic, 2003.

TI. "Be Easy." Single. Grand Hustle, Atlantic, 2003.

———. *Trap Muzik*. Album. Grand Hustle. Atlantic, 2003.

Trouble. "Bussin." Single, 2011.

Tyga. "Rack City." Single. Young Money Records, Cash Money Entertainment, Republic Records, 2011.

UGK. "Pocket Full of Stones." *Too Hard to Swallow*. Song, Album. Jive Records, 1992.

Usher featuring Juicy J. "I Don't Mind." Single. RCA, 2014.

Usher featuring Nicki Minaj. "Lil Freak." Single. LaFace, 2010.

Waka Flocka Flame. *Flockaveli*. Album. 1017 Brick Squad, Brick Squad Monopoly, Asylum, Warner Bros, 2010.

———. "Hard in da Paint." Single. 1017 Brick Squad, Asylum, Warner Bros, 2010.

Young Jeezy featuring Mannie Fresh. "And Then What." Single. Corporate Thugz, Def Jam, 2005.

Young Thug. "Best Friend." Single. 300, Atlantic, 2015.

———. "Stoner." Single. 1017 Brick Squad, Asylum, Atlantic, 2014.

Young Thug featuring Birdman. "Constantly Hating," *Barter 6*. Song, Album. 300, YSL, Atlantic, 2015.

INDEX

2 Chainz, 116, 118–120
50 Cent, 74
69 Boyz, 106
808. *See* Roland TR-808

ableism, x, 16, 18, 23–31
Ace Hood, 93
Adeyemi, Kemi, 96–97
Afrofuturism
    as antihumanism, 16–17, 20–26, 32
    in funk and hip hop, 92
    See also posthumanism
Agamben, Giorgio, 33, 41. *See also* bare
    life; habeas viscus
alternative humanisms, 19–20, 27–31
Anderson, Marian, 72
antiblack, 27, 94
antihumanism
    as class of ontologies, 19–22
    in Eurocentric posthumanism
        discourse, 17–19, 25, 26, 32
    See also posthumanism
Aronowitz, Stanley, 103–104. *See also*
    postwork
Auner, Joseph, 38
AutoTune, 75–78, 123, 135n4

Banks, Tyra, 56
Banner, David, 90
Barad, Karen, xiii, 18
bare life, 30–33, 41–42. *See also*
    habeas viscus
Barker, Hugh, 66
Barthes, Roland, 64
bass
    in car culture, 91–93
    Miami Bass, 83–87, 106–109

sub-, 129–131
    in trap music, 83–84, 91–93, 108
Battaglia, Andy, 106–107
Big Daddy Kane, 60–62
Big Ghost, 65
Big K.R.I.T., 83, 129–131
Big Sean, 118
Big Tuck, 130, 137n1
biopolitics, 23–25, 30–33, 116–128.
    See also neoliberalism
birth control, 126–127
Biz Markie, 73
Bland, Sandra, 96
bodies
    and flesh, 33–34
    and orthodox knowledge, 26–34, 131
    raced and gendered, 8, 56, 71–73,
        89–90 (*see also* sonic blackness)
    transitional, 115–117
Bogazianos, Dmitri, 66–67, 93–95,
    111–112
Bonecrusher, 106, 136n1
bounce, 70, 85, 106–110
Bourdieu, Pierre, 64
Braidotti, Rosi, 16–31
Brown, Adrienne, 92, 113
Brown, Michael, 52, 55–56
Bun B. *See* UGK

capitalism, 16, 23, 65
Caramanica, Jon, 107
Césaire, Aimé, 24
Child, 21, 125. *See also* Edelman, Lee;
    reproduction
cishetero-
    normativity, 52
    patriarchy, x, 10, 16–21, 28–29, 42

Civil Rights, 52, 56, 57
clap
    booty clap, 115–122, 136n5
    in trap percussion, 84–87
club
    in crunk music, 105–109
    in Rae Sremmurd's music, 101–102,
        118–131
    strip club, 113–122
    as work, 110–112
Common, 65
compression
    in car culture, 91–92
    sidechain, 124–131, 137n8
    in trap, 77–79
Compton, 45–46, 53–55
crack governmentality, 58–63
creative destruction, 61–62
critical race theory, 16, 33–38, 42.
        See also post-racialism
crunk, 105–112. See also Rae Sremmurd

David, Marlo, 38
Davis, Angela, 126–127
Davis, Jenny, 111
de Beauvoir, Simone, 19
Desiigner, music of
    critical press about, 87–94
    instrumentals in, 82–87
    vocals in, 73–82, 97–100
deviant, 113–115, 126. See also Iton, Richard
DJ Mustard, 98–100
DJ Screw, 96–97
DJ Toomp, 82–87
Dr. Dre, 90–92, 108
Drake
    as meme, 64–67, 15nn3–4
    "Tuesday," 111–112
drugs
    as authenticity metaphor, 95
    as entrepreneurial, 58–64, 111–112
    in trap music, 82, 93–97
    War on, 59, 63, 90, 128 (see also prison
        industrial complex)
Duct Tape Army, 69–70

East Side Boyz. See Lil Jon
Edelman, Lee
    on antireproduction, 123–127
    No Future as antihumanism, 20–21

Eidsheim, Nina Sun, 71–73, 90,
        94, 99
Ellis, Nadia, 85, 106–107, 109–110
embattled humanism, 21–26, 31–35.
        See also Wynter, Sylvia
Eminem, 90–91
EQ, 77–79. See also frequency
Eshun, Kodwo, 20
exceptions
    in black parallel publics, 31, 48,
        58–67
    definition of, 29–31
    in political economy of popular
        music, 40
    in posthumanism, 42–43
    produced by postwork, 105
    trap rappers as, 67–68, 115, 128
        (see also sonic blackness)
    See also habeas viscus; neoliberalism
existentialism, 22
eugenics, 126–127

Fanon, Franz, 19, 24, 35
Ferguson, 54, 63
flesh, 33–42, 128–131. See also habeas
        viscus; Spillers, Hortense
Font-Navarrete, David, 83–86, 109
Foucault, Michel, 19, 23, 33
Fraser, Nancy, 23
frequency
    in popular music analysis, 12
    in trap music, 77–78, 83–87, 124

Gangsta Boo, 81
gangsta rap, 55, 58–59, 106
Garner, Eric, 52, 96
Gates, Kevin, 96, 110–112
gay marriage, 29–30, 125
gender
    and flesh, 33–38, 42
    in parallel publics, 48–56
    performance, 7–9, 113–122
    in post-identity politics, 28–31
    See also queerness; race
Gilroy, Paul, 22, 92
Glissant, Édouard, 24
Goodman, Steve, 129–130
Goveia, Elsa, 24–25
Gray, Freddie, 63
Gucci Mane, 69, 80, 95

habeas viscus, 10, 30–35, 37–42, 101
Hagstrom-Miller, Karl, 66
Hall, Stuart, 27, 36, 39
Haraway, Donna, 18
Harvey, David, 61
Hayles, N. Katherine, 18–19, 27, 37
hi-hats, 84–97, 107, 112–114, 131
hip hop
    authenticity in, 49–60, 93–94
    and car culture, 91–92
    and clubs, 109–128
    criticism about, 47–53, 73–75, 90
    and imagination, 113
    and politics, 6–9, 38–41, 45–55,
        63–68, 101–102
    as popular music, 36–38
    Southern, 69–71, 75–87, 94–100
Hofer, Sonya, 38
humanism
    liberal, 16–26
    neoliberal, 26–32, 34–43, 58–71, 127–131
    See also posthumanism

IloveMakonnen, 111–112, 119
Indeep, 131
irony, 94–100, 115–118
Iton, Richard, 113–115, 131

James, Robin, 28–29, 35, 112, 136n3
Jay Z, 2–9
Jones, Ralkina, 96
Joseph, Ralina, 55–56
Juicy J, 114–117

Kajikawa, Loren, 71–73, 90–92
Kelley, Robin, 59
kick drum
    in crunk music, 107–108
    in "Monster," 3–9
    in trap music, 83–87, 91, 95, 98
Killer Mike, 52–54, 65
Krims, Adam, 80

Lamar, Kendrick, 45–68, 72–73,
        88–89, 93
Lex Luger, 83, 136n11
Lil Jon, 105–112, 136n5
Lil Yachty, 80
Lord Infamous, 81, 135n7
Lynch, Marc, 50–68, 89, 135n2

Mais, Roger, 24
Manchard, Michael, 113
Marshall, Wayne, 83, 85
Martin, Trayvon, 52
mass incarceration. *See* drugs; prison
        industrial complex
Menace, 83–89, 136n10
Metro Boomin, 112
Middleton, Richard, 38
Migos, 79–81, 135n6, 135n7
Mike Will Made-It
    "Bandz a Make Her Dance," 115–117
    "Bugatti," 93
    "Move That Dope," 95–96, 112
    "Safe Sex Pay Checks," 117–128, 137n8
    "Turn on the Lights," 83–87, 136n10
Minaj, Nicki
    "Monster," 1–9, 71
    and queerness, 7–9, 120–122, 128
    "Throw Sum Mo," 118–122, 137n7
Mississippi, 129–131
Morrison, Toni, 17
Morton, Thomas, 69–72
Mos Def, 39–41, 134n5
multiracialism
    as anti-black, 57, 64–67
    and post-identity, 28–30
Mulvey, Laura, 35, 120

Nelson, Alondra, 20
neoliberalism
    and biopolitics, 23–25, 30–33,
        116–128
    creative desctruction, 61
    neoliberal humanism, 26–32, 34–43,
        58–71, 127–131
    and parallel publics, 47–48
New Orleans, 69, 106–109, 110
NoFuturism. *See* Edelman, Lee
Noisey Atlanta, 69–71
nontheism, 22
normativity
    in biopolitics, 28–30
    in Kendrick reception, 52
    politics against, 119–121, 125
    in postwork discourse, 105

Obama, Barack, 29–30
OJ Da Juiceman, 83–87
Outkast, 82

parallel public, 47–62, 89, 98–100
pariah groups, 30
patriarchy, 28–29
Pecknold, Diane, 66
Pharrell, 95
pitch correction, 76–78, 123, 135n4
police violence, 56, 122–128
political economy, 38–41
politics
    illegible, 62–68, 87–100, 113–128
    ironic, 94–100
    legible, 47–58, 62–68
    in popular music, 36–41
    post-identity, 19–22, 28–30
    See also biopolitics; neoliberalism
popular music analysis, 12–13, 36–41
popular music industry, 38–41, 66,
    95, 111
posthumanism
    overview and definition of, 15–43
    posthuman vestibule, 33–43, 101–131
    in trap music, 68–73
    See also Afrofuturism; antihumanism;
    humanism
post-racialism, 53–67, 71–73, 89–100
postwork, 102–105, 112–128
prison industrial complex, 33, 45, 59–60
Pusha T, 95

queerness
    in hip hop, 101–105, 113–128
    Nicki Minaj, 1–9, 118–122
    and posthumanism, 16–21, 35–43
    See also habeas viscus

Rae, Issa, 114–115
Rae Sremmurd
    the crunk aesthetics of, 117, 124, 130
    the queer performance of, 117–128
    "Safe Sex Pay Checks," 117–122
    "Throw Sum Mo," 122–128
rap. *See* hip hop
reproduction, 21, 30, 105, 125–128
rhythm
    in crunk music, 105–109
    in "Monster," 1–4, 133n2
    in trap muisc, 78–87, 135n8
    See also popular music analysis
Rich Boy, 83, 92
Rich Homie Quan, 97, 99

Rihanna, 2–3, 74, 114–115
Robinson, Zandria, 130
Roland TR-808, 1, 84, 114, 136n10
Rose, Tricia, 90, 109

Sarig, Roni, 67–68
Sartre, Jean-Paul, 19–22
saturation, 77–79
Schoolboy Q, 96
Scott, David, 134n2. *See also*
    Wynter, Sylvia
Sedgwick, Eve, 9
Sexton, Jared, 28–29, 57–64,
    71–73, 89–94
Shange, Savannah, 7–8, 118–121
Shaviro, Steven, 38
Sheth, Falguni, 30
Sinker, Mark, 20
Skinny Pimp, 81
snare drum, 84–87
social media, 27, 111, 118, 125
sonic blackness, 69–75, 87–99, 105–107,
    114–116, 126–128
Sonny Digital, 112, 117
Spence, Lester, 27–30, 47–64, 95–100,
    115–116
Spillers, Hortense, 30–35, 116, 128
Stallings, L.H., 112–128, 136n3
sterilization, 126–127
strategic queerness, 7, 118, 126
structure (music), 2–8, 12–13
subwoofer, 129–131
Sun Ra, 20
synthesizer, 2–8, 83–84, 112–124

Taylor, Chris, 20
Taylor, Yuval, 66
texture, 12, 98
Thompson, Derek, 102–104
Thompson, Robert Farris, 92
Three 6 Mafia, 81, 88, 105–107, 135n7
TI, 82–83, 90
timbre, 12, 72, 77, 84–85, 90
Tompkins, Dave, 76
T-Pain, 76
trap
    aesthetics, 73–87, 105–109
    politics, 70–73, 87–102, 109–128
Trouble, 69, 90
Tyga, 98

UGK, 58–59
Uncle Murda, 73

VICE, 70
voice
    background, 98–100, 108
    of Desiigner, 73–82, 89
    of Future, 73–82
    of Nicki Minaj, 1–8, 120
    processing, 73–79, 135n4
    of Rae Sremmurd, 117–128
    See also sonic blackness

Waka Flocka Flame, 80–87, 99
Weeks, Kathi, 104–105, 109, 112, 127

Weheliye, Alexander, 32–43, 94, 101–102
West, Kanye, 1–9, 76, 78
white supremacy, 17–29, 33–34, 46–49, 64
Williams, Justin, 91–92
Wynter, Sylvia, 15, 19–35, 134n2

Ying Yang Twins, 105
Young Jeezy, 80
Young Thug
    "Throw Sum Mo," 119–122
    the vocal aesthetics of, 80–81, 97–99

Zaytoven, 83–87, 136n10